International
Perspectives on
Lifelong Learning

SRHE and Open University Press Imprint
General Editor: Heather Eggins

International Perspectives on Lifelong Learning

From Recurrent Education to the Knowledge Society

Edited by
David Istance, Hans G. Schuetze
and Tom Schuller

The Society for Research into Higher Education
& Open University Press

Published by SRHE and
Open University Press
Celtic Court
22 Ballmoor
Buckingham
MK18 1XW

email: enquiries@openup.co.uk
world wide web: www.openup.co.uk

and
325 Chestnut Street
Philadelphia, PA 19106, USA

First Published 2002

A catalogue record of this book is available from the British Library

ISBN   0 335 21003 1 (hb) ⊢

Library of Congress Cataloging-in-Publication Data is available

Typeset by Graphicraft Limited, Hong Kong
Printed by St Edmundsbury Press, Bury St Edmunds, Suffolk

For Jarl Bengtsson

Contents

Notes on Contributors

Martin Carnoy is Professor of Education and Economics at Stanford University, California, where he directs the International and Comparative Education Program and the Social Sciences, Policy and Educational Practices Department. He has published extensively in economics of education and economic development. His latest books are *Faded Dreams: the Economics and Politics of Race in America* (1994); *The International Encyclopedia of the Economics of Education* (ed.) (1995); and *Sustaining Flexibility: Work, Family and Community in the Information Age* (1999).

Pierre Caspar is Professor at the Conservatoire Nationale des Arts et Métiers, (CNAM), Paris, one of France's oldest adult education institutions. He has written widely on continuing education and training, and been adviser to French governments in these fields. He directs *Quaternaire Education*, a private training consultancy.

Chris Duke worked for many years in university adult education in the UK and Australia, at the universities of Leeds, Canberra and Warwick, where he was founding Professor of the Department of Continuing Education. He was until recently Deputy Vice-Chancellor of University of Western Sydney, and is currently Professor of Lifelong Learning at the University of Auckland, New Zealand. He is the author of *The Learning University* (1992) and *Managing the Learning University* (2002), and is a consultant to OECD's higher education management programme.

Bill Ford's employment journey began at the age of 15 and traversed through a number of low-skilled jobs in a range of traditional industries. Much later he entered academia, became Professor of Organizational Behaviour at the University of New South Wales, Australia, and carried out cross-cultural action research on four continents. He then left academia to become a player-coach, leading enterprises through workplace renewal and developing learning organizations. He is currently in an Internet start-up enterprise and is organizational mentor for the Sydney Opera House.

David H. Hargreaves was, until recently, Chief Executive of the UK Qualifications and Curriculum Authority. Before that, he was Professor of Education, University of Cambridge, England. Between 1984 and 1988 he was Chief Inspector of the Inner London Education Authority (ILEA), and has held university posts in Oxford and Manchester. His main research interests are in institutional and professional development and knowledge management, and he writes regularly on the need to change the nature of education research.

Tom Healy is a research associate with the Institute for the Study of Social Change (ISSC) at University College, Dublin. His research interests relate to the link between learning and social networks and norms and their impact on well-being and social cohesion. He worked at OECD for four years and was the principal author of two publications there: *Human Capital Investment: An International Comparison* (1998) and *The Well-being of Nations: The Role of Human and Social Capital* (2001). He has also worked as a researcher with the Economic and Social Research Institute in Dublin and the Northern Ireland Economic Research Centre in Belfast.

Donald Hirsch is a national and international policy consultant (to the British government, OECD, the Rowntree Foundation, and others) and has been Visiting Fellow at the University of London Institute of Education since 1994. Before returning to England, he was at the OECD's Centre for Educational Research and Innovation, working on a wide portfolio including school choice, non-formal lifelong learning, school–business partnerships, and learning cities and regions. Previously, he was Education Correspondent at *The Economist.*

Torsten Husén is Emeritus Professor and former Director at the Institute of International Education, University of Stockholm, Sweden. He was a founding organizer and first Chairman of the International Association for the Evaluation of Educational Achievement (IEA); Trustee of the International Council for Educational Development (ICED) in the 1960s; Chairman of the Governing Board of the International Institute of Educational Planning (IIEP) in the 1970s; founding President of International Academy of Education in the 1980s; Co-editor of the second *International Encyclopaedia of Education* from 1991 (the first edited by Torsten Husén and Neville Postlethwaite appeared in 1985). He has published extensively across many educational fields, and has frequently worked with the OECD, including as author of *Social Influences on Educational Attainment: Research Perspectives on Educational Equality* (1975) and (with James Coleman) *Becoming Adult in a Changing Society* (1985).

David Istance rejoined OECD's Centre for Educational Research and Innovation (CERI) in 1997, after a period in Wales as a consultant, teacher and researcher. He has written international reports on a wide range of educational topics, including OECD reports for occasional meetings of ministers of education. His current interests include the future of schooling, lifelong learning, human capital, and equity.

Denis Kallen is a former professor at the Universities of Paris VIII and Amsterdam. He is now active in several European comparative education societies, and as a consultant (Council of Europe, UNESCO, OECD and the European Union). When at OECD's CERI in the 1960s and 1970s, he wrote extensively on recurrent education. He was Director of the Council of Europe project 'A Secondary Education for Europe'. His publications cover a broad range of educational issues, including schooling, lifelong education and training.

Terri Kim was Visiting Research Scholar in the International Relations Department at the London School of Economics and Political Science (LSE) for the academic year 2000/01. After the completion of her PhD in Comparative Higher Education at the Institute of Education, University of London in 1998, she worked as a consultant for OECD, CERI, and for the Korean National Commission for UNESCO (KNCU), and for the ASEAN University Network (AUN); and also taught as a part-time lecturer at Yonsei University in Seoul, Korea. She has a strong comparative research interest in the university academic profession, the social construction of merit in different cultural and knowledge traditions, and globalization and its impact on the uses of the university and knowledge. Her book *Forming the Academic Profession in East Asia: A Comparative Analysis of Korea, Malaysia and Singapore since Colonial Times* was published by Garland Publishing in 2001.

Lisa M. Lynch is William L. Clayton Professor of International Economic Affairs at the Fletcher School of Law and Diplomacy at Tufts University, Massachusetts. She is also a research associate at the National Bureau of Economic Research and the Economic Policy Institute and is currently a co-editor of the *Journal of Labor Economics*. From October 1995 to January 1997 she was the Chief Economist at the US Department of Labor. Her many publications have covered issues such as private-sector training and its impact on productivity and wages, youth unemployment, the school-to-work transition, and the impact of technological change on employment.

George Papadopoulos is a former Deputy Director for Education at OECD in the Directorate for Social Affairs, Manpower and Education, and a senior consultant to the Council of Europe, OECD, UNESCO and various national governments. He has written a history of educational policy analysis and exchange at the OECD, contributed to the UNESCO International Commission on 'Education for the 21st Century', and has published particularly in the fields of lifelong learning, higher education, and vocational education and training.

Kjell Rubenson is Professor of Adult Education in the Department of Educational Studies and Director of the Centre for Policy Studies in Higher Education and Training (formerly the Centre for Policy Studies in Education) at the University of British Columbia, Canada. He was educated in Sweden and held the chair of Adult Education at the University of Linköping before moving to Canada in 1986. His main academic interests and publications are in the relationships between education, learning and work, adult education and learning, and educational policy studies.

Hans G. Schuetze is a professor at the Department of Educational Studies and a Research Fellow at the Centre for Policy Studies in Higher Education and Training, University of British Columbia, Canada. Previously, he has been a practising lawyer, policy analyst and researcher at the Centre for Educational Research and Innovation of the OECD in Paris, and counsellor on human resource policies to the Minister of Economic Affairs and Technology, Lower Saxony, Germany. His recent research is in the fields of knowledge management and learning in firms, the collaboration between universities and industry, organization and finance of post-secondary education and training, labour market issues, and the role of human resources in innovation and economic development.

Tom Schuller is Professor of Lifelong Learning and Dean, Faculty of Continuing Education, Birkbeck College, University of London. Previously, he was Director of the Centre for Continuing Education, University of Edinburgh, and has held posts in the Universities of Glasgow and Warwick and at the Institute of Community Studies, London. He worked in OECD's CERI in the 1970s and has since been a regular consultant for the OECD. He has written on lifelong learning, educational and related policies, social capital, and the organization of work and time.

David Stern is Professor of Education at the University of Berkeley, California, and former Director of the National Center for Research in Vocational Education, in Berkeley's Graduate School of Education. Having joined the Berkeley faculty in 1976, he worked in the OECD's Centre for Educational Research and Innovation between 1993 and 1995. His publications and research interests include the relationship between education and work, training, and resource allocation in schools.

Albert C. Tuijnman is Professor at the Institute of International Education, University of Stockholm, Sweden, and School of Continuing Education, University of Nottingham, England. During the 1990s, he worked at the OECD, and was responsible for the First International Adult Literacy Survey and the report to the 1996 meeting of Education ministers on 'Lifelong Education for All', and has been a consultant to the European Commission, World Bank and UNESCO. He has written extensively on adult education and lifelong learning, adult literacy, and policy analysis and edited the *International Encyclopaedia of Adult Education and Training*.

Daniel A. Wagner is Professor of Education and Director of the International Literacy Institute and National Center on Adult Literacy at the University of Pennsylvania, Philadelphia. As well as US-based posts, he has worked and studied in Europe, having been a visiting fellow at the International Institute of Educational Planning (IIEP), Paris and a visiting professor at the University of Geneva. His publications have covered many international and national fields, including literacy, adult learning and school-to-work transition.

Foreword

Nearly thirty years ago Denis Kallen and Jarl Bengtsson's pathfinding report on lifelong learning changed my views about the nature and purpose of education. Two or three years afterwards, Tom Schuller invited me to contribute to his work with Jarl Bengtsson on developing the meaning of recurrent education, as lifelong learning was then called. They wanted to talk to me about the work I had been doing on pre-school education across Europe because they wanted 'the cradle to grave' maxim to have real meaning at the beginning of people's lives. Jarl challenged me to think more imaginatively about how lifelong learning could be applied to extending educational opportunities 'down' to very young children as well as 'up' to older people, just as he challenged many others to think about the ideas he was developing.

The introduction to this volume shies away from any claim that it is intended as a formal celebration of Jarl's work. In this foreword I want to make an exception. On behalf of all the authors in this book and thousands of others who have in one way or another interacted with Jarl or simply been influenced by his writing, I want to salute his extraordinary contribution to the debate on lifelong learning over three decades.

Optimism is what makes the world a better place. We have made phenomenal progress since 1973. More dramatic progress than is often conceded has taken place across many OECD countries in extending educational opportunities far beyond the conventional age range of formal education from five or six years of age to the early twenties. This includes the rapid expansion of nursery education, the huge increase in the numbers of part-time mature students in higher education and the greater emphasis on education and training at the workplace for all age groups. Over a decade or so, a transformation of political attitudes and provision has been taking place. The opportunity has been grasped and not missed. By the turn of the twenty-first century the importance attached to lifelong learning by European Union governments was reflected in the agenda at the Lisbon Summit. Jarl Bengtsson deserves acclaim for helping make this happen. Of course there is still much to be done. Above all, access to all forms of life-long learning must be extended to those social groups currently excluded from it. This poses an enormous challenge: to provide the necessary re-sources; to shift the focus of policy further towards providing opportunities for learning outside conventional age groups, and to change social attitudes so that age is no longer seen as a barrier to learning.

I hope politicians, educational managers and all those concerned with lifelong learning across the world will read this book and reflect on its findings. But they can be optimistic that a great movement has begun on which they can build. For that they should be grateful to Jarl Bengtsson and his colleagues at the OECD for pointing the way.

Tessa Blackstone
Minister of State for Education
and Employment, UK, 1997–2001

1

From Recurrent Education to the Knowledge Society: An Introduction

Tom Schuller, Hans G. Schuetze
and David Istance

This book is a hybrid. Its main aim is to provide a multi-stranded perspective on policy research in the field of lifelong learning over the past three decades. The rationale for such an exercise is that in the febrile world of contemporary political debate it is worth stepping back to trace out the trajectory of ideas; to remind ourselves of how persistent the main themes of the debate are and assess how many of the claims to novelty are overblown; and to retrieve ideas that might otherwise have fizzled unjustly into obscurity merely because they failed to take root first time round.

The contributions commissioned for this volume were given a common framework, around the twin themes of the knowledge society and lifelong learning, whether viewed historically or through a particular disciplinary literature or in terms of policy agendas for the future. The central thread running through all is the illumination of the nature of a society in which learning is central to its economic, social and democratic life. This introduction re-examines the ideas set out in the OECD's original comprehensive conceptualization of the notion of recurrent education, and explores how these have broadened and developed through subsequent analysis.[1]

The book's second aim is a more personal one: to acknowledge the seminal energies of Jarl Bengtsson in promoting and animating international debates on lifelong learning. It is not formally a *festschrift*, since publishers have an aversion to such things. *Recurrent Education: A Strategy for Lifelong Learning* was written by Bengtsson and Denis Kallen and published in 1973. The latter (the author of Chapter 3) left OECD soon after the report's publication to return to academia while Bengtsson remained for the rest of his professional life in the Centre for Educational Research and Innovation (CERI), the OECD's educational think-tank. He has used his Paris base to foster – and to challenge – so much thinking and analysis in the areas covered by this book. The contributors to this volume have all taken part in that process of developing and challenging ideas, as either

OECD/CERI staff members or consultants on one or another of its numerous projects, or sometimes both.

We are sure there is no conflict between the two aims.

From recurrent education . . .

Recurrent Education: A Strategy for Lifelong Learning was one of the key educational policy documents of the last quarter of the twentieth century. The 'Clarifying Report', as it came to be known in the OECD, can reasonably lay claim to seminal status although it did not score highly for its immediate appeal or impact. We operate now in a world where 'lifelong learning' is almost a cliché, but it was indeed new 30 years ago. The Clarifying Report, along with *Learning To Be*, a volume published around the same time by another Paris-based international body UNESCO (1972), opened the way for a flow of policy analysis and prescription in countries across the world.

Recurrent Education was written before the end of the post-World War II decades of uninterrupted economic growth and the accompanying dominant ideology of steady social progress, though oil shocks were soon to disrupt that. Torsten Husén, in the next chapter, acknowledges how tempting it was to assume indefinite steady progress, a view he had revised sharply by the end of the 1970s. The cold war was still very much under way, but this hardly affected the stability of daily life, dominated by the assumption of continuing linear development. Serious environmental concerns were articulated only at the very margins of political debate; much more attention was devoted to the immediate vagaries of fashion and the youth culture. But there was genuine contestation, and not only in dramatic scenes of the 1968 student revolt in the streets of Paris.

In education, the 1960s had seen radical changes in school systems in many countries. Even more strikingly, the elite husk guarding higher education had been cracked open as post-compulsory provision expanded, generating all kinds of uncertainties about whose knowledge and whose standards should prevail. One major debate centred around 'more means worse', as mainstream progressive thinking sought to scale the ramparts of traditional conservatism by encouraging more young people to stay in education. A more exotic argument developed around the 'de-schooling' thesis of Ivan Illich (1971) as an alternative to institutional expansion: schools should not so much be rearranged as dismantled altogether.

But education was unambiguously equated with schooling – if not with schools, then certainly with young people – and few ever paused to ask what happened to the innate human drive to learn once people had left the school system. There were occasional nods in the direction of adults – Sweden's U68 Commission being an unusually substantial exception – but the institutions serving adults were primarily seen as marginal adornments to the main business of socializing young people and equipping them for a future life, mainly as male full-time employees.

In the light of this, there can be no doubt of the radicalism of the 'recurrent education' concept as it was articulated in the Clarifying Report. The report stated the twofold claim of the new concept, namely 'to offer an alternative to the unlimited further expansion of the formal and youth-oriented educational system, as well as making possible earlier participation of the individual in society' (p. 2). This alternative proposed replacing a 'front-end' model of education, where organized learning is overwhelmingly concentrated in childhood and adolescence, with the principles of recurrence and alternation. Thus:

> recurrent education is a comprehensive education strategy for all post-compulsory or post-basic education, the essential characteristic of which is the distribution of education over the total life-span of the individual in a recurring way, i.e. in alternation with other activities, principally with work, but also with leisure and retirement.
>
> (p. 24)

The authors and the OECD (which made this proposal its own by publishing it under the organization's, not the experts', names) were aware of the scale of the project and the audacity of their proposal. The report maintained: 'the conversion of the present educational system into a system of recurrent education is a vast and ambitious undertaking, much greater than anything that has yet been undertaken in educational planning, policy and reform' (p. 88). It was not the only proposal that emerged during this era arguing for a shift towards lifelong principles. The early chapters in this volume outline how the educational and cultural international organizations each proposed their own version – 'lifelong learning' for UNESCO and 'education permanente' for the Council of Europe. But the Clarifying Report offered a distinctive radicalism: it was more ambitious in its proposed reform strategy than its Council of Europe and UNESCO counterparts, and it was the most visionary and ambitious of all the models put forward at the time (see the chapters by Kallen and Papadopoulos).

The Report posed questions both unfashionable and contentious in education systems wedded to the idea that 'more education' should translate into growing numbers staying on at schools, colleges and universities in their late teens and early twenties:

> Is a continuous process of schooling, from pre-primary through primary, secondary and higher education, the best way to prepare all individuals for their future role in society and to provide optimal opportunities for self-development; and secondly, is a continuous lengthening of the schooling period, and hence a further expansion of the conventional education system, the best way to respond to the increasingly important role of knowledge and abilities in modern society?
>
> (pp. 10–11)

In our view, these questions remain wholly apposite, and the overarching question about the need for more flexible, imaginative and individualized lifelong learning opportunities for all is as powerful as ever.

It is often disconcerting to return to historical documents and discover how many apparently newly minted ideas have been around for a while. This is another reason why the Clarifying Report can claim seminal status. Anyone who thought that notions such as the knowledge society or even globalization are products of the 1990s is referred to this 1973 volume where the contours of the knowledge society are clearly sketched out:

> Society is becoming more and more a 'knowledge society' . . . The old capital–labour relationship is being replaced by a capital–knowledge–labour relationship, with competence and skills based on knowledge playing an increasingly important role.
>
> (p. 44)

It also anticipated the importance of demand patterns when, for many, educational development was conceived in terms of traditional supply-led tramlines: 'recurrent education is by definition consumer-oriented' (p. 78). This was not so much early support for the market-based ideas that emerged in the 1980s as affirmation that the potential participants, as an unorganized population, would require 'frameworks of consultation and participation' to be set up. Although unelaborated, it points to a more citizenship-based solution to the paradox that those who most oppose market-based solutions are often the strongest supporters of learner-centred approaches.

The Clarifying Report is very strong in its commitment to equality. This was nothing peculiar at that time, of course, as Husén's chapter and others underline. He was particularly concerned about how to make the radical step from a focus on equality of opportunity to equality of results, but worried about the widening gulf between educated expertise and the large body of citizens. Although this was not ignored in the Clarifying Report, its particular concern was intergenerational inequality, and the risk that mere expansion of the system will exacerbate the problem. In this, it has broadly been proved right: cohort analysis shows clearly how later generations have benefited from educational expansion, largely paid for by their fathers and mothers without these latter gaining access to anything like the same opportunities.

The report is strong in the way it urges interconnection between policy spheres – a constant OECD message over the years, but one that most countries have found hard to take on board effectively. It also provides a salutary, and often-ignored, message that education on its own will not be effective in tackling broad social objectives. It was a policy document that suggested a fundamentally different way of looking at educational provision and participation. It was radical indeed, and had a hard time making its voice heard.

Recurrent education as a product of its time – gaps and limitations

Politically, the report reads as a distinctively social democratic document – unsurprisingly given the authors' origins and the disproportionately strong influence of Scandinavians on the policy analysis and debates within the OECD. The complexion of those countries has changed somewhat, but the features have not sagged unrecognizably. The stress on union–management arrangements for handling recurrent education in the workplace looks curious in an age when trade union membership has shrunk dramatically from its postwar heights. Yet, bipartisan approaches to training as part of organizational life are still significant. More generally, the link between education and democratic participation is assuming a higher profile, as concern grows about the health of political institutions. The stress on learning by adults to enable an informed participation to flourish both in civic affairs and in workplace decisions, is as salient as ever.

However, there are some striking gaps. Perhaps the most glaring was the absence of gender in the analysis – the half of the population that already in very large measure deviated from the education–work–retirement lockstep. Only at the end of the report, and almost as an *obiter dictum*, are women given a specific mention in a consideration of priorities, where they come fourth in the list. It said:

> Increasing the educational and occupational opportunities given to women will have to be one of the priorities of any recurrent education policy. However, the priority given to this objective will have to be weighed against other, notably socio-economic, objectives and constraints.
>
> (p. 90)

So, in other words, 'girls, you're in line, but only if someone else doesn't show up ahead of you'. Ethnic divisions received no attention at all.

There were other limitations in the recurrent education concept. It was seen as a strategy applying to post-compulsory education, though it did have things to say about how schooling would need to change to implement this approach to lifelong learning. Limiting the strategy to post-compulsory education may be explained by pragmatism, evidence of a realistic approach towards implementation rather than lack of full understanding of the crucial role of initial education in the lifelong learning concept. But it perpetuated the notion of schooling as separate, whereas more recent proponents of lifelong learning, including the OECD itself much later (OECD 1996), emphasize the very importance of a strong foundation for any learning later in life. Many studies have shown how adults with the most extensive initial education are much more likely to participate in learning activities later than those who had a shorter school career. Without integrating schooling fully within a truly lifelong strategy, recurrent education would always stumble over these critical *intra*generational inequalities.

The Clarifying Report also oversimplified the relationship between education and work, though it represented an unusual position in the debate of the time about whether the economy held any relevance for educational policy. This debate ranged functionalists, who gave priority to preparing young people for work, against both the guardians of a more liberal approach, seeing school as a necessary protection from and counterbalance to the future demands of employment, and the radical separatists who challenged any liaison between schooling and the capitalist work system. The Clarifying Report incurred suspicion from all sides: its analysis was critical of existing systems and their resistance to change, but, on the other hand, with the OECD as an organization primarily charged with economic development, it held little appeal for either the liberal-humanist or the Marxist orthodoxies. In fact, the OECD as an international organization contained its own political tensions, accommodating the widely different political complexions of its member governments as well as sharply contrasting ideological and disciplinary traditions among its own sections. Free market doctrines jostled with corporatist tendencies arguing for social intervention and equalization.

The simplified education/work nexus is found in the essential feature of the recurrent education approach as 'alternation'. The alternation envisaged was mechanistic, as well as suffering from acute gender-blindness, principally envisaging periods of full-time education interleaved with paid employment. At its simplest, it would be known in the UK as a sandwich course, with a slice of work placed between the beginning and end of the course; the recurrent education model transforms this sandwich into a *mille-feuille*. The view that there would be redistributed phases of education and work or other activities assigned an important role to (paid) educational leave. As Kallen notes in his chapter, advocating such leave was one of the most controversial aspects of the Clarifying Report; he also notes the failure to implement the principles of recurrence and alternation over the past quarter century. It remains a radical vision, but it oversimplified the relationship between education and work.

Fully developed educational leave quickly proved to be politically unrealistic in view of the operation of the labour market, in spite of much debate and support from the International Labour Organization (ILO) and the labour unions in many countries (Schuetze 1992; Schuller 1999). With the economic crises of the 1980s and the upheavals and developments of the labour markets, part-time work – voluntarily sought or imposed – grew. More adult learners were combining part-time education and part-time work, and in some countries such as the United States, part-time numbers in post-secondary education grew to almost similar levels as full-time enrolments (OECD 1987; Schuetze and Slowey 2000). Companies, especially those caught up most by scientific and technological change, greatly increased their investment in the continuing education and training of at least sections of their workforces. This led to the emergence of many new learning opportunities at the level of the enterprise, and to new forms of on-the-job and job-related training, most of them organized not in alternation, as the Clarifying Report had imagined, but in combination with work. David Stern's chapter provides more recent thinking on different combinations of activity and learning, with 'social enterprise for learning' as a sector where education, social activities and private enterprise all intersect.

Entrenchment of the 'front-end' model – the enduring resonance of the Clarifying Report

The tensions between the positions outlined above about how education and the economy relate can be illustrated by reference to the varied connotations of the single word 'investment'. For mainstream humanists, the notion of education as investment epitomized economism at its most instrumental. Education for the young should be regarded as a good in itself and for individual development, with little direct connection to working life. For many economists, by contrast, investment in education was desirable but it should be an investment to pay off over as long a period as possible; according to this argument, 'front-loading' in the early part of the life cycle made economic sense since deferring any of the investment reduced overall returns. The simplistic nature of the underlying assumption – that the same quantum of learning keeps paying off directly and indefinitely – did not disturb the technical modelling which was based heavily on it. For diverse reasons, therefore, both camps remained committed to education as essentially a preparatory phase in the life-course.

Why did the Clarifying Report challenge the 'front-loaded' system? The main reasons as perceived in the early 1970s were:

- the malaise in secondary education: poor efficiency, high drop-out rates, low teacher morale, and problematic transition from school to work;
- the isolation of individuals from the world outside the 'protective educational environment', and especially the disconnection of school-based learning from the context in which knowledge is applied;
- the imbalance between supply of and the increasing demand for highly qualified personnel;
- limited learning opportunities for adults, both in what is offered by education institutions and in the inflexibility of working life;
- the rapid expansion and change of knowledge, and continuous need for updating and relearning;
- the intergenerational imbalance caused by the massive increase of educational opportunities concentrated among the young.

Several of these reasons still feature strongly in today's rationales for lifelong learning, and others (such as teacher problems) have become acute even if not linked explicitly to lifelong arguments. *Yet, policy-makers throughout the OECD have preferred – consciously or not – to expand the system without fundamentally changing its shape.* The 'front-end' model has, if anything, become even more entrenched as it has expanded. Recent OECD analysis on transitions from school to working life has suggested that between 1990 and 1996 the international average duration of young people's initial transition to working life grew by nearly two years (see OECD 2000b). In many countries, over 90 per cent of the age group are enrolled in education for 12 or more years, and in some it is higher than this: in Sweden, the figure is 13 (from ages 6 to 18); in Japan and the Netherlands (between ages 4 and 17) it is 14 years, rising to 15 in Belgium and France (between ages 3 and 17). Over three-quarters of the 15–19-year-old population across the OECD are now students, and in a number of countries more than 85 per cent are enrolled. Even the proportion of 20–29 year olds who are students stands at 1 in 5 for OECD as a whole (20.7 per cent), and is one-third or more in Finland (36.1 per cent) and Sweden (33.7 per cent) (OECD 2001b). This strongly suggests a further reinforcement of front-end initial education.

Far-reaching demographic changes have been taking place in the context of an ageing society. As Husén points out, the generational balance of numbers has shifted markedly over the past forty years: 'by 1999 the proportion of under-15s had fallen to less than 1 in 5 of total population in 22 of the 30 OECD countries, with only Mexico and Turkey significantly above; in 1960, in no OECD country was it as low as this.' One issue this raises is how well education systems respond to the different generations as the younger ones shrink and the older ones expand – a point anticipated in the Clarifying Report list above. Another is the growing dependency ratio implied by continually squeezing the 'active' generation into an ever-tighter age range in the middle of people's lives. Growing calls on the expenditure purse (for education, and especially health) unmatched by growth in the tax-paying base are adding economic arguments to the social and educational ones about re-examining the 'continued extension of adolescence' (OECD 2001a).

It was probably too much to have expected the lifelong learning principles to have led to recasting education systems in the early 1970s when the Clarifying Report and similar manifestos first appeared. They were ahead of their time. The same cannot be said now. Governments line up to interpret and reinterpret their policies as contributing to this umbrella aim. Schooling has been brought within its ambit, and hence so has the main business of education authorities. The need to respond to rapid change, the knowledge society and ageing populations is now mainstream to debate, not peripheral. Will the opportunity at last be taken to rethink the front-end system, with radical not incremental shifts towards lifelong learning? Our sombre conclusion is that the signs are yet few that this challenge has been thoroughly accepted.

. . . to the knowledge society

The defining features of a knowledge society, or a knowledge-based or learning one, are still emerging into solid form. OECD begins its recent analysis of knowledge management in a learning society (2000a) by reaching back to Aristotle's taxonomy of knowledges – *episteme, techne* and *phronesis*; others take a more socio-political approach, raising issues of power and control (e.g. Coffield 2000). From the contributions to this volume a set of overlapping themes emerges. These deal especially with:

- broadening the focus from education to knowledge, and developing a more extended set of notions of capital;
- the need to understand learning in context – including the organizational (whether in education or enterprises) – and to bridge the divide between micro and macro levels;
- the changing geopolitical environment: globalization, democracy and equity, especially in relation to educational institutions and the making of policy in such complexity;
- the pioneering role of one country, Sweden, which has challenged traditional views and thinking on all these.

As we synthesize, we identify the challenges our authors pose, to policy-makers, practitioners and researchers.

Lifelong learning has become an all-encompassing concept. Yet in spite of this scope, or probably because of it, there is no master concept of lifelong learning to be found among the many policy documents that have been written in the 1990s, whether by international organizations (European Commission 1996; OECD 1996; UNESCO 1996) or by national governments (for example, Denmark, UK, Finland, Ireland, Netherlands, Scotland, Slovenia and Wales). One reason for this rather unconditional acceptance of lifelong learning by policy-makers, employers and educational institutions is that many different policy agendas are pursued under the new umbrella. If we apply a more critical perspective to the discussion, the implementation of such a lifelong learning concept actually poses serious policy dilemmas (Rubenson and Schuetze 2000). Disturbingly high levels of illiteracy, the asymmetric distribution of learning opportunities, and crises in professional identity are examples of such dilemmas in the emergent knowledge society addressed in subsequent chapters.

Learning for what? From education to knowledge and competence

The simplest of all assumptions is that learning is an unambiguous good, but that somehow this message has failed to get through to enough people. If only we could market it more effectively, almost everyone would come to see that learning pays. Simple propositions are often the most effective and profound, but the policy debate and the accompanying research agenda has had a lot of difficulty in stepping out beyond this rather cloying notion. On the one hand there are structural factors which prevent people from realizing the potential benefits of their learning, such as discrimination in the labour market or cultural attitudes which place a low value on education. On the other, some types of learning have a tremendous and positive impact but others can be inhibiting or actually damaging. Which types are which depends on the learner's context and biography. Retaining young people in formal education may very well fall into the less productive category, inhibiting them from personal or professional development, even if they are gaining formal qualifications, perhaps even at a high level. No one would reject the idea that people learn outside the education system as well as within it, but in practice it is learning within the system that is given all the attention. Could it be otherwise, as Hargreaves explicitly and Healy implicitly suggest it should? Can human capital be effectively measured in ways that go beyond years of schooling or levels of qualification, as Tuijnman proposes in this volume? How can we broaden the scope of analysis – and save education from becoming again the victim of excessive expectation?

We pointed out above that the Clarifying Report had some interesting, if sketchy, things to say about the process of research and knowledge creation. One of the key trends, dramatically accelerated in recent years, has been the way in which the production of recognized knowledge has shifted away from the education sector. There are both material and cultural forces behind this. Universities struggle to compete, nationally or internationally, with the private sector in the recruitment of knowledge-producing staff, and to maintain the technical capacity needed for cutting-edge research (not only in the hard sciences). As a result not only of this but also of wider changes in social attitudes, the status of academic knowledge and its relationship to other knowledge sources has changed.

Intellectually challenging work is being carried out in, and made available from, a much wider range of places than used to be the case. As Terri Kim's chapter demonstrates, moreover, these 'places' are not always physical institutions. The era of the university as the hallmarker of knowledge is waning. A professorial title is a diminishing guarantor of authority – not necessarily because what professors have to say is any less true, but because of the proliferation of alternative sources of information, and because of heightened competition for the attention of consumers of information.

At a more functional level this can be seen in the widespread questioning of qualifications and the trend towards basing these on competence criteria. This is one of the areas that Husén identifies as pivotal for the next quarter-century. As opportunities for learning outside formal education continue to flourish, he sees this as putting increasingly in question what is understood as 'merit' in meritocracies and how it is to be recognized and accredited. As individuals are called on to demonstrate competence in ways that go well beyond the proxies and status conferred by attainment in formal education (completion of high school, the university degree etc.), so will its former monopoly over certification be eroded. This may yet prove to be one of most powerful pressures for educational change, in particular in rethinking the entrenched front-end system.

Literacy and competence

Attention to literacy and competence among adults represents a major shift in the landscape of issues since the Clarifying Report appeared in 1973, even if it has been hard-fought. Major institutional interests are at stake once it is admitted that simply keeping students longer in education is no guarantee that competences will be acquired. The competences that are gained may be rapidly eroded or found to be ill-fitted to a rapidly changing world. Earlier hopes that educational expansion would abolish skills problems simply with the passage of time, as yesterday's students become today's workers and parents, have not materialized. Both Albert Tuijnman and Dan Wagner paint the broad contours of the problem. Tuijnman's data from International Adult Literacy Surveys show *inter alia* how many adults scored at less than Level 3 on prose literacy – an accepted cut-off of low achievement. Of the 24 countries or communities included in Table 14.3, in 13 of them more than half the adults surveyed fell into this category. Wagner argues that, serious though literacy problems are in the OECD countries, they are far worse in the poor countries of the world.

Definitional problems are legion, but such surveys serve the essential purpose of asking about what people can do, not what they are meant to be able to do. At one level, poor literacy can be interpreted, as certain analysts and some sections of the media are wont to do, as a massive indictment of the education system: that despite enormous financial outlays, many leave school or college with few tangible learning gains and a determination never to return. At another level, however, it is confirmation of what the Clarifying Report had predicted many years before. Simply extending the front-end model is neither efficient nor effective in addressing the learning needs of contemporary societies. Far more flexible and individualized pathways are needed, where competence is recognized and accredited in diverse ways, and where a prominent place is given to non-formal and informal as well as formal education.

Despite its growing priority, however, literacy constitutes another major example of how difficult it is to develop a coherent knowledge base. Tuijnman's account of the development of the International Adult Literacy Survey is a singular insider story, which contains a mix of political and technical issues. From economic, social and cultural viewpoints, the case for ensuring that basic skills such as literacy and numeracy are adequately developed looks *prima facie* enormously important. Yet it has been a constant struggle in most countries, to say nothing of internationally, to secure commitment to developing a proper understanding of the reasons and the impact of low basic skills, let alone of how to address the problem. And even when the commitment is there, there are considerable technical problems in assessing the actual levels of apparently quite straightforward concepts such as literacy and numeracy.

The introduction of the notion of technological literacy does nothing to ease the problem – a point made in Dan Wagner's chapter – but, on the contrary, adds another dimension to the complexity of the problem. Do our education systems appropriately reflect the gamut of the differing learning needs of our populations? It is not only the age distribution of access to learning that is skewed, but also the access which different groups have to different forms of learning opportunities.

A key issue is to do with human communication. We are told incessantly that teamwork and communication are key employment competences. But formal qualifications are not the key to this: more education does not necessarily mean more communicative competence. How far are educational institutions really moving away from old traditions of individual, often secretive behaviour (other perhaps than on the sports field) towards genuinely communicative forms of learning? What will the overall 'bilan' or balance sheet of the new communication technologies be in respect of collective communication? There is still a reluctance to confront established educational practice to ask how far it is conducive of key competences that all may agree are important but which do not fit neatly into school and college syllabuses.

Given that the case for lifelong learning is based on the importance of people, skills and knowledge, surprisingly little attention has been paid to the implications for the competences and professional identity of those responsible for delivering learning opportunities. Technological change is having a major impact on modes of delivery. But, as Pierre Caspar observes, it is people who make up systems, and it is they whose roles and competences are challenged. One of Caspar's key phrases is the 'mutualization of competences'. By this he means the sharing of knowledge or expertise, linking to the discussion of social capital by focusing attention on the interdependent relationships that exist between different players in the knowledge game. Caspar goes on to explicate a number of gallic trinities in his analysis of the implications for professionals involved in knowledge activities – such as the roles of administrators, trainer-tutors and experts; or the functions of managing training systems, networking and project management, and specialist technical expertise. His piece is the only one not originally written in English, and it is well worth reflecting, in an era of globalized anglophonia, on how different linguistic constructions affect the structure and dissemination of knowledge, in respect of our understanding of lifelong learning itself as well as more generally.

Measuring human and social capital

The concept of human capital was used from the 1960s onwards to buttress arguments for increased levels of spending on education, and to reinforce the front-end model on the basis that returns to young people's education were higher because dividends were paid over a longer period of time. Lisa Lynch summarizes some of the most salient evidence on the relationships between age, education and earnings. As an economist of education and labour markets and a senior policy adviser in the United States, she knows the value of quantified evidence. She grapples with the relationship between demographic and economic change, and how both employers and employees respond (or do not respond) to this in their propensity to train older workers. Her chapter addresses one aspect of what is now being perceived as one of the biggest challenges to economic and social policy throughout the industrialized world: the ageing of the population. In the learning context, how does this square with lay prejudices about age, intelligence and learning capacity, and with professional economists' calculations about returns to investment. She concludes on the need to capture the variety of investments made in human capital if we are not to generate policy on the basis of what is easy to measure rather than what is necessary to measure.

Martin Carnoy, epitomizing the tradition of evidence-based analysis, provides sweeping evidence on the impact of education on life chances and economic outcomes. Like Lynch, he deploys traditional tools of economic analysis but is equally aware of their limitations, conceptually and politically. Even where concepts such as human capital are relatively well established as tools for thought (Waddington 1977), they have deficiencies that are often ignored. Yet, there are now discernible shifts in the way learning is conceptualized and the policy implications explored, in which the notion of social capital is prominent and the role of social relationships is reaffirmed as critical to the success of education and of economic progress. Carnoy's analysis raises key issues to do with the role of education in promoting, or dissolving, community bonds. In this respect it connects with the notions of bridging and bonding within the social capital literature – the former referring to cross-network and cross-community linkages being forged and the latter to the strengthening of ties within networks and communities.

The introduction of social capital as a key concept is a central shift in thinking about research and policy analysis, and in this case the measurement problems are still more imposing. This is the main theme of Tom Healy's chapter, which charts the thinking behind the publication of the *Well-being of Nations*, another brief OECD volume which may come close to the Clarifying Report in its long-run impact on thinking (OECD 2001c). It espouses social capital as a concept for policy-makers and researchers to run with alongside human capital. Healy accounts for this in terms of the limitations of narrow human capital approaches, causing the shift away from excessively individualistic approaches to knowledge and skill acquisition in order to locate education, and the measurement of its effects, in the wider context of social relationships. It acknowledges the interdependence of the economic and the social. This broadening of perspective is significant, including for our understanding of the notion of lifelong learning and how it should be analysed and promoted, yet we are still far short of an effective set of indicators and measurement instruments. It will be a further major step to blend these into an appropriate process of analysis that recognizes the diversity and the dynamism of lifelong learning.[2]

The notion of social capital is still highly contested, at both the intellectual and the political level, and its operational relevance is still being tested (Baron *et al.* 2000). But there seems little doubt that it has a direct lineage to a different notion of human capital which is closer to the ideas developed in the Clarifying Report than to the narrow economic concept that is commonly associated with this term. It challenges educationalists to move beyond a focus on their own institutions and investment by, and returns to, the individual, and to look as well at the networks and relationships in which learning is embedded.

Organizations and culture – the importance of the 'meso' level
The general issue of the changing character of knowledge generation and use is beyond our remit here (see Gibbons *et al.* 1994). We focus instead on the way knowledge is or may be used to illuminate our understanding of educational practice and policy. (The importance of better understanding the production, mediation and use of knowledge in all sectors including education has also been taken up by CERI in its more recent work (OECD 2000a).) A key feature of many of the contributions is the inclusion of organizations – educational, economic and social – as a meso level of analysis lying between the individual and the broader society.

In his chapter, David Hargreaves offers a theory-based model for school improvement. Hargreaves is demanding about what should count as an effective model – and implicitly critical of many existing claims to theoretical or modelling quality. Unusually, his chapter visibly builds up the model step by step, and offers propositions for testing. Alongside this very explicit approach to modelling, he deploys four master concepts – outcomes, leverage, intellectual capital and social capital – of which all except the first have tended to be left out of conventional models. The challenge posed is to those concerned with the central institution of the formal education system, and is to go beyond prevailing notions of effectiveness and to engage with concepts and issues which have a much wider application. While an organizational focus on schooling itself is not new (see, for example, Handy and Aitken 1986), it challenges us to think of effectiveness and improvement rigorously in terms which go well beyond the usual boundaries.

Recasting the education and work relationship involves a reconsideration of how different activities are valued, and of the way in which people communicate with each other in organizations. Why do we do what we do when we do? What forms of reward do we and others derive from our different activities? How well do we engage in collective as well as individual activity? David Stern addresses one aspect of this clutch of issues head on, by conceiving of education as a form of activity to be considered alongside, and as being of the same order as, other forms of activity, economic and social. His is a broad-brush overview of the interrelationships between different spheres of activity. It turns some of the traditional economistic approaches to education on their head by conceiving of enterprise as itself a fundamental form of learning.

One issue this raises is the pedagogical notion of learning by doing. The effectiveness of existing teaching and learning modes is coming under increasing scrutiny. There is some interest – but not on the same scale – in how more of organized learning, whether by schoolchildren or older students, could be directly integrated with activities which count in the outside world, socially or commercially. 'Social enterprise for learning' encapsulates that. It challenges not only the divisions between learning and work, but also the boundaries between work which is paid for because it serves commercial interests and work which is valued by the community. It therefore raises basic political questions about values, and how far market-driven activities can and should be allowed to dominate the other spheres. These are wholly familiar questions in themselves, but the notion of social enterprise introduces a fresh perspective on them.

How people in organizations learn and how organizations themselves learn is very much the concern of Bill Ford's contribution. Strikingly illustrated, his chapter makes in one sense a familiar case for the integration of learning into organizational thinking. But he allies this with a strong plea for variety in the way this is presented. Explicitly this takes the form of visually re-presenting the case in diagrammatic form; Ford reports that in his extensive experience of working with organizations this mode of representation has done much to give the case for learning purchase on the minds of participants, even sceptical hardhats.

But the line of argument has wider implications, not only for pedagogy and communication but also for notions of collective learning. The idea of 'learning organizations' has become a familiar theme, ever since Senge (1990) published his treatise on the 'fifth discipline'. Ford further consolidates this concept and extends it to include the cultural dimensions that are particularly important in a globalized economy: he sees himself as a 'reflective practitioner' in the Donald Schon mould, and stresses continuous and shared learning as key to organizational learning and success. Ford believes that he has Darwin on his side – only the learning organizations will survive. Yet there seems to us to be no guarantee of this, especially in the globalized economy. In many countries many organizations still depend on low-skill, low-paid work to provide many of us with cheap goods and taken-for-granted services. A major challenge to education as a labour-intensive industry is how to manage the improvements that are achieved elsewhere mainly by technological innovation.

The geopolitical dimension

Globalization and local diversity

A major shift in the world in which lifelong learning is now located, and that in which the Clarifying Report was written, is the pervasive trend of globalization. Technology is generally seen as the major driver behind it, especially in relation to knowledge-based organizations and economies. As Martin Carnoy points out, at the producer level, the capacity of organizations to integrate labour in different parts of the world on a daily basis gives a new sense to the notion of a global division of labour. Information is routinely processed 'overnight' in one hemisphere so that colleagues in the other half can wake up and pick up the threads immediately. For consumers, access to information in massive quantities is instantly available. But this is no lotusland of infinite and costless supply. Dan Wagner's chapter also reminds us that access to ICT (information and communication technology) and to the links that this brings is badly lopsided, globally and even within industrialized societies. Those excluded from the widening circle of access find themselves in far worse positions than before, relative to the rest of the population.

In one sense, OECD and the other international organizations are quintessentially instruments for global cooperation and convergence. They provide common frameworks for the gathering and dissemination of data and information and sometimes for policy prescriptions which are based on the assumption that what seems to work in some countries will apply more widely. But, nations – and units within them – cannot all operate successfully to the same formula. Indeed, given a global division of labour, success comes in part from achieving adequate differentiation. This is a paradox discussed in Donald Hirsch's chapter. The notions of learning regions and learning cities may have some kind of universal appeal, but they depend for their success on those units giving their own distinctive local branding to these notions. Can lifelong learning legitimately be seen as some kind of universal, decontextualized good, or are its forms and its impact only meaningfully analysed in specific cultural contexts?

Terri Kim gives a sharp historical and political science angle to the debate on globalization. She reminds us of the way in which forms of higher education defined according to the traditions of western nations penetrated Pacific Rim countries, and how these are now being overtaken by fresh waves of change. One question here is how far any reverse influence has occurred or might occur: what can western education systems learn from Asia or elsewhere? She argues that the global spread of large-scale higher education can be seen as cultural colonialism, and links this to what might be called the corporatization of higher education. Here the scene is changing fast, with technology and global capital remorseless drivers making education a global business in its own right – although events after 11 September 2001 have shaken many of the underlying financial assumptions about continued growth. What is the role of universities in a drastically changing global environment? Chris Duke believes that they must concentrate on core missions which include social context and service to the community. He sees a double threat from the forces of globalization and competition, fearing that they can lead eventually to fragmentation and what he calls competitive homogenization. Like Ford, he believes that universities are no different from other organizations in that they must learn and develop in order to survive.

Martin Carnoy also addresses the question of how communities are defined within the globalizing process. All three – Kim, Duke and Carnoy – bring sharply into focus the changing context within which enormously diverse institutions of higher education are having to define their goals and priorities. Carnoy's analysis of higher education developments is very broad, covering ethnicity, gender and religion in an international context. He conveys acutely the jagged dynamics of educational growth, as some but by no means all groups benefit from expansion, within and between countries. Technology is indeed a massive promoter of knowledge-based employment, but this does not mean that people who attain given levels of education will secure employment of the kind which used to be associated with the use of the head rather than the hand. The loss of local context and culture – which is more than just local colour and vernacular – is particularly worrying when we know that all knowledge is socially and culturally constructed and best learned in the context with which the learner is familiar.

Making lifelong learning policy for global knowledge societies?
The arguments about the nature and difficulties of making policy, especially in the knowledge of growing complexity and interdependence, coalesce broadly around the unending struggle between analysis and prescription based on evidence and logic, on the one hand, and inertia and dominant interests on the other. Kallen identifies the view surfacing in the swell of international interest in lifelong learning thirty years ago that, 'policy-making had become an activity based on rational-scientific analysis rather than a more "political" ideological undertaking'. But since then, the heyday of educational planning has come and gone, and the limits of science-based decision-making remain daunting.

One question is how much research has been driven by what is most easily available to measure, as Lynch observes; another is how far policy has then built on the research. We can note without undue cynicism that the relatively low level of the second to some extent counterbalances the high level of the first. This raises the perennial issue of the relationship between knowledge and power, and specifically the use of social sciences research by policy-makers. The relationship has been recast in the three decades since the Clarifying Report was written, especially in the light of the shifting boundary between public and private spheres, but remains even more pertinent today. It is fundamentally to do with control, and with the values which permeate educational provision.

Policies and practice can change for a number of reasons. Arguably, effective change has been limited by the absence of strong, articulated models for improvement, at institutional or policy level. The knowledge base of much educational thinking has been only patchily developed and applied. Hargreaves cogently argues, at least as regards schools, that they have lacked a well-developed evidence base with which to inform practice, and the organizational and professional structures within which that knowledge can be applied. The relationship between evidence and policy is nevertheless an uncertain one, which is why certain authors, such as Hirsch and Papadopoulos, focus strongly on learning *culture* – complex compounds of history, values and structures that defy reduction to simple measures and policy levers.

If change is difficult within education systems, what scope is there for policies that influence the employment sector so that the returns to education can be more equitably distributed, at different levels and across different groups? One problem is that where markets are heavily internationalized the policy levers available to nation states are weakened, at least in their capacity to bring about precise distributive results. For educational institutions, a major question is how far they see themselves as operating in a national or international rather than regional or local contexts. Globalization and corporatization give a wholly new complexion to the debate about curriculum – including the hidden curriculum.

It is no coincidence that the discourse on lifelong learning has flourished most at the international level, detached from the structures of power and decision-making that dominate national systems. It can be described as an international concept that increasingly strikes chords in national arenas, but it is not clear that either the policy channels or sufficient consensus of purpose exists in many countries to translate the enthusiasm into coherent action. Papadopoulos's contribution sounds warning bells about the extent to which recurrent education or lifelong learning may in reality (though not in rhetoric) be allocated a residual role in national policy-making – scooping up all the bits that do not fit into conventional categories in order to give an impression of policy coherence. The bells are not sounded cynically, although it may be so interpreted by conspiracy-minded readers.

It is not a matter of simply pitting the forces of enlightenment against conspiratorial irrationality, but the stubborn, almost banal difficulty of bringing about change at systemic as well as institutional levels. It applies with particular force to lifelong learning, as this is conceived to take place in much more diverse, complex, often informal settings than any single 'system', for which the agencies of change are highly diffused. If systemic change has been elusive in schools, as Hargreaves argues, how much more elusive is it in knowledge societies as a whole. Earlier we argued that progress has been made in understanding lifelong learning by the growing focus on the organizational and 'meso' levels, rather than either the overly-individualized or overly-socialized perspectives of micro and macro analysis. The challenge now remains of reintroducing these insights into broader models of change, which can 'scale up' local and network innovation.

Sweden: paradigm or peculiar?

Jarl Bengtsson's native Sweden has undoubtedly been at the forefront of much of the new thinking about educational policy over the past decades. It is arguably a nation *par excellence* possessing the elusive qualities that allow for society-wide consensus on change to emerge. Papadopoulos characterizes Sweden as the exemplification of learning and training culture, and Hirsch singles out its distinctive tradition of study circles, relying on informal and voluntary endeavour rather than policy design. There is sometimes a tendency for outside observers of any country to romanticize achievements, though as Tuijnman describes in his chapter, Sweden has scored remarkably highly across all the dimensions on which the adult literacy has been tested internationally. There are thus objective reasons for taking note of the Swedish example. The Swedes, moreover, are known for their willingness to engage in international policy debate – and not necessarily as straightforward proselytizers of their own practice.

Kjell Rubenson's chapter gives a detailed historical account of the twists and turns in the Swedish policy story, seen from his semi-exile position on west coast Canada. The account is typically political in tone. The context within which educational policy is forged is an ideological one. This is more explicit in the Swedish context than in most cases – somewhat ironically, given the relatively high level of consensus that prevails there. It reminds us that governmental values shape policy, and to some extent articulate the values of the wider society. In many countries relationships between the governing classes and the mass media now tend to be particularly mistrustful and stressed, so that such articulation may not always be straightforward, but the role of policy-makers in laying down the values and benefits of learning should not be dismissed. The politics reaches into the workplace: with its Scandinavian sisters Sweden has pushed forward thinking on healthy working conditions, including mental health. But the politics extends well beyond this, to basic questions of power and democracy.[3]

Yet while the particular tradition that anchors learning so firmly in Swedish culture is stressed by several authors in this volume, the long-term trend might be one in which it is converging to a sort of OECD norm. Rubenson describes how, over the past forty years, the very distinctive popular adult education sector has not fared as successfully as either formal education, or, most especially, employer-sponsored activities.

It is thus not clear that the example of Sweden is a paradigm in the sense of offering a universal model. What it does is embody at a higher level the boldness that the Clarifying Report proposed. Swedish policy and ideology, at least for long periods, espoused redistribution of time, money and power to an extent not seen elsewhere and – most significantly for us – in ways which at least partly fashioned links between these three forms. They may not yet have entirely succeeded, but they have tried more than most.

Our aim in this introductory chapter has been to give some perspective to the continuing debate on lifelong learning. We have identified challenges thrown down thirty years ago that have still not been met and have traced lines of conceptual and policy development opening up new directions. It is, we acknowledge, a perspective heavily shaped by the OECD agenda; we leave it to the reader to decide how far that has constrained our analysis. We have argued, above all, that the lifelong learning agenda not only is not accomplished, particularly for the many who never really start out on a learning career; but is still to be addressed in its most radical form, of restriking the balance in the distribution of learning throughout people's lives.

Notes

1. The Organization for Economic Cooperation and Development (OECD) is a major intergovernmental organization, established in 1961 and based in Paris. Originally established after World War II as the Organization for European Economic Cooperation to administer the Marshall Plan, its members comprise the world's most advanced industrialized countries. It draws on work done by its own secretariat, officials in its member states and by individual analysts, collecting data and providing policy-related analysis and advice on a wide range of fields, from basic economic policy to environment, energy and social affairs. It has worked on education and learning since the early 1960s, and the Centre for Educational Research and Innovation (CERI) was established in 1968.
2. In the UK, a recently established Wider Benefits of Learning Research Centre is grappling with both this kind of issue, and how to relate different types of learning to different types of social benefit such as better physical and mental health, higher levels of civic engagement or improved quality of life (Schuller *et al.* 2000).
3. It is appropriate here to refer to another of Jarl Bengtsson's Swedish mentors, Gosta Rehn. He spelt out a clear case for the redistribution of time over people's lives and put forward ambitious schemes for the reform of social security as well as work-life practices to allow this to happen, including education and training in the equation (see e.g. Rehn, 1983). His ideas maintain their relevance today, when demographic changes are more apparent, and when 'work-life balance' is a common theme (see also Milner and Wadensjö, 2001).

References

Baron, S., Field, J. and Schuller, T. (eds) (2000) *Social Capital: Critical Perspectives*. Oxford: Oxford University Press.

Coffield, F. (ed.) (2000) *Differing Visions of a Learning Society*. Bristol: Policy Press.

European Commission (1996) *Teaching and Learning: Towards the Learning Society*, White Paper on education and training. Brussels: European Commission.

Gibbons, M., Limoges, C., Nowotny, H. *et al.* (1994) *The New Production of Knowledge: The Dynamics of Science and Research in Contemporary Societies*. London: Sage Publications.

Handy, C. and Aitken, R. (1986) *Understanding Schools as Organisations*. London: Pelican.

Illich, I. (1971) *Deschooling Society*. New York: Harper & Row.

Milner, H. and Wadensjö, E. (eds) (2001), *Gösta Rehn, the Swedish Model and Labour Market Policies: International and National Perspectives*. Aldershot: Aldgate.

OECD (1973) *Recurrent Education: A Strategy for Lifelong Learning*. Paris: OECD.

OECD (1987) *Adults in Higher Education*. Paris: OECD.

OECD (1996) *Lifelong Learning for All*. Paris: OECD.

OECD (2000a) *Knowledge Management in the Learning Society*. Paris: OECD.

OECD (2000b) *From Initial Education to Working Life: Making Transitions Work*. Paris: OECD.

OECD (2001a) *What Schools for the Future?* Paris: OECD.

OECD (2001b) *Education at a Glance: OECD Indicators*. Paris: OECD.

OECD (2001c) *The Well-being of Nations: The Role of Human and Social Capital.* Paris: OECD.

Rehn, G. (1983) Individual drawing rights, in H. Levin and H.G. Schuetze (eds) *Financing Recurrent Education: Strategies for Increasing Employment, Job Opportunities, and Productivity.* Beverly Hills: Sage.

Rubenson, K. and Schuetze, H.G. (2000) Lifelong learning for the knowledge society: demand, supply, and policy dilemmas, in K. Rubenson and H.G. Schuetze (eds) *Transition to the Knowledge Society: Policies and Strategies for Individual Participation and Learning*, pp. 355–76. Vancouver: UBC (Institute for European Studies).

Schuetze, H.G. (1992) Paid educational leave through legislation and collective bargaining, in A. Tuijnman (ed.) *International Encyclopedia of Adult Education and Training*, pp. 303–10. Oxford: Pergamon.

Schuetze, H.G. and Slowey, M. (eds) (2000) *Higher Education and Lifelong Learners: International Perspectives on Change.* London: Routledge/Falmer.

Schuller, T. (1999) Educational leave in a lifetime working-hours policy, in J-Y. Boulin and R. Hoffman (eds) *New Paths in Working Time Policy*, pp. 159–80. Brussels: European Trade Union Institute.

Schuller, T., Field, J. and Baron, S. (2000) Social capital: a review and critique, in S. Baron, J. Field and T. Schuller (eds) *Social Capital: Critical Perspectives*, pp. 1–38. Oxford: Oxford University Press.

Schuller, T., Bynner, J., Green, A. *et al.* (2001) *Modelling and Measuring the Wider Benefits of Learning.* London: Institute of Education.

Senge, P. (1990) *The Fifth Dimension: The Art and Practice of the Learning Organisation.* London: Century Books.

UNESCO (1972) *Learning To Be* (Faure Report). Paris: UNESCO.

UNESCO Commission on Education for the Twenty-first Century (1996) *Learning: The Treasure from Within* (Delors Report). Paris: UNESCO.

Waddington, C.H. (1977) *Tools for Thought.* St Albans: Paladin.

Part 1

Historical Reflections on
Policy-making

Part

2

Education in 2000 and 2025:
Looking Back to the Future

Torsten Husén

Introduction – the future then and now

One of the advantages of being an old professor with more than half a century in the social sciences – and you must be grateful for these advantages when they come along – is that you may have the possibility to verify your predictions about the future by being there when it arrives. The readiness to see advances into the future was typical of the *zeitgeist* of the 1960s. I was commissioned by the Swedish National Board of Education in the late 1960s to run a study which was published under the title 'Education in the Year 2000' (Husén 1971a).[1] With these reflections fresh in my mind, I gave the Peter Sandiford Memorial Lectures at the Ontario Institute of Education in Toronto on present trends and future developments, and it is on these I draw specifically in summarizing how the future looked to me then (Husén 1971b). As so much of my work has been devoted to studying the school in western societies, I will focus particularly on this level of education.

The first of the three lectures dealt with the purpose of futurological studies in education, in which I emphasized the need to identify the medium- and long-term consequences of contemporary policy decisions. I stressed in particular that it is important to consider what *could* happen in the future – 'possible futures' or *futuribles* as these are known in France – rather than focus exclusively on what *should* happen. While normative visions are an essential part of shaping worthwhile futures, we need also to consider what plausibly may happen based on actual trends. Not only does this provide a much firmer base with which to shape our visions; it helps to clarify whether contemporary developments are working at cross-purposes with the futures we want to see unfold.

Looking back on my forecasts, I am not sure how well I followed my own advice. I, like others, may have been tempted by an over-optimistic view of the future both for the economy and society, on the one hand, and for education, on the other – emphasizing positive features that would need to be strengthened rather than looking at the trends with a colder analytical eye. Certain predictions turned out to be well wide of the mark, though others have stood the test of time. In offering in conclusion of the chapter some ideas on how education might be in another quarter of a century from now, the rather sobering exercise of scrutinizing my earlier predictions leads me to present these as open questions for the future rather than as confident forecasts.

The year 2000 viewed 30 years ago – economy and society . . .

The analysis in the 1971 Peter Sandiford Memorial Lectures began with trends and assumptions about the development of the industrial, and increasingly post-industrial, western society at large. The following eight assumptions summarized the world at the new millennium as I saw it then:

- Economic growth will offer opportunities for increased consumption in different respects (better material standards, more leisure, more education and more cultural participation).
- The process of change will accelerate in such essential respects as the manufacture of goods and the provision of services.
- Greater international exposure is to be expected by virtue of the increased use of the mass media and more extensive travel.
- An accelerating flow of information will have to be coped with, both on the production side (scientific research) and on the distribution side (mass media, computer technology).
- Gainful employment as a means of obtaining life's necessities will become increasingly unimportant. An overabundance of goods and services in the highly industrialized countries will be made available to the masses.
- There will be a marked increase in the influence of experts, with a tendency towards meritocracy.
- Increased pluralism will be experienced, at least for a transitional period, as regards life outlooks and values.
- It will be increasingly difficult to maintain a balance between the ecological system and technology (owing to pollution and man's ravages of nature).

Certain of these assumptions have, I believe, survived well the passage of time. The burgeoning production of information, and the need to cope with overload, have indeed become critical issues. Growing ecological problems and the importance of sustainability, anticipated 30 years ago, are a very recognizable part of today's world of global warming, Rio and Kyoto Summits, and so forth. The assumption of the increasing influence of 'experts' was broadly on target as various studies have charted the continued growth of 'knowledge workers' in our societies, even if it begs questions such as who 'experts' are, the organizations they work for, how their knowledge is communicated and legitimated, etc.

The acceleration of change, the marked increase in levels of consumption levels, and the growth of pluralism contingent on international movements of population – all listed above – were also justified assumptions, but they are examples where we were possibly guilty of over-optimism. Whatever the many benefits of higher standards of living and consumption, for instance, affluence has brought its own 'problems' of sustainability just as it has been a 'solution' of want. Nor have growing consumption levels been associated with any direct increase in measured happiness (Inglehart 1997). And, while I was focusing specifically on western post-industrial societies in my 1971 lectures, we cannot now ignore, as perhaps we were tempted to do then, the yawning and widening gaps between the richest and poorest in the world.[2] The economic change we assumed in 1971 would continue to accelerate may be a sign of dynamism, but it also brings insecurity and exclusion for those left behind by the processes of change. Greater ethnic and cultural diversity may foster a spirit of pluralism, but our recent world experiences are replete with reminders that it may also strengthen xenophobia and narrow nationalism. So, even if certain of these predictions were broadly on target, we may have underestimated the problems they would bring with them.

In certain other important respects, the assumptions I made about society at large proved to be wide of the mark. At the end of the 1960s, after a decade of spectacular growth on both sides of the Atlantic, it was generally assumed that this would go on uninhibited for the foreseeable future and that gainful employment of goods and services would be plentiful. Only a few years later, however, the oil crisis and 'stagflation' had occurred, and in the 1980s and early 1990s mass unemployment became a major problem in many countries. The confident prediction of decline in the importance of gainful employment has not occurred either, except in the life cycle sense whereby more time tends to be spent in education at the beginning of people's lives and more in retirement (often in relative affluence) during the later years. Alternative mechanisms to distribute societal rewards have not taken the place of gainful employment: the problems confronting those in our knowledge societies who are outside or on the margins of the job market are now, if anything, even more visible than before.

There were other assumptions that were importantly missing. We did not say anything about demography, especially fertility and birth rates, which so strongly affect educational planning and financing, and the burden shouldered by the working generation in providing the means for the rest, including those in school. For instance, by 1999 the proportion of under-15s had fallen to less than one in five of the total population in 22 of the 30 OECD countries, with only Mexico and Turkey significantly above; in 1960, in no OECD country was it as low as this (OECD 2001). Nothing was said about the role of the family, in particular about its relationships with the school as an institution. Thirty years ago we did not realize the extent of the change in the structure and function of the family that was imminent. The 'normal' household with two adults and one or several children is today not the most frequent one. The number of mothers with children of school age working outside the home has, in some countries, trebled or quadrupled since the late 1950s, with divorces rocketing similarly. This has had important repercussions on the school which, despite lacking relevant resources, is expected to shoulder more responsibility for taking care of children in ways that extend well beyond teaching them certain cognitive competences. We did not foresee just how significant this would be by the year 2000.

. . . and education and learning

As regards future educational systems, we made a variety of assumptions. We predicted that education in the year 2000 would be a lifelong process, with far-reaching implications for both formal and informal education. The institution labelled 'school' and associated with youth would not be able to provide the fare on which people could subsist for the rest of their lives. Education would not be bounded by the clear 'cut-offs' it had been in the past – beginning with an entrance test and ending with the near-dramatic climax of a secondary school examination or university degree. It would become a much more continuous process, both as regards access and participation over time and its integration as part of the other functions of life. Formal education of the type that had conventionally been available in schools would, as it became accessible to many more persons, become more meaningful and relevant to learners.

In this process, education would take on a more informal character. In addition to multimedia 'learning centres', facilities would be provided for learning at home and at work by means of computer terminals. To an ever increasing extent, education would come to depend on large supporting organizations or systems. These, whether public or private, would be needed to produce systems of teaching aids, information processing and multimedia instructional materials. The information systems involved would consist of tried-and-tested storage and retrieval components, and one of their main challenges would prove to be in creating 'compatibility' between the medium and the receiver.

We identified the importance of creating the broadest frame of reference in terms of knowledge, skills and attitudes, given the risks to democracy of information becoming increasingly specialized leading to rule by experts alongside alienation of the many. With a growing premium placed by society on scientific research and advanced education, so would there be a strengthening of meritocracy. The development of communications skills would need to be a very high priority so that as many citizens as possible would be able to speak the same language and understand one another. The school would have to prepare its pupils to live in a pluralistic society, meaning *inter alia* the development of their ability to be selective on the basis of criteria of authenticity. Schooling for internationalism, and the demise of educational provincialism, would be prerequisites for world survival.

Education must address the balance between the ecological system and technology, and hence the whole complex of problems relating to pollution and the wanton destruction of natural resources.

In order to establish common values and frames of reference, initial educational provision would need to take the form of a common liberal schooling, with vocational specialization to follow only much later. Basic schooling ought to lay the groundwork for relearning – learning to learn – by providing a sound basic repertoire of skills and the ability to assimilate further knowledge. It should go further than this by instilling openness to change, a flexible attitude and a willingness to continue one's education. It should convey the realization that the whole lifespan will be one long continuation school. Schooling should be a preparation for life in which gainful employment and recreation (in the traditional sense) decline in importance and in which 'work' is increasingly self-realization. Schooling will be necessary for the ability to live as an independent individual, without necessarily relying on some primary group, such as the family, for support. We predicted the necessity for schools to build skills to deal with the torrential flow of information if people are not to be swept away by it; skills which include computer literacy and general technology.

Again, I believe the predictions and prescriptions from that time have enjoyed a mixed track record. The value of lifelong learning we so emphasized 30 years ago is very familiar in the rhetoric of today's policy discourse. But beyond the rhetoric, how far have we come? I believe we correctly anticipated the growing part played by informal education in its manifold guises – in some countries the expenditures made today by enterprises on knowledge and worker competence are of similar magnitude to outlays on the public system of education itself – but we went too far in predicting lifelong learning as the norm by 2000.

We were surely on target in identifying the growing importance of ICT (information and communication technology), the potential of new media and support systems, and the need to tackle 'information overload'. But, did we place undue faith in the power of technology itself to provide the answers? We had, for instance, surprisingly little to say about teachers and the other professionals responsible for learning. And, despite the undoubted importance of ICT, has it yet changed the fundamental culture of education institutions? Probably not, for we underestimated the sheer inertia of the dominant models of schools and were unduly optimistic about their capacity to embrace new values – such as flexibility, tolerance and 'learning to learn' – into their core business.

We did not foresee the institutional crisis that gradually hit the public sector in the industrialized countries, which was not only financial in origin but also the result of enormous growth, bureaucratization and loss of close human contacts. Whatever the merits of developing autonomy in people to cope with rapid change and mobility (in 1971 we had advocated that individuals be prepared to live independently from primary groups such as families), at that time we seriously underestimated the social aspects of schooling, and what came to be called 'social capital'. Schooling increasingly took place in 'pedagogical factories', as units merged into larger ones and as big-city pathologies moved within school walls. The revision of my 1960s optimism to reflect this had already taken place by 1979 (Husén 1979), in the study I jointly wrote for OECD/CERI with Jim Coleman in the mid-1980s (OECD 1985), and the Academia Europaea study published in 1992 (Husén *et al.* 1992).

Schooling in 2025

A major challenge for schooling over the next couple of decades will be how to balance the tasks and responsibilities between, on the one side, the informal settings of the home, community, enterprise, ICT and so forth, and, on the other, the formal institutions of school and pre-school. How to achieve a proper balance between collective and individual endeavours in educating the young? What kinds of balances should we seek between learning for cognitive competence and expertise, for values and attitudes, and for social purposes generally, and how should responsibilities divide in striking these balances between the formal and informal settings? And, if further strides are really to be made in the direction of lifelong learning, what will be the specific role of schools in contributing to this? The questions themselves may not be new, but fresh solutions will emerge as informal education grows and lifelong learning spreads more widely.

In moving towards new solutions, I would like to single out three areas that deserve close attention. First, we have already seen major shifts away from the pursuit of equality of educational opportunity, if not of results, since the 1960s. As new relations are forged between the school, the home and the community, will this lead back towards greater equity and equality through a stronger emphasis on the social goals of education? Or will it instead widen inequalities as those with favoured home and community environments forge ahead? Sadly, more meritocracy can lead directly to more inequality as those with a favourable start (genetically or socially) profit from their advantage, with an 'underclass' left behind in a competitive knowledge society. Equality and equity issues are thus just as relevant in the early part of the twenty-first century as they were post-World War II.

Second, while the march towards meritocracy may continue, burgeoning opportunities for learning outside formal education may well cause searching questions to be asked about the meaning of 'merit' and how it is to be recognized and accredited. Increasingly, individuals may be called on to demonstrate competence in ways that go well beyond the proxies and status conferred by attainment in formal education (completion of high school, the university degree etc.) As the monopoly formally enjoyed by the education system over the certification of merit declines, where does this leave the school? It is just possible that it will become reinvigorated, if it is able to focus especially on socialization into culture and preparation for life and learning rather than trying to do everything.

Finally, recasting the relationships between formal and informal education, and the spread of lifelong learning, increases the complexity of policy-making. Who is responsible for social decisions when so many different agencies are involved? The unbridled market is not the answer, especially to address the problems confronting the 'underclass'. But neither is the bureaucracy of large public bodies that failed to deliver in the 1970s and 1980s. These questions are already acutely relevant today. They are likely to become critical over the next quarter century.

Notes

1. Later in the 1970s, the Aspen Institute for Humanistic Studies invited me to undertake another study: 'School as an institution and its future in western societies', which resulted in six seminars on both sides of the Atlantic and the book *The School in Question*, published in 1979 by Oxford University Press. A further taskforce that I chaired was for the Academia Europaea; this was published as *Schooling in Modern European Society* in 1992.
2. The inequality between the rich and poor countries of the world has been widening at an alarming rate as summarized by Jolly (2000). He refers to modestly growing inequalities over the first half of the twentieth century, that quickened and then soared after 1960: 'from 30 to 1 in 1960 to 60 to 1 in 1990 and 74 to 1 at present'.

References

Husén, T. (1971a) *Utbildning ar 2000 [Education in the Year 2000]: En framstidsstudie*. Stockholm: Bonniers [published in six languages].

Husén, T. (1971b) *Present Trends and Future Developments in Education: A European Perspective*, The Peter Sandiford Memorial Lectures, no. 8, occasional papers. Toronto: Ontario Institute for Studies in Education.

Husén, T. (1979) *The School in Question: A Comparative Study of the School and its Future in Western Societies*. London: Oxford University Press.

Husén, T., Tuijnman, A. and Halls, W.D. (eds) (1992) *Schooling in Modern European Society: A Report of the Academia Europaea*. Oxford: Pergamon Press.

Inglehart, R. (1997) *Modernisation and Post-modernisation: Cultural, Economic and Political Change in 43 Societies*. Princeton: Princeton University Press.

Jolly, R. (2000) Global inequality, human rights and the challenge for the 21st century, in *The Creative Society of the 21st Century*. Paris: OECD.

OECD (1985) *Becoming Adult in a Changing World*, report prepared for OECD/CERI by J.S. Coleman and T. Husén. Paris: OECD.

OECD (2001) *OECD in Figures: Statistics on the Member Countries*. Paris: OECD.

3

Lifelong Learning Revisited

Denis Kallen

This chapter explores the history of lifelong learning as it has been promoted by the three international organizations that have been most responsible for its development: Council of Europe, UNESCO and OECD.

The history of an idea

Learning has been a lifelong activity ever since humanity has existed, or even since the earliest origin of living beings. In its institutionalized form, it is of recent origin. Organized lifelong learning was given a strong impetus by the nineteenth-century industrial revolution with its aftermath of social and cultural upheaval. But there is another, less often mentioned root: the evolution of civil society towards democratic participation and self-management, spurred by a tidal wave of political unrest and protest against domination, whether from above or abroad. Denmark in the nineteenth century showed the way, and under the leadership of Grundvig gave birth to lifelong learning for participatory democracy. These two origins determined the conceptualization and development of lifelong learning over the next century. Although they have to some extent blended, they still represent two distinct strands of thinking concerning the purpose of lifelong learning and its role in community and society.

General awareness of the need for national and international policies for the development of lifelong learning dates from the period immediately after World War II. Postwar economic reconstruction of national economies and the spectacular development of science and technology impelled larger firms to offer in-house training opportunities. Parallel to this, a rapid expansion of socio-culturally oriented adult education took place, most of it initiated by private and communal initiative, but often also supported by public money. It took some time before the public and private actors realized that vocationally oriented further training provided only a partial answer to the new needs for qualified personnel and the updating of the competences of the existing labour force. It took more time before it was recognized that the above two currents basically served the same purpose, that of enabling the individual to participate fully in social, political and economic life on his/her own terms. Nevertheless, culturally and socio-politically oriented lifelong/adult education continued on the whole to follow its own course, catering mostly for other clienteles than work-oriented programmes. It usually did not lead to recognized qualifications and was almost allergic to the whiff of prescribed curricula, examinations or any other restrictive influence. Only in the postwar years could a certain *rapprochement* be noticed here and there – for example, in the German *Volkshochschulen*, courses leading to vocational qualifications were no longer systematically excluded.

The rapid growth of initial education and training generated another incentive for reshaping and rethinking lifelong learning. In itself, it generated massive new demands for further learning. But, it also soon became obvious that initial education alone, owing to its slow pace of innovation, could not meet the growing demand for qualified personnel. In addition, the knowledge and competences acquired in school needed to be renewed and brought up to date at a rapidly increasing pace.

The expansion of initial education was, however, accompanied by a disconcerting degree of failure, grade repeating and drop-out, particularly among the newly recruited pupils from less advantaged social groups. One of the main arguments for investment in initial education had been that it would create more educational and social equality. On this score, however, the performance of educational systems was persistently disappointing. The need for 'second chance' education and training came to be generally recognized and soon a wide variety of such programmes appeared. Literacy courses were offered to large numbers of those with basic and functional literacy problems, secondary education programmes provided for adult learners, and 'open universities' were created in many countries.

A further stimulus to national policy came from the policy-making scene itself. Policy-making had become an activity based on rational-scientific analysis rather than a more 'political' ideological undertaking. Systems analysis and planning had made their entrance in ministries, and parliaments tended to follow, though not always whole-heartedly. The many earlier, uncoordinated and unregulated initiatives in the domain of lifelong learning fell well short of the newly elaborated criteria for 'rational-empirical' policy-making. A climate had thus emerged that was favourable to the more articulate national policies for lifelong learning. The international organizations responded each in their own way to this need, in line with their specific mandates and clienteles. At the same time, however, the concepts and paradigms for lifelong learning that they developed responded to their own needs as organizations, for coherence and systematization of their programmes in the various sectors covered by their mandates.

The three major concepts

The main concepts and policy guidelines that were put forward by the Council of Europe, the OECD and UNESCO all originated in the 1960s. Each of these organizations had, of course, its own agenda, and the concepts and paradigms that were put forward reflected their particularities. In retrospect, however, the differences were more of tactics and strategies to be followed than they were inspired by different philosophies. It was agreed across all three that initial education and training needed to be followed by lifelong opportunities accessible to all citizens, irrespective of their social or economic status or by such conditions as gender or age.

It was also generally thought that the existing programmes of lifelong learning should be integrated in a future 'system', but one in which a large place would be given to new initiatives, to non-traditional approaches, and to new contents and methods. The programmes should in this respect have more in common with those that had already been put in place in the world of work and in the culture–leisure sector, and be much less subject to the standardizing and constraining regulations common in initial education. Contrary to the current practice in lifelong and adult education and training, the state would be given a significant role in policy-making, financing and quality control and create the necessary conditions for the basic goals to be attained.

The Council of Europe had already placed '*education permanente*' at the centre of its educational and cultural programmes in the 1960s: 'the introduction of the general theme of permanent education during the CCC's [Council for Cultural Cooperation] general policy debate in 1966 marked a turning point in the history of educational policy within the Council of Europe framework' (Council of Europe 1970: 9). The Council had in the past rather unsuccessfully attempted to accelerate the harmonization and adaptation of traditional education systems. Permanent education was considered to be 'a fundamentally new and comprehensive concept' to attain ambitions considered beyond the reach of initial education; 'an overall educational pattern capable of meeting the rapidly increasing and ever more diversified needs of every individual in the new European society.' Three principles were to guide this Council policy: equalization, participation and globalization.

In UNESCO, much importance was attached to the potential of lifelong education to reduce the rapidly widening gap between the education of the younger and the older generations. Many of its member countries had largely illiterate adult populations. Democracy and economic development required that at least a majority of them be equipped with a minimum of knowledge and competence. Furthermore, lifelong learning would, it was thought, offer a common frame of activities for the Organization's cultural, educational and socio-cultural programmes that had hitherto followed separate agendas.

In *Learning To Be* (UNESCO 1972), prepared under the chairmanship of Edgar Faure, the philosophy of the new policy was brilliantly elaborated, though the Faure Report, as it became known, had been preceded by others outlining contours of the new approach. Lengrand's 1970 *Introduction to Lifelong Education* in particular had described the 'new humanism' that was to guide UNESCO's lifelong learning policy, paving the way to a more humane world order, peace, and universal tolerance and understanding.

The OECD's 'recurrent education' paradigm (OECD 1973) had, in one way, a more modest thrust in political and socio-cultural terms as it focused primarily on the relevant educational and economic issues. But it did not eschew the underlying social and political problems, in particular those of equality and social justice. And, it was more ambitious in its proposed reform strategy than its Council of Europe and UNESCO counterparts. Its subtitle, 'a strategy for lifelong learning', is in this respect deceptive. Recurrent education referred to all education, initial as well as lifelong or for adults. Its main aim is to assign to them their place in a global strategy of recurrence.

This would require a profound modification of initial education. The ever lengthening period of initial education needed to be reversed, given ample proof of its ineffectiveness in spite of ever rising costs. The school was, in Coleman's terms, 'information-rich but action-poor', and alternation between school and work or other social activity should become the main principle of the new education policy. All forms and levels of education and training would be brought under a single policy-making framework. One of the main benefits would be a better response of education and training to the economic and socio-cultural needs of society and of the individual. A vigorous plea was also made for paid educational leave, to be guaranteed by relevant legislation. Together with the recurrence principle, the leave issue proved to be one of the most controversial proposals of the report.

Over 30 years have passed since these international policy concepts were proposed. During this period, a fourth international organization, the European Commission (EC), came to play an important role in terms of implementing the proposed strategies, or at least aspects of them. But, contrary to the three other organisations, the EC has not yet put forward a new paradigm or proposed a coherent and comprehensive strategy for lifelong learning (but see below). Some would say it is not its mission to do so.

Policies for lifelong learning

The necessity of lifelong learning in modern society has in the past three decades become widely recognized, by policy-makers, by the 'world of work' and by public opinion. The developments that led to the early policy concepts have since gained pace and intensity. Lifelong learning activities have enjoyed a spectacular development in terms of programmes offered and participant numbers. To this extent, the high expectations of the past have been met. EC data showed that in spring 1994, 16.7 per cent of all 15–64 year olds took part in lifelong learning programmes. However, the figures for the age-groups above 25 are much lower. Of the 35–64 year olds, only 2.9 per cent participated. Furthermore, rates differed strongly between countries, with Denmark at the top and Greece at the bottom (Davis 1996: 33–4).

Surprisingly, there was little difference between female and male rates of participation, and among the younger people the economically inactive showed much higher rates than the active, probably due to the many retraining programmes for the younger 'risk groups'. Also, the part-time employed participated more than their full-time equivalents. Sector of activity was important: the highest rates occurred in the service sector and the lowest in agriculture. Occupational level also proved to be an important variable.

Among the basic policy goals that have not been attained is that of 'recurrence' – the essential element of the OECD concept. No attempt has been made to impose alternation between periods of education and of work or other social activity, at the completion of compulsory education. The period of uninterrupted initial learning has grown unceasingly. In the 1990s, the average time that 5-year-olds could in most developed countries expect to stay in school increased by another two years and there is no reason to suppose it will not further increase. Implementing the 'recurrence' concept would have met with strong opposition and required far-reaching changes and innovations, not only in the educational system, but also in employment practice and qualification systems.

Another essential goal of the earlier models was not attained either: creating a comprehensive education and training system covering all learning, initial and lifelong, school- and out-of-school-based. Neither the schools nor the universities (with very few exceptions) offered places to 'second chance' or other lifelong learning adults alongside those for their traditional clienteles. In particular, the universities missed the opportunity to reorganize their teaching so as to make real 'recurrence' possible and to open their doors to a new clientele (Kallen 1980). Not that this goal of an all-inclusive educational service (or system) was clearly formulated in the earlier lifelong learning concepts. Its implementation would have required at least a close coordination between all forms and places of learning and a policy-making structure that would cover all of them.

Implementing lifelong learning policies would also have demanded a strong commitment in public policy-making to regulating and financing lifelong education. This would have raised the sensitive issue of public versus private initiative and of public control and financing. On the whole, governments have not directly tackled this question, leaving the private sector mainly to manage its own programmes, while the state has reduced its activity and interference. Over time, by means of educational leave of absence and the financing of courses out of company funds, the amount of money available for work-related lifelong learning has increased spectacularly, whereas public money and initiative has progressively been reallocated in favour of special needs and specific groups, to the detriment of a great part of traditional 'liberal' adult education.

One overriding conclusion emerges: the lifelong learning idea has been fully implemented in as much as its economic dimension is concerned, but this has largely been to the detriment of the other dimensions (Kallen 1996). Moreover, the safeguards that were included in the most pointedly economic concept – OECD's recurrent education – have only very partially been put in place. On the whole, lifelong education nowadays leads to more inequality. It mainly benefits those who are already the 'winners' in the game for desirable and stable jobs and good incomes. It has become a powerful and willing instrument in the hands of the neo-liberal economy that it provides with a qualified, available and flexible workforce. It has also eagerly adopted the rules and practices of the globalized economy and it ensures the transferability of skills and competences across national borders and continents (see Preston 1999).

Unfortunately, not all abilities, competences and skills serve this purpose. A clear hierarchy has emerged between the profitable, innovatory and 'international' occupations and those that are in these respects on the losing side. The former have generous access to qualifying lifelong learning programmes, most of them financed by the firms, but many also, while created by private initiative, benefiting from generous public aid. The 'losing' groups, on the other hand, have to rely on publicly financed programmes that may bring them into the mainstream economy but may also perpetuate their status as 'socially excluded'.

Towards new concepts and paradigms?

Probably the most remarkable, as well as remarked on, recent policy text giving prominence to lifelong learning is the EC White Paper *Teaching and Learning: Towards the Learning Society* (European Commission 1995). It largely reflects dominant ideas about economic growth and the key role of education and training in that growth. The quality of continuing economic growth, and of scientific progress and technological innovation, is not seriously questioned, nor are the necessity and benefits of globalization. In the White Paper, lifelong learning should serve to bring the learning and the productive systems closer together. It thus assigns to lifelong learning a key role in bringing about the new society with its free flows of information, knowledge, goods and persons, and with a flexible and disposable labour force. It acknowledges that there are also 'losers' in these processes, but assumes that on the whole the 'winners' prevail. For the 'losers', the at-risk groups, there should be special public funds for financing publicly controlled education and training programmes. Private associations should also help to bring an element of solidarity in a system in which this is not a first priority.

The White Paper has been severely criticized for its 'contradictions between the accepted foundations for action and the objectives assigned to that action' (d'Iribarne 1996: 23). One may, however, reasonably submit that these contradictions are inevitable, and indeed even inherent to the neo-liberal philosophy. Why should firms invest in lifelong learning that they do not need? And why should the state take corrective measures in order to assure access to lifelong learning to those whom the economy does not need – except when this either complements firms' efforts and builds up a reserve of qualified, flexible labour or where it targets groups that are excluded from the mainstream of society and could threaten democracy and security or excessively burden the public conscience?

On this reasoning, the EC paper provides the basis for a new concept or paradigm of lifelong learning, that is perfectly adapted to the needs and expectations of the neo-liberal worldwide society. It is a vision endorsed by the EC and most of the EU member countries in which qualifications are a global commodity and the labour force serves the interests of the global economy.

References

Council of Europe (1970) *Permanent Education.* Strasbourg: Council of Europe.
Davis, N. (1996) Who participates in education and training: an overview at European level, *Vocational Training, European Journal,* 8/9 (May–December II/III): 32–6.
European Commission (1995) *Teaching and Learning: Towards the Learning Society,* White Paper. Luxembourg: Office for Official Publications of the European Communities.
d'Iribarne A. (1996) A discussion of the paradigms of the White Paper on education and training, *Vocational Training. European Journal,* 8/9 (May–December II/III): 23–31.
Kallen, D. (1980) University and lifelong learning: a crisis of communication, *European Journal of Education,* 15: 1.
Kallen, D. (1996) Lifelong learning in retrospect, *Vocational Training: European Journal,* 8/9 (May–December II/III): 16–22.
Lengrand, P. (1970) *An Introduction to Lifelong Education.* Paris: UNESCO.
OECD (1973) *Recurrent Education: A Strategy for Lifelong Learning,* report by Denis Kallen and Jarl Bengtsson. Paris: OECD.
Preston, R. (1999) Critical approaches to lifelong education, *International Review of Education,* 45(5–6). Hamburg: UNESCO Institute for Education.
UNESCO (1972) *Learning To Be* (Faure Report). Paris: UNESCO/Harrap.

4

Lifelong Learning and the Changing Policy Environment

George Papadopoulos

Lifelong learning – expectations and risks

Consensus on the value of lifelong learning has been one of the most remarkable features of the education policy discourse, nationally and internationally, of the past decade. Equally remarkable has been the widespread endorsement of the view, reaching up into the highest government levels, that lifelong learning can resolve many of the economic, social, cultural and even political, problems that confront our twenty-first-century societies. This is a tribute to the dominant role that education has come to occupy in the development of western societies over the past 50 years or so, a role that is periodically reinterpreted as changes occur in education's broader context. An aspect of this dominance has been a growing tendency for education to be used as an instrument in the pursuit of the broader policy objectives seeking to address the contextual changes. The extent to which education thereby influences the directions of the change is an open question, and one of special relevance to contemporary lifelong learning policies.

There is, however, an important gap between the acceptance of a concept and its application in policy. Recent history is replete with examples of governments endorsing concepts that imply drastic educational change but finding the translation of bold pronouncements into educational action thwarted by such factors as the lack of new resources or the corporatist behaviour of established systems, buttressed by vested interests and ideologies. There is a real danger that this fate may already have beset lifelong learning. The alacrity with which governments have endorsed it has been only palely reflected in concrete measures, let alone the implementation of overall strategies. There is a tendency in many countries to put under this umbrella all the disparate initiatives that have been introduced in different parts of their education and training systems, loosely rationalizing them as responding to the objectives of lifelong learning.

Partly as a result of this ad hoc approach, the lifelong learning concept is in danger of being hijacked by various interests – traditional adult education, community and popular education groups, the vocational training and apprenticeship sector, entrenched schooling protagonists, universities and other higher education institutions – in order to secure additional resources and political support for their own aggrandisement. The resulting educational segmentation would militate against the systemic approach that is of the essence for the realization of lifelong learning (Papadopoulos 1999). The latter approach calls not merely for more of what is already on offer in the various sectors and levels of education and training systems, but rather for systemic change of a different kind that develops an articulated vision of lifelong learning.

The importance of history, culture and context

That educational thinking and policies develop in cycles, shaped by prevailing socio-economic, cultural and political conditions, is amply demonstrated by the evolution of the lifelong learning concept to its present dominant position. Its prehistory reaches back into the nineteenth century with the rise of 'popular education' and workers movements, originating in Scandinavia and spreading across Europe. These movements were defined primarily by cultural, social and political, rather than overtly work-related, goals, and this remained the case even with the later expansion and institutionalization of adult education. It was only after World War II that there was serious recognition of the need for the organized retraining of workers and in turn scrutiny of the role of formal education in contributing to this. From the 1960s onwards, in a new climate fostered by burgeoning social and economic demands and the massive educational expansion this brought, new models began to emerge – described variously as 'continuing education and training', '*education permanente*' and 'recurrent education' – all with lifelong learning as their *leitmotiv*. The title of the 1973 OECD report, *Recurrent Education: A Strategy for Lifelong Learning* speaks for itself (OECD 1973; Kallen 1996).

These models, with recurrent education as the most visionary and ambitious, emerged at a time of unprecedented growth – economic, demographic and educational. With full employment and rising national and family incomes, these were the halcyon days of expansion, when public educational expenditure rose faster than economic growth itself. This made possible the pursuit of all the diverse educational objectives more or less simultaneously, with a particular accent on social and equality objectives. There was a great deal of experimentation in educational structures, content and pedagogy, seeking to optimize their relevance to the needs of a larger and more diversified school population. While the importance of education for the economy was acknowledged, education was allowed by and large to develop through its own dynamics, with governmental efforts concentrating on marshalling the necessary resources and setting up the structures through which to meet the social demand for education.

This euphoric educational cycle was dramatically altered in the mid-1970s. The onset and deepening of the recession consequent on successive oil crises resulted in constraints being imposed on public resources and in high unemployment levels, particularly among the young. A new educational cycle was thus initiated in which social and equality objectives receded to the background. Economic goals moved centre-stage. The focus shifted on to the allocation and deployment of scarcer public resources. New answers were offered as to the purpose of education, and it came to be assigned the unrealistic task of combating unemployment. Demand-led gave way to supply-driven thinking, in which factors exogenous to education systems entered into the equations used for setting educational objectives and targets. This process reached down into the very contents and methods of education, with the monitoring of systems' performance and the quality of their outcomes. Eventually, this led to the market approaches for funding and organizing education, particularly at the post-secondary level – a *fin-de-siècle* prelude to the present situation (Papadopoulos 1994).

Against this changed context we can identify the distinctive features of current policies for lifelong learning. In contrast to previous paradigms driven by cultural and social objectives, the driving forces behind the current advocacy of lifelong learning are economic-cum-technological imperatives and the needs of increasingly knowledge- and information-based economies, operating in globalized markets. Where objectives such as social cohesion and democratic values are taken into account, they are subsumed as products of a learning-intensive economy rather than as the prime movers in the strategy. In consequence, education understood broadly as lifelong learning is receiving unprecedented political endorsement, both nationally and internationally. Within the OECD, for example, the precepts of 'lifelong learning for all' have been recently endorsed not only by education ministers but also by ministers of employment, of social affairs and even of finance. The Secretary-General of this economic international organization has gone so far as to state that education 'should be our priority of priorities' (OECD 2001: 7).

Education thus advocated is more broadly conceived than in many of the earlier paradigms. It extends well beyond formal education to encompass all learning activity wherever it may take place. It includes enterprise-based training and individual learning, especially that gained through the new technologies. The emphasis is on the individual and his/her needs and the propagation of self-directed learning. The imaginative use of information technologies is an integral part of policies for lifelong learning. Inevitably, this perspective raises a host of complex questions concerning overall planning, management and coordination, and the role of the various stakeholders, all of which extend well beyond the traditional remit of education authorities. It calls for the development of partnerships at all levels and brings to the fore new relationships between the public and private sectors, particularly in relation to resources. The long-established view of education as a public service largely publicly financed, epitomized in the Scandinavian countries, is being increasingly eroded by private-sector initiatives and the shift of costs to the individual, especially in post-school education and training. These are among the most significant contextual changes for education.

As in previous historical cycles, however, too much may be expected of lifelong learning as *the* remedial instrument. 'Learning' is not synonymous with 'education', and risks being interpreted narrowly to refer merely to the mastery of specific bits of knowledge or skills. This danger is heightened by the force of the economic/technological arguments, and may be revealed by the powerful emphasis on training in many present policies for lifelong learning and by a common willingness to judge educational achievements in those terms amenable to quantifiable measurement. Lifelong learning strategies will need to serve multiple purposes and reach well beyond such narrow, instrumental definitions. This applies particularly to the place of training in such strategies, which too often continues to be treated in isolation from the broader humanistic culture instead of being an integral part. For example, with the main exception of the Scandinavian countries, general education tends to be conspicuously missing from the much-expanded adult education and training programmes, whether public or enterprise-based, that have been generated under the impulse of lifelong learning.

An overview of the lifelong learning policy landscape

Progress towards lifelong learning in OECD countries over the past decade remains patchy and difficult to assess. There has been a flourishing of policy statements and experimental initiatives in the different sectors and an equally flourishing body of policy analysis and research. The momentum has been importantly sustained by international cooperative efforts. European Union programmes in support of pilot experiments have played a key role, as well as the OECD contribution through the analysis and monitoring of country progress towards lifelong learning policies (OECD 2001).

As regards *access policies* within formal education and training, the concern, in high-income countries at least, is no longer one of numbers. One exception in some countries is pre-primary schooling, which is not yet generalized although its importance for subsequent educational careers is increasingly recognized. Another is in countries with strong systems of apprenticeship, where problems relating to trainee numbers may arise depending on the (un)employment situation. In general, however, instead of numbers the issue has rather become identifying the changes needed to the objectives and functioning of the various levels to align them to the achievement of lifelong learning. Within this broad issue is the concern to improve access to both formal and post-formal learning opportunities for specific groups in society, particularly the socially and educationally disadvantaged. Enrolment rates in formal education of those aged 30 years and over are also rather limited and vary significantly from country to country.

This fact highlights the importance of *adult education and training* as the focus of remedial policies, particularly in the fight against low levels of adult literacy, which represent a major hurdle to the successful achievement of lifelong learning. Parallel and related problems arise for unemployed adults. Governments are providing a variety of schemes to enhance their employability and job opportunities, ranging from information and guidance services to programmes for retraining, skills enhancement and job search, funded principally from central government sources. Over recent years, some countries have developed active labour market policies, seeking to make unemployment benefits more constructive by making entitlement to them conditional on participation in further education and training. The levels of direct government support for access to lifelong learning opportunities have been raised by these means.

Enterprise-based training is now widely recognized internationally as a critical area of lifelong learning policies, and again there are wide differences – among countries, firms and population groups – as to the volume of training and who benefits most. The common pattern is that those with more education and higher levels of literacy benefit most. The strong link between national levels of educational attainment and the levels of workforce training suggests that a strategy for strengthening schooling is a potent means of encouraging participation in lifelong learning (see OECD 1999: chapter 3).

This underlines the more general challenge of establishing effective systems of *basic educational preparation for all* as the cornerstone for the subsequent development of individuals and for laying the foundation of a culture of lifelong learning. An essential part of such preparation is to give individuals the propensity for continuous learning – to learn how to learn – that once in place remains operational throughout life. Basic educational preparation now extends from pre-primary education, through initial compulsory schooling, upper secondary education (including vocational education and training under apprenticeship schemes), and often into higher education studies. The prolongation of basic preparation is distinctive to the modern era, as the knowledge and skills required before entry into working life rise and as the competition for jobs intensifies. Both factors result in the need for ever rising levels of qualifications and competences.

In improving basic education preparation, two major problems stand out. The first is the continued phenomenon of school failure, affecting in particular the socially disadvantaged, which no system has yet adequately resolved. Until *all* children attain the 'starting qualifications', chances for lifelong learning will always be stacked in favour of the already well educated. The second problem is the dichotomy that has traditionally prevailed between general education on the one hand, and vocational education and training on the other, that is particularly marked in systems characterized by a strong apprenticeship component. There is now general recognition that apprenticeship schemes should be reformed so as to give trainees greater flexibility through more advanced generic skills and to open possibilities for further studies (Federal Ministry of Education, Science, Research and Technology 1997).

National political cultures and lifelong learning

Under the shared pressures exerted by the new environment, there has been a degree of educational convergence among countries. This relates primarily, however, to general objectives and the directions of future policies, of which lifelong learning is a good example. It applies far less to the underlying processes, approaches and methods through which such objectives are pursued or priorities set, for education and training represent *par excellence* national policies, embedded in the political and cultural traditions of individual countries and their particular systems of governance. This national determination of the educational physiognomy of individual countries is formally recognized in the 'subsidiarity' rule within the EU. The resulting insularity of national education systems is one factor that has so far kept education outside the contemporary boisterous anti-globalization protests, in notable contrast to the events associated with May 1968.

Such profound cultural differences render difficult any comparative assessments of how well educational systems meet economic and social objectives. Japan offers a case in point. During the period of its strong economic performance, it was customary in the West to attribute this to the organization and rigour of its education system and the success of Japanese students in international achievement tests. With the decline of the Japanese economy such reasoning is now out of fashion; the Japanese themselves are the first to admit to what they term the 'desolating effect' that their traditional system has exerted on its young people, society and the economy. A parallel example is provided by the German apprenticeship system. During the period of high youth unemployment beginning in the 1970s, it was the envy of many in the education and employment fields in other European countries. Yet now there is growing recognition of its rigidities even in Germany itself, leading to efforts to revitalize the apprenticeship system. Where stronger apprenticeship elements have been introduced in other systems, these have tended to be assimilated into school-based programmes as against the employment-based system that prevails in Germany.

These examples highlight both the difficulties of international comparisons, despite the clamour for them in today's global world, and the importance of cultural influences on education change strategies being adopted in individual countries (Kearns and Papadopoulos 2000). Sweden, for instance, exemplifies a learning and training culture embedded in national social, economic, cultural and political history. It has one of the highest rates of participation in both formal and post-formal education and training in the world, among young people and adults. Current policies seek to bolster the connections between education, the labour market and industry in order to consolidate a coherent infrastructure for education and training across the whole lifespan. Key to this is the development of a comprehensive system of adult education that brings together three strands: the popular social movements and adult education; active labour market policies based on tripartite (government, labour and industry) responsibility for employment training; and the well-established tradition of education for adults at primary, secondary and tertiary levels. Such approaches can properly be described as part of the Swedish way of life (Sohlan 1998).

The pluralistic and consultative nature of society and decision-making in the Netherlands is amply reflected throughout its education and training system. There is considerable involvement of the social partners (trade unions and business associations) in vocational education and training (VET) policies and administration and in the employment service, which powerfully shapes policy developments. Dutch industrial relations arrangements lead to collective agreements that are legally binding; these often specify funds or schemes for training, and they cover around three-quarters of private-sector employees (Down 1999).

The English situation may be an example of how the political culture can generate a national commitment, marshal resources and develop instruments and partnerships in a coordinated endeavour to build the learning society. The measures adopted do not replace the existing education and training system but are being simply – and skilfully – grafted on to it. While the objectives are radical, change is incremental and may thus be more acceptable to the key stakeholders (see for example DfEE 1999).

Conclusion

This chapter has located lifelong learning within its broader policy environment, of which it is both a product and, ideally, a source of sustenance. It has argued the importance of the social, economic and political circumstances prevailing at the time in shaping educational thought and policies, in this and in earlier paradigms. It has also described the difficulties that have been encountered in bringing about change in education and training systems to meet the expectations of governments and society, which often result in disappointment. As yet at least, lifelong learning is proving no exception to these difficulties: the policy environment is favourable but can such strategies be translated into action? On this question the jury is still out.

The chapter has also drawn attention to pitfalls to be avoided in the application of lifelong learning strategies. One of these is an excessively narrow interpretation of learning, focused on the acquisition of fragmented pieces of knowledge and skills, at the expense of broader education. There is an irreducible plurality of purposes to be served by education in twenty-first-century societies that lifelong learning strategies cannot afford to ignore.

References

DfEE (1999) *National Targets Action Plan.* Sheffield: Department for Education and Employment.

Down, T. (1999) *Developing Skill Policies in Six Countries.* Leeds: Leeds Metropolitan University.

Federal Ministry of Education, Science, Research and Technology (1997) *Vocational Training in the Dual System in Germany.* Bonn: Federal Ministry of Education, Science, Research and Technology.

Kallen, D. (1996) Lifelong learning in retrospect, *Vocational Training: European Journal,* 8/9 (May–December II/III).

Kearns, P. and Papadopoulos, G. (2000) *Building a Learning and Training Culture: The Experience of Five OECD Countries.* Adelaide: National Centre for Vocational Education and Research.

OECD (1973) *Recurrent Education: A Strategy for Lifelong Learning.* Paris: OECD.

OECD (1999) *Employment Outlook.* Paris: OECD.

OECD (2001) *Education Policy Analysis.* Paris: OECD.

Papadopoulos, G.S. (1994) *Education 1960–1990: The OECD Perspective.* Paris: OECD.

Papadopoulos, G.S. (1999) Policies for lifelong learning: an overview of international trends, in P. Kearns, R. McDonald, P. Candy, S. Knights and G. Papadopoulos (eds) *VET in the Learning Age: The Challenge of Lifelong Learning for All.* Adelaide: National Centre for Vocational Education and Research.

Sohlan, A. (1998) *The Culture of Adult Learning in Sweden.* Paris: OECD.

Part 2

Building Human and Social Capital

5

Effective Schooling for Lifelong Learning

David H. Hargreaves

Introduction – the need for better theory[1]

For over 20 years, researchers have been developing models for school effectiveness. As many countries have sought to improve the quality of schooling through sustained reform, there has been parallel work on models of school improvement. In the UK, and much of the English-speaking world, the literature has been dominated by *Fifteen Thousand Hours* (1979) by Michael Rutter and his associates, which sought to make sense of the correlations between a number of school-related process variables and four educational outcomes, including academic achievement. Much subsequent work has consisted of an elaboration of this input–process–output conceptualization, which has become the conventional model.

The accumulated results of this line of enquiry have been summarized by Sammons *et al.* (1995) in terms of 11 characteristics of effective schools. Despite being attacked as platitudinous or tautological, the findings are reasonably robust. It may be fruitful to treat the model's limitations as desiderata for a better model, as follows.

- A model should derive from a theory: it must be more than a set of measured variables that correlate with educational outcomes. A useful theory contains a relatively small set of concepts in explicit relationships, and measured variables should be capable of being contained within the concepts. When integrated into a coherent whole, the concepts become a theory from which testable hypotheses can be derived to guide research.
- Concepts that are basic to educational discourse, such as curriculum, must find a place in the theory, since *what* is taught in school is one of the goals of schooling and therefore cannot be ignored.
- Outcomes of effective schooling have been progressively narrowed and are often reduced to test results of academic knowledge. Social and moral outcomes, including motivation and the commitment to lifelong learning, need to be restored.

• It is desirable that a model be derived from a shared theoretical base for both school effectiveness and school improvement. A key idea for linking school effectiveness to school improvement is that of *capacity for improvement*, which is assumed to characterize a school that sustains its effectiveness by successfully managing change in a context of instability and reform. Attempts to define this capacity usually invoke additional variables – for example, a commitment to staff development or a culture of enquiry – rather than building capacity into the concepts that define effectiveness itself.

This chapter deals with some limitations of the conventional model, while retaining some of the input–process–output features, by providing a theory of a limited yet integrated set of concepts from which a better working model can be derived.

An outline of the theory

The theory has four master concepts – outcomes, leverage, intellectual capital and social capital – only the first of which is central to the conventional model. The following definitional statements may be regarded as testable hypotheses.

The *outcomes* of schooling represent both the extent to which overt goals are achieved. Two main outcomes are assumed: cognitive and moral, defined here in essentially Aristotelian ways. For Aristotle, the very purpose of the state is to enable its citizens to lead the good life. On his view, it is *eudaimonia*, the Greek word usually translated into English as happiness, but perhaps better rendered as well-being, which is the complete end or purpose of life. *Eudaimonia* is not a state of mind or set of feelings, but a quality of conduct or disposition to act in a certain way. Well-being consists in virtuous activity. Here is a second intractable problem of translation: the Greek *arete*, usually translated as virtue, is perhaps better rendered as excellence. In Aristotle's view, there are two kinds of excellence, namely *intellectual excellences* such as science, art and practical wisdom, and *moral excellences* such as courage, justice and self-control. The purpose of education is to initiate the young into these excellences through which they acquire the disposition to make sound intellectual and moral judgements and choices. From their teachers' example and their own habits based on practice, they learn how to make the right decisions in their lives and so achieve well-being (*eudaimonia*) and become good citizens. Human beings are naturally disposed to live together in society, and by participation in community as citizens they realize their natural dispositions, achieve full humanity and live the good life. The principal outcomes of schooling thus refer to the quality of the intellectual and moral life of students.

Leverage (Senge 1990) concerns the relation between teacher input and educational output, and is defined as the quality and quantity of effected

Figure 5.1 Leverage

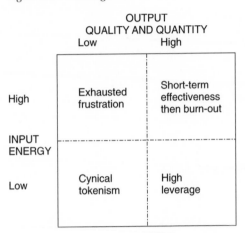

change on students' intellectual and moral state as a function of the level of teachers' invested energy. There are four possible relationships. Teachers often put considerable effort into making changes with relatively little impact on students and so become frustrated and exhausted. At other times a high input produces a high level of positive change, but the improvement is liable to be short-term since the high input cannot be sustained for long. A low input yielding a low output may be a rational response of teachers to mandated change of which teachers disapprove. *High leverage*, the desirable relation between input and output, leads to a large impact on effectiveness or improvement from low levels of teacher effort (Figure 5.1). The highest leverage occurs when single high-leverage strategies are combined. Teachers in effective schools share and regularly apply combinations of high-leverage strategies: they respond to demands for change by working smarter, not harder. Outstanding schools discover how to combine high-leverage strategies and to sequence their implementation over time so that the quality and quantity of their outcomes are unusually high in relation to the investment of energy.

An improving school learns how to identify and apply effective, efficient and ethically justifiable leverage points to enhance the intellectual and moral excellences as outcomes. Many schools do not know how to increase their leverage, that is to learn how to work smarter. Understanding school improvement means discovering how schools can learn to implement, that is combine and sequence, the high-leverage strategies of effective schools. Mastery of the art and science of leverage requires an understanding of, and a professional ability to apply the evidence for, 'what works' on the basis of research or personal experience, and a capacity to innovate and experiment in novel situations and where evidence is lacking.

The two forms of *capital* central to the theory, intellectual and social, are among other forms of capital, of which the best known are physical and

Figure 5.2   The master concepts and subsidiary concepts

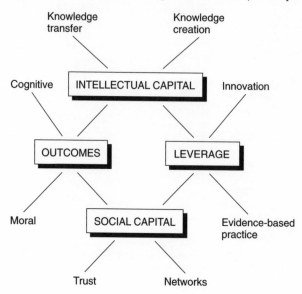

financial – the value of a firm's property or money in the bank. Human capital is usually measured as the level of education and skill of a company's staff. *Intellectual capital* was originally defined as the organized knowledge that can be used to produce wealth, the sum of everything everybody in a company knows to give it competitive edge (Stewart 1997). Here it is defined as the sum of the knowledge and experience of the school's stakeholders that they could deploy to achieve the school's goals. Intellectual capital grows by two important processes: the *creation* of new knowledge and the capacity to *transfer* knowledge between situations and people.

Social capital (Fukuyama 1995, 1999; Nahapiet and Ghoshal 1998; Putnam 2000) is here defined in terms of its cultural and structural components. The cultural part is mainly the level of *trust* between people and the genera- tion of norms of reciprocity (mutual favours) and collaboration. The struc- tural aspect refers to the *networks* in which the people are embedded. In a school rich in social capital, the high levels of trust generate strong networks and collaborative relations among its members and stakeholders. High levels of social capital in a school strengthen its intellectual capital.

The four master concepts, each with two subsidiary concepts, may be represented diagrammatically, in a simplified model form, as shown in Figure 5.2.

In this theory, the concepts of school effectiveness and school improve- ment are reformulated as follows.

- An *effective* school mobilizes its intellectual capital (especially its capacity to create and transfer knowledge) and its social capital (especially its capacity to generate trust and sustain networks) to achieve the desired educational outcomes of intellectual and moral excellences, through the successful use of high-leverage strategies grounded in evidence-informed and innovative professional practice.

- An *improving* school increases its intellectual capital (especially its capacity to create and transfer knowledge) and its social capital (especially its capacity to generate trust and sustain networks) to achieve the educational outcomes of intellectual and moral excellences, by learning successfully to use higher-leverage strategies based on evidence of 'what works' and/or innovative professional practice.

In the light of these formulations, a more elaborate definition of some of the purported characteristics of effective schools becomes possible. For example, the leadership of the school's principal is commonly cited simply as 'purposeful'. This is worryingly bland. It is not *any* purpose that matters: the nature and perceived legitimacy of the goals involved is critical to the purposefulness that a leader demonstrates. Moreover, leadership is concerned with the means of realizing the goals, both their efficiency and morality, not only the goals themselves. The conventional model lacks sufficient theory to specify the goals or means of effective school leadership. Whereas, derived from the above definitions, it is evident that, in the present theory, the leader of an effective or improving school is:

- committed to achieving high levels of intellectual and moral excellences in students as main institutional outcomes;
- able to achieve commitment to such outcomes in the school community; and
- able to mobilize the community's intellectual and social capital and apply the principle of high leverage to those ends.

The rest of the chapter presents a more detailed outline of the theory to show how the master and subsidiary concepts relate to one another and to a range of further concepts. For lack of space I neglect the task of subsuming other models within the present one (see Teddlie and Reynolds 2000).

The theory elaborated

Relationships between the four master concepts are complex – which explains why there are no simplistic and potentially misleading arrows in the diagrams. These are now set out as propositions or hypotheses. The relationship between social capital and intellectual capital is fundamental, for there are severe limits to the extent to which a school's intellectual capital can be mobilized if social capital is low. High social capital entails high levels of trust among the stakeholders – between principal and staff, among the teachers, between teachers and students, between teachers and parents, and among the students. There are thus strong networks with norms of reciprocity and mutual aid. In these circumstances people readily share their knowledge, both intellectual and moral. The sharing is of different kinds – for example, teachers share their knowledge of what works professionally in classrooms. Social capital is an important lubricant of knowledge transfer on which the mobilization of an organization's intellectual capital depends.

School effectiveness and improvement do not simply have two aspects, cognitive (or intellectual) and social (or moral), which are independent of one another or inherently in conflict. Rather, the moral domain needs to be cultivated to provide the conditions of successful knowledge transfer needed to sustain the optimum mobilization of intellectual capital. An effective school might be one in which all the teachers have individually developed the knowledge and skill of teaching effectively. But this school will be more effective, and certainly have greater capacity to improve, if there is sufficient social capital for the teachers to share and improve that professional knowledge. Low social capital among teachers entails lack of trust and networking among colleagues, who thus fail to share their pedagogic knowledge and skills. Failure to recognize that social capital supports the knowledge transfer essential to the maximal mobilization of intellectual capital damages the school's capacity for *any* kind of improvement.

In highly effective or improving schools, there is substantial investment in social capital among teachers because this supports the transfer of high-leverage teaching strategies among them, which enhances student achievement. Teachers look outside their own school and trust in research evidence or the experience of other teachers in the same specialism as potential sources of ideas and practices for boosting leverage, and such knowledge feeds back through internal staff networks, which support knowledge transfer through coaching and mentoring. Such a culture also promotes internal innovation or knowledge creation of many kinds (OECD 2000).

In the conventional model of effectiveness and improvement – and much current public policy – the impact of the moral excellences and the underpinning social capital on the optimization of intellectual capital remain badly neglected. The interactions between the two forms of capital, leverage and student outcomes, as in Figure 5.3, now require more detailed study, as suggested in Figure 5.4, in which each of the four master concepts is linked to a set of subordinate but explicitly educational concepts. The curriculum is linked to outcomes; learning to intellectual capital; teaching to leverage; and social capital to the school as a community.

Curriculum can be divided into its formal and hidden aspects. The formal curriculum is primarily the knowledge, skills and understanding that teachers intend students to acquire. This consists of disciplinary bodies of knowledge and of ways of thinking and behaving. Although the formal curriculum deals predominantly in the intellectual excellences, the moral excellences also play a part. The hidden curriculum consists of what students learn from their participation in school but which is not planned as the official curriculum. This curriculum also has an elaborate content – the art of

Figure 5.3 Relationships between master and subsidiary concepts

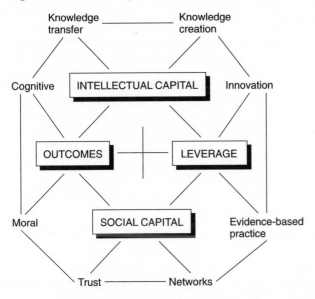

Figure 5.4 Master concepts and their subordinate educational concepts

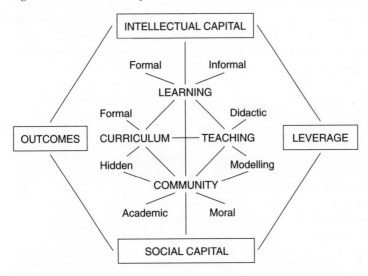

pleasing teacher, the skill of coping with the constraints of institutional life, the ability to control relationships with peers, and so on, some of which is not necessarily educationally desirable.

Learning is divided (for convenience) into formal and informal. Formal learning is that which is intended to take place in classrooms and other

Figure 5.5 The main educational components of intellectual capital

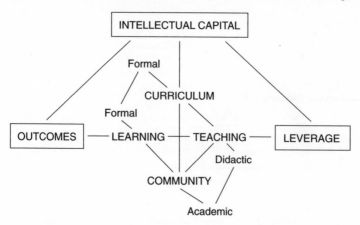

settings where students deal with the formal curriculum. Informal learning is that by which the hidden curriculum is acquired but also includes learning that is indeed intended by the teachers but which is unrelated to formal teaching. The extracurricular life of the school is certainly intended, but much of this learning is informal, not a direct result of teaching.

Teaching is divided (again for convenience) into two major forms. Formal, or didactic, teaching consists of explicit and verbal interactions between teacher and student directed to student learning of the intended curriculum. Modelling is concerned with the student learning that is patterned on teacher conduct, for example, by imitation, whether conscious or not. Modelling may be intended, as when teachers expect to be exemplary in their conduct in the presence of students, but much is unintended, non-verbal and unnoticed.

The school as a *community* has two main aspects that reflect its major outcomes. It is an academic community aiming to inculcate intellectual excellences and also a moral community seeking to promote moral excellences. These elements are linked in particular combinations. Intellectual capital is mainly (but not exclusively) linked to particular patterns of the elements (as suggested in Figure 5.5). Similarly the dominant pattern of the components of social capital is outlined in Figure 5.6. Because in this case the outcomes tend to be less valued, the concept of social capital is less well understood, and the processes involved frequently fall outside teachers' purposes and escape their attention. In consequence, less is understood about leverage in this domain than in that of intellectual capital and excellence.

In summary, it is possible to specify from the theory the conditions under which one would expect schools to improve. A test of the value of any innovation, pedagogical or curricular, is the extent to which it contributes not only to student outcomes in terms of the excellences, but also to the school's capacity by enhancing intellectual capital, social capital and high

Figure 5.6 The main educational components of social capital

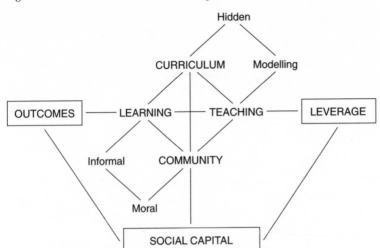

leverage. When the theory is expressed in the form of (an inevitably simplified) model, as in Figure 5.7, any innovation will have its major impact at one or more points. The power of the innovation will be measured by the strength of the flow from the points of impact to other components; and its overall effectiveness or improvement value will be a function of the extent to which it enhances the four major elements – outcomes, social capital, intellectual capital and leverage – not just cognitive outcomes.

School effectiveness and improvement in the knowledge economy: a test of the theory

The conventional model of school effectiveness and improvement is weakly related to issues arising from a nation's entry into a knowledge economy and the role of education therein; arguably, the model is relatively narrow and parochial, legitimizing a highly limited view of the outcomes and processes of schooling. The nature of work changes in a knowledge economy and this is reflected in organizational changes in how companies manage and exploit the intellectual assets of the workforce. Knowledge management, which includes the creation, use and transfer of knowledge, has radical implications for how firms achieve success. There is a rapidly growing literature on knowledge management, the educational implications of which are now being analysed (OECD 2000). In a knowledge economy, the knowledge and skills that schools seek to develop in students must include creativity and innovation, not as a substitute for traditional knowledge and skills, such as literacy and numeracy, but as an addition to them.

Figure 5.7 The theory expressed in the form of a simplified model

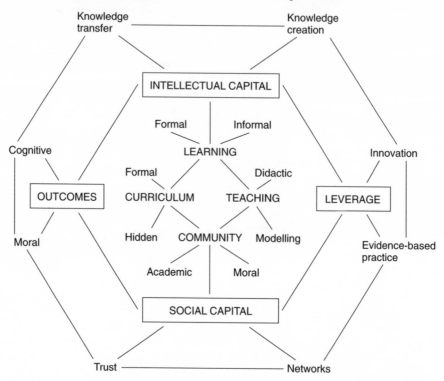

Schools, like businesses, must find new ways in which to manage and exploit their intellectual assets, especially of the teachers. Since teachers have a weak knowledge base on how to develop the new knowledge and skills required by pupils, they must learn how to create this professional working knowledge and then transfer it rapidly and effectively through the teaching force. This will require new ways of engaging in research and development work for teachers as well as new forms of collaboration with professional researchers (Hargreaves 1998). In a knowledge economy, schools are the beginning of lifelong learning in which people develop flexibility and innovativeness. By means of knowledge creation, innovation and transfer, teachers generate new forms of high leverage to improve their teaching (upper right of Figure 5.7) and also promote knowledge creation and transfer to support new forms of intellectual excellence for their students (upper left of Figure 5.7). Such concepts are at the heart of a theory of school effectiveness and improvement in the age of lifelong learning in a knowledge economy.

Like the literature on intellectual capital, that on social capital has grown exponentially in the last decade. Here I focus mainly on the work of the

American political scientist Robert Putnam (2000), who treats social capital as close to civic virtue, both a private good that helps individuals succeed in life and a public good that builds communities. Social capital serves as a *bridge*, the 'connections' or networks that help people to get ahead; it also serves as a *bond* that attaches people to groups. If groups are strong in social capital, they resolve collective problems more easily; the wheels of communal life turn more smoothly, and people become more tolerant and empathetic in their social relationships.

Putnam's book documents the power of social capital to make people 'healthy, wealthy and wise', and demonstrates in detail that social capital has a powerful impact, second only to poverty, on education and children's welfare. States with high social capital have measurably better educational outcomes. Putnam then marshals impressive evidence of a serious decline of social capital in late-twentieth-century United States, with consequential social damage. However, renewing the stock of social capital is no simple task. Putnam's prescription for reversing the decline of social capital is less convincing than the analysis of the causes of the decline. Putnam sees a role for the school, in the form of improved civic education, community service and richer extracurricular activities, but the injunctions are vague and the understanding of the process of schooling is superficial. By not acknowledging the potential power of social and intellectual capital to interact in mutually supportive ways, he underestimates the potential of schools to be institutions that generate high levels of both forms of capital as private *and* public goods (Leadbeater 1999).

Financial capital is lost if it is given away: you cannot keep money and spend it. When intellectual capital is given away, it does not deteriorate, but becomes shared knowledge. That, if done on a reciprocal basis, means mutual learning and gain. Social capital increases when it is given away: if I give you my trust, you are more likely to trust me in return and our mutual trust grows progressively. In a situation of mutual trust, we share our intellectual capital, which in turn confirms our relationship of trust. In schools, as trust and networking build social capital, it is easier for teachers to share professional practice and innovate and thus to improve teaching. It also means that the community of teachers enhances the school as a moral as well as an academic community and generates social capital in students as an educational outcome. The creation of the civic and social entrepreneurs who are essential to a successful knowledge economy depends on such a theory of schooling.

The theory thus changes what should be measured in research on school effectiveness and what should be the target of school improvement projects. For example, it is not simply a matter of measuring moral outcomes, but of measuring them as a stock of social capital with added value. Moreover, social capital should be measured as a 'process variable'. Most urgently needed here are measures of trust, a central component of social capital, between principal and teachers, teachers and students, teachers and parents, and among students themselves. Lifelong learning in a knowledge economy thus requires new indicators and performance measures to track new models of schools' effectiveness and school improvement.

From an Aristotelian point of view, friendship is the true root of community and politics, and measuring its existence among students and teachers is relevant to assessing social capital. More structural aspects of social capital can also be measured, such as the extent and quality of extracurricular provision and the nature and strength of networks among students and among staff. The rich literature on community is a resource for ideas on what might be measured. When researchers measure these variables they will illuminate the role of the moral in school effectiveness and improvement and persuade policy-makers to act on the findings, for example by incorporating these aspects of education into schemes of student assessment.

Action to improve schools should now turn to neglected phenomena which are crucial to the model and which could also be measured. For example, the theory emphasizes informal and social learning, thus making mentoring and coaching, both intellectual and moral – among teachers, between teachers and students, and among students – vital mechanisms for sharing intellectual capital and building social capital. This entails rehabilitating apprenticeship theories of teaching and learning, in educational as well as workplace settings.

Teacher effectiveness – a further test of the theory

School effectiveness research has recently emphasized teacher effectiveness at classroom level. However, there is a lack of conceptual coherence in integrating these two levels of analysis and their associated literatures. This final section examines the work of Stigler and Hiebert (1999) to show how the present theory can incorporate some of the key features of teacher effectiveness.

Their book is based on the Third International Mathematics and Science Study (TIMSS the video study) and a comparative analysis of eighth grade mathematics teaching in the United States, Japan and Germany. What do German and Japanese mathematics teachers do that results in students achieving at a higher level than in the United States? American students, it seems, are invited by teachers to memorize definitions and then practise procedures; they are shown what to do and then practise doing it on relatively simple problems by following rules. In Germany, teachers lead students through the development of procedures for solving problems; students participate directly in the development of the procedures. In Japan, students are presented with problems and have to invent procedures for solving them; teachers provide the scaffolding that helps students devise methods for solving challenging problems. In particular, Japanese students do more of the mathematical work and spend more time inventing new procedures than do their peers in Germany and the United States. In Japan and Germany, the parts of mathematics lessons are carefully connected to create a smooth, narrative flow.

These (and other) findings are used to argue that teaching is a *system*, and that teaching systems vary from country to country and in the quality of their effectiveness. Teaching, argue Stigler and Hiebert (1999),

> is not a loose mixture of individual features thrown together by the teacher. It works more like a machine, with the parts operating together and reinforcing one another, driving the vehicle forward ... [This] means that individual features make sense only in terms of how they relate with others that surround them. It means that most individual features, by themselves, are not good or bad. Their value depends on how they connect with others and fit into the lesson.

Here, in effect, is a neat description of the principle of leverage and how high leverage can be achieved. These teaching patterns or *scripts* are deeply embedded in teachers. Changing just one or two of the elements in the whole system is not likely to produce a marked improvement in quality, in part because the change is superficial, leaving most elements of the original script undisturbed. To improve teacher effectiveness, the whole script must be examined and improved. In the language of the proposed theory, high leverage is achieved only by devising powerful combinations of teachers' classroom practices, not by changing just one or two selected for closer attention.

How, then, is teacher effectiveness improved? According to Stigler and Hiebert, participation in school-based professional development groups is part of a teacher's job in Japan. These groups provide a context in which teachers are mentored; they also provide a laboratory for the development and testing of new teaching techniques. Teachers devise 'research lessons' which they take time to design, test and improve – and then share and implement collectively. They observe one another at work and develop a language in which to talk about what they do. Because the outcome is owned collectively, teachers can constructively criticize one another without causing offence. In the terms of the theory, teachers form a community with high social capital, in which mentoring is part of teachers' social learning, and collaboration to solve shared professional problems is common. This provides not only the basis for knowledge transfer of 'what works' but also the potential for knowledge creation and innovation. All this contributes to high leverage strategies of teaching that shape classroom teaching and ensure high cognitive outcomes. A school's capacity for improvement depends not on *general* provision of continuing professional development or spirit of enquiry, but on *specific* versions as built into the present theory.

In summary, the proposed theory incorporates the evidence about the effectiveness of Japanese teaching more adequately than does the conventional model. It has two other advantages. First, while it is unclear whether Japanese schools can at the same time use the relatively high social capital among teachers to create a moral community to yield moral excellences as outcomes of schooling, the theory points to those processes which would repay investigation to test relevant hypotheses. Secondly, it indicates what action might need to be taken to increase school and teacher effectiveness in other national contexts. Like the Japanese, but unlike the Americans, the British have a national curriculum with the potential for devising effective lessons around that curriculum and then sharing them widely. Continuing professional development is currently being redesigned in the UK and many aspects of educational research and development are being reconstructed. It is an opportunity to develop new methods for professional knowledge creation and transfer, ones closer to the Japanese way, in the interests on improving schools in which teachers teach more effectively to sustain a philosophy of lifelong learning in a knowledge economy.

Note

1. This chapter is a revised version of 'A capital theory of school effectiveness and improvement', first published in the special issue of the *British Educational Research Journal*, summer 2001.

References

Fukuyama, F. (1995) *Trust: The Social Virtues and the Creation of Prosperity*. London: Hamish Hamilton.

Fukuyama, F. (1999) *The Great Disruption: Human Nature and the Reconstitution of Social Order*. London: Profile Books.

Hargreaves, D.H. (1998) *Creative Professionalism: The Role of Teachers in the Knowledge Society*. London: DEMOS.

Leadbeater, C. (1999) *Living on Thin Air*. London: Viking.

Nahapiet, J. and Ghoshal, S. (1998) Social capital, intellectual capital and organizational advantage, *Academy of Management Review*, 23 (2): 242–66.

OECD (2000) *Knowledge Management in the Learning Society*. Paris: OECD.

Putnam, R.D. (2000) *Bowling Alone: The Collapse and Revival of American Community*. New York: Simon & Schuster.

Rutter, M., Maughan, B., Mortimore, P. and Ouston, J. (1979) *Fifteen Thousand Hours*. London: Open Books.

Sammons, P., Hillman, J. and Mortimore, P. (1995) *Key Characteristics of Effective Schools*. London: Institute of Education.

Senge, P.M. (1990) *The Fifth Discipline: The Art and Practice of the Learning Organization*. New York: Doubleday.

Stewart, T.A. (1997) *Intellectual Capital*. London: Nicholas Brealey.

Stigler, J.W. and Hiebert, J. (1999) *The Teaching Gap*. New York: Free Press.

Teddlie, C. and Reynolds, D. (2000) *The International Handbook of School Effectiveness Research*. London: Falmer Press.

6

Too Old to Learn? Lifelong Learning in the Context of an Ageing Population

Lisa M. Lynch[1]

Overview

As workers age across the OECD they will encounter a labour market that places an increasing premium on investments in human capital. As shown in Figure 6.1, employment growth for the G7 countries over the period 1970–93 was concentrated in higher educational attainment sectors. These trends are forecast to intensify over time. For example, in the United States the Bureau of Labor Statistics (see Fullerton 1999) predicts that over the period 1998–2008 employment growth in occupations that generally require two years or more of post-secondary education will grow faster than the average of all occupations.

Furthermore, over the years to 2025 the proportion of the population that will be over the age of 65 as a fraction of those aged 20–64 will rise substantially in all of the G7 countries. As shown in Figure 6.2, all of the G7 countries by the year 2025 will see increases in their elderly support ratios anywhere from 40 to 160 per cent, with the largest growth in Japan. The impact of this trend on the age distribution of the workforce is profound. For example, Fullerton (1999) shows for the United States that by the year 2008 over 60 per cent of the workforce will be aged 35 or older. This predicted pattern of an ageing workforce is forecast to occur in all of the other G7 countries. It should be noted that this ageing of the workforce is not a new phenomenon. In fact, the projected ageing of the workforce could be described as a return to the 1960s, before the baby boom made the workforce of the past 20 years relatively young.

Nevertheless, in an increasingly skills-driven economy a key issue is the extent to which the growing number of mid- and late-career workers are able to refresh, expand and redeploy their job skills. We know that, in general, the returns to investments in human capital are large and have grown over recent years in many OECD countries. Within the OECD, more

Figure 6.1   Employment growth by higher and lower educational attainment sectors, 1970–93

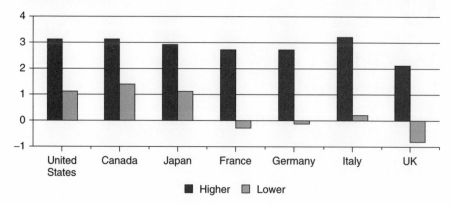

Source: Bureau of Labor Statistics 1995

Figure 6.2   Elderly support ratio, 1990, 2010 and 2025*

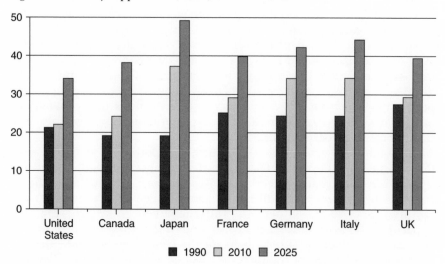

* Elderly support ratio is the number of persons 65 years and over per 100 persons 20–64 years
Source: US Bureau of the Census 1993: 122

educated workers are more likely to participate in the labour market, are less likely to become unemployed, and on average earn more. In addition, investments in human capital are positively associated with economic growth at the macroeconomic level and establishment productivity at the micro level. Returns to education and training compare favourably with rates of return on business capital (see OECD 1998).

An example of both the size and the growing importance of education can be seen in the United States. In 1980, the average full-time male(female) worker with only a college degree earned 44 (35) per cent more than the average full-time male(female) worker with only a high school degree. By 1999, the gap had widened to 78 (71) per cent. While the size of the earnings advantage varies across country, as shown by the OECD (1998), it remains true that a university education offers a substantial boost to earnings compared with just having a secondary degree in virtually all of the countries in the OECD.

Recent evidence indicates that the returns to schooling occur because more educated students are more productive as employees and not because higher education screens out low-ability individuals. In the United States, Kane and Rouse (1995) and Ashenfelter and Rouse (1998) find that a year of post-high school education increases earnings by 5–10 per cent. In addition, micro-level studies of firms and establishments show significant gains in productivity associated with human capital investments. For example, research by Black and Lynch (1996) finds that increasing the average educational level of workers in a firm by one year raises productivity as much as 8 per cent in manufacturing and 13 per cent in non-manufacturing.

The evidence on the returns to education and training in general, then, suggest that they are large. But what evidence is there on the returns to investments in older workers and how might the returns to human capital investment be affected by an ageing workforce?

Potential problems for the education and training of older workers

In spite of all of the potential benefits associated with investments in education and training there are two key issues that may affect the optimal level of investment, especially for older workers. These issues are the possibility of a market failure in the provision of post-schooling training for older workers and the impact of technology on the probability of older workers to retrain or retire.

Potential market failures

If firms invest in general skills of workers and workers then leave a firm (either to work for another employer or to retire), employers may end up investing in a sub-optimal level of training. This is because employers worry that the workers that they train in portable skills may be 'poached' by competitors or that they retire from the firm before they have been able to recoup the investment costs associated with the training. One of the largest costs associated with employer-provided training are the wages of workers who are involved in training programmes rather than in actual production. If compensation plans are structured so that there is a great deal of 'back load-ing' (i.e. deferred compensation that is obtained towards the end of a work-ing career) then these costs can be quite high. If, on top of this, the potential period of time over which a firm can recoup its training costs is short because of retirement, then firms may be reluctant to invest in older workers.

At the same time, employees who have already shown an aptitude to learn new skills by having completed more years of schooling are more likely to receive additional human capital investments provided by an employer. Studies by Lillard and Tan (1986), Barron *et al.* (1987), Mincer (1988), Brown (1989), Lynch (1992), and Bishop (1994) show that firm-provided training is much more likely to be obtained by more educated employees. This results in the creation of both a virtuous and a vicious circle of human capital accumulation. Individuals who acquire more schooling are also more likely to receive post-school employer-provided training, while those with minimal education find it extremely difficult to make up this deficiency in human capital once they enter the labour market. New entrants into the labour market have typically higher levels of educational attainment than previous entrants. If education and training investments are complements, then employers may end up investing more in younger workers than in older employees even if there is not the issue of shorter horizons over which to recoup the investment in human capital.

None of these issues would necessarily result in underinvestment in train-ing if capital markets were perfect so that workers could borrow to finance more general training, if the government subsidized general training, or if workers accepted lower wages during training spells. However, capital markets are far from perfect, and workers differ from employers in their attitudes towards risk and time horizons. In particular, older workers may be much more risk averse and certainly have shorter time horizons than younger workers. As a result, there may be a market failure in the provision of general training, especially the proportion of older workers trained in more general skills.

New technologies and training

Changes in the workplace, including new technology and organizational structure, can have a substantial impact on the human capital investments of older workers. In particular, if new technology increases the depreciation rate of both physical and human capital owing to obsolescence and the pay-off period to investments in human capital is shortened, older workers may become more marginalized in the workforce. However, human capital theory does not provide an unambiguous prediction of the effect of technological change on the optimal level of on-the-job training. As discussed by Bartel and Sicherman (1993), technological change may be positively or negat-ively correlated with training. The eventual sign will be determined by the degree of complementarity or substitutability between schooling and training and the impact of technological change on the marginal returns to training. In addition, new technologies themselves may lower the cost of providing training to workers. One example of this is the new capacities associated with Internet II that will allow new forms of more interactive distance learning at substantially lower costs to employers.

If there is a positive correlation between technological change and on-the-job training, human capital theory would predict that workers in industries that have been characterized by higher technological change will retire later. This is because industries that do a lot of continuous on-the-job training will offer steeper wage profiles that reward work in later years relative to earlier years. As a result, those industries which offer more on-the-job training because of high technological change will end up attracting workers who plan to retire later. So technological change can actually result in some workers retiring later than others.

However, if there are unexpected changes in the rate of technological change in a firm or industry, this will increase the depreciation rate of previously acquired skills and make new human capital investments less attractive for older workers and firms employing them. As a result, workers in these types of firm or industry would be predicted by human capital theory to retire earlier.

Bartel and Sicherman (1993) examine both of these effects using individual data on the United States. They find that workers in industries that have higher permanent rates of technological change have longer careers than those employed in sectors with lower rates of technological change. This is due in part to the fact that they find that workers in sectors with high but expected rates of technological change are also more likely to receive employer-provided on-the-job training. Conversely, they find that if there is an unexpected increase in the rate of technological change then workers in a sector experiencing this type of technology shock are induced to retire earlier.

These results suggest that concerns need to be tempered that technological change combined with an ageing workforce are bound to create skill shortages because workers are more likely to retire earlier. What seems to matter most is not technological change *per se* but unexpected shocks in technological change. This empirical work may also help in policy discussions on the possible role of government in providing training for older workers. Workers in sectors experiencing unexpected technological shocks may be better served by subsidies for their training than those in sectors that have a permanently high rate of technological change.

Mincer and Higuchi (1988), in a comparison of human capital investments in the United States and Japan, argue that while increasingly rapid technological change results in less human capital investment at any point in time, more investment in training may be repeated over the working life. In other words, obsolescence of human capital does not necessarily imply obsolescence of workers. Using the example of Japanese workplace practices of flexibility and job rotation, Mincer and Higuchi show that potential obsolescence is overcome without having to change who is employed within a firm. As they state: 'If the new cycle of training builds on the partially obsolete previous cycle and both contain elements of firm specificity then skills adjustments are accomplished at lesser cost using the existing workforce rather than new hires.' So, experienced older workers can actually lower training costs for a firm even in a world of rapid technological change. This seems to work, however, only in what researchers have labelled 'high performance' workplace systems.

What is the impact of these new forms of work organization on older workers? Lindbeck and Snower (1996), building on a large industrial relations and human resource management literature, argue that reorganization of firms from Tayloristic task-oriented production processes to customer-oriented teams has resulted in a breakdown of occupational barriers within companies. They predict that the movement to more horizontal work organizations with greater emphasis on cross-training will result in a labour market that is segmented into three parts: an expanding, flexible, 'high performance' workplace where wages are rising; a contracting Tayloristic sector where wages are stagnant; and an expanding pool of jobless with longer durations of unemployment and lower re-employment wages. These three segments will not necessarily be industry- or occupation-specific.

One of the implications of Lindbeck and Snower's model is that when researchers talk about a relative demand shift away from unskilled to skilled labour, skill may now also include the ability to be versatile and 'learn how to learn'. A worker could be 'higher' skilled in the sense that s/he can do several semi-skilled jobs rather than a single, specialized one. This versatility is presumably positively correlated with education, but there will certainly be variation within education groups in the ability of individuals to adapt to change. The concern is that older workers may be the least versatile even given their education level, and as a result end up in the latter two sectors of Lindbeck and Snower's model.

Current patterns of investments in human capital by age

Given the above discussion, what do we know about the current distribution of skills by the age of workers already in employment? In particular, some have argued that the ability to deal with quantitative issues and computers are two skills that not only have become increasingly important but are also less likely to be acquired by older workers. If older workers have weaker quantitative skills they may be left behind by the computer revolution.

The International Adult Literacy Survey (OECD and Human Resources Development Canada 1997) provides some interesting information on the skill capacities of workers in different countries of different ages. Figure 6.3 presents information on the proportion of employed workers aged 16–65 with minimal mathematics skills (for example, unable to complete simple

Figure 6.3 Employed individuals with minimal mathematics skills: minimal quantitative score.

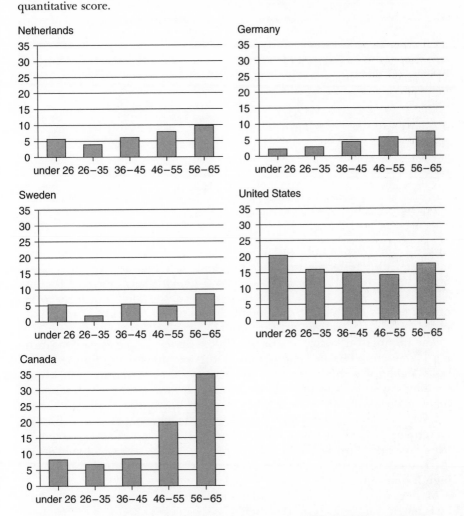

Source: OECD and Human Resources Development Canada (1997) Adult Literacy Survey

addition or subtraction on a bank deposit form or an order form) for five OECD countries. There is some modest evidence that older workers are more likely to have limited mathematics skills than new entrants. But what is most striking in this figure are the differences across countries, irrespective of age, in the skill ability of workers. For example, in the United States, one in five young employed workers has only minimal quantitative skills. This is ten times larger than the number for Germany. The proportion of employed workers with minimal quantitative skills actually declines with age

Table 6.1   Percentage of population at various literacy levels

Mathematics level	Very high 4/5	Medium 3	Low 2	Minimal 1
Australia	19.1	37.7	26.5	16.8
Belgium (Flanders)	22.6	37.8	23.0	16.7
Canada	22.2	34.8	26.1	16.9
Germany	23.5	43.2	26.6	6.7
Ireland	16.2	30.7	28.3	24.8
Netherlands	19.9	44.3	25.5	10.3
New Zealand	17.2	33.4	28.9	20.4
Sweden	35.8	39.0	18.6	6.6
UK	18.6	30.4	27.8	23.2
United States	22.5	31.3	25.3	21.0

Source: OECD and Human Resources Development Canada 1997

in the United States until the 56–65 year old age range. These numbers may even underestimate the skills problem in a country like the United States since they are for those who have actually succeeded in finding employment. So the 'skills' problem across countries does not seem to be one of age as much as of the potential within each country to raise skill proficiency across the ability distribution.

The numbers in Figure 6.3 for the United States are particularly disturbing if one considers the implication of this picture for the future. If the skills ability of young workers is low, unless there is massive post-school training investments by firms, it is unlikely that these workers with minimal mathematics skills will ever be able to catch up. But as shown in Lynch (1994), the United States and Canada seem to have much lower rates of employer-provided formal on-the-job training than many other OECD countries. So, barring workers returning to school, the percentage of workers in the United States with minimal mathematics skills may become disturbingly high in the future.

More generally, as shown in Table 6.1, the variation in mathematics ability is much smaller in countries such as Germany, Sweden and the Netherlands than it is in the United States, UK, Ireland, New Zealand or Canada. For example, there are about three times as many people with zero or minimal reading and mathematics skills in the United States as there are in Germany. In Germany, basic educational standards are set for all students to attain, and students know that their performance will be a critical factor in the probability that they attend university or obtain a good apprenticeship. In other words, the German educational system sets high minimum standards for all and there are incentives in place to do well in school, and not just for those going on in higher education. School systems that set and achieve a high level of performance for those in the bottom half of the ability range combined with a comprehensive post-school vocational training

Figure 6.4   Any training since 1993, by age

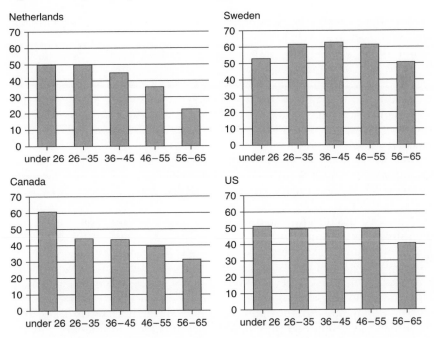

Source: OECD and Human Resources Development Canada (1997) Adult Literacy Survey

system can help to minimize many of the negative consequences of a relative demand shift away from the unskilled.

Human capital theory would lead one to suspect that on-the-job training would be significantly 'front-loaded' in a worker's career so that there is a sufficiently long period to recoup the costs of training. Figure 6.4, again using data from the OECD International Adult Literacy Survey, shows the probability of employed workers receiving any education or training by age. (Note these data suggest much higher 'training' incidence in the United States than do previous surveys on the American workforce but these figures include returning to school to take a course that may or may not be provided by an employer.) What is striking about these figures is the lack of evidence of front-loading in any of the countries examined. While this may seem to be inconsistent with human capital theory, it is not. Employers' concerns about having a sufficiently long period to recoup their investment costs means that they worry about two types of exit from the firm: resignations and retirements. High turnover rates of young workers is a well-documented phenomenon in the United States so it may make sense for employers to wait before investing in training. Work by Lynch (1991, 1993) using the National Longitudinal Survey Youth Cohort found that nearly three-quarters of young workers who were post-school left their first post-school employer within their first four years in employment. The average duration of the first job was a year and a half. So employers may be delaying their investment in training until they are sure that the employment relationship is likely to last.

However, as discussed above, when workers are closer to retirement, employers may be much less likely to invest in their training given the shorter expected horizon over which they can recoup the costs of the investment; the length of the required horizon being a function of the size of the investment. Therefore, we need to know something more about the average size of employer investments in human capital in order to predict the impact of an ageing workforce on the probability of older workers receiving training. Unfortunately, measuring the costs of training investments is not straightforward. There is no universally accepted accounting standard for training costs. While direct costs such as the expense of hiring an outside training consultant/teacher and materials may be easy to quantify, indirect costs such as lost production time by workers in training or supervisors doing informal training are not. These indirect costs are likely to be the largest component of training costs, especially for smaller firms.

Given these caveats, the American Society for Training and Development estimates that in 1995 US$55.3 billion was spent by US employers on formal training, of which 52 per cent was on indirect costs including wages, salaries and fringe benefits. For the months of May through October 1995, the US Bureau of Labor Statistics found that small establishments (50–99 employees) spent an average of US$159 per employee on direct training costs (tuition reimbursements, wages and salaries of in-house trainers, payments to outside trainers, contributions to outside training funds, and subsidies for training received from outside sources) and US$110 per employee on indirect wage and salary costs for formal training. The corresponding numbers for medium establishments (100–499 employees) were US$248 on direct costs and US$215 on indirect costs, and for large establishments (500 employees or more) US$466 on direct costs and US$308 on indirect costs of formal training.

These are not large amounts of money, although they are for a country where employers spend relatively little on their workers compared with France, Norway or Sweden. Nevertheless, these numbers for the United States suggest that the horizon necessary to recoup these costs does not need to be that long. Again, an ageing workforce will mean that the horizon to recoup investments will be shorter, but the key is the scale of those investments to determine whether an ageing workforce will really mean a reduction in the amount invested in training.

What to do

This chapter has tried to show that although there are reasons to be concerned about the interaction between an ageing workforce and an increasingly skills-driven economy, an ageing workforce is not necessarily an obsolete workforce. There are reasons to be concerned about possible market failures in the delivery of training to older workers, however, especially those that have been displaced by the patterns of trade or a sudden technological change in their industry. What might be some of the policy responses?

The role of government training programmes

Some have argued that expenditures for government training programmes should be cut in countries such as the United States since they do not work or they even have a negative impact on the wages and earnings of displaced or disadvantaged youths and adults. However, a review of the evidence on the effectiveness of government training programmes (see US Department of Labor 1995) suggests that at least some types of government-funded training and employment programmes have been successful. In particular, studies of dislocated workers and older college students have found significant positive impacts of long-term training. For example, Jacobson *et al.* (1994) examined displaced workers in Pennsylvania who had lost jobs that they had held for at least three years and whose average age was 35. Workers who received between one and two years of community college training showed earnings gains of 6–7 per cent per year of education received. These returns did not appear to diminish over time. However, displaced workers in short-term skills training (three to six months of classroom training or on-the-job training) showed no significant increase in earnings or employment compared with displaced workers who just received job search assistance. This is just one study and there has been very little empirical work on the returns to government training programmes for older workers (see Leigh (1995) for a comprehensive international overview on the effectiveness of programmes targeted at displaced workers). However, these results suggest that simply writing off older works as 'too old to learn' may misjudge the potential benefits of substantial investments in these displaced workers.

Hand-in-hand with the demographic trend towards an older workforce is the increasing participation of women in the labour market in all of the OECD countries. Unfortunately, in many of the OECD countries where there are data on the incidence of post-school investments, women traditionally have received much less employer-provided training (especially when measured by hours of training). This may mean that countries that are concerned about skills shortages associated with an ageing workforce may have to pay special attention to women workers and target some programmes towards their skills development.

If there is a market failure in the provision of more general skills training, then other policies such as tax credits for employers who invest in their employees, or training vouchers to workers to acquire new skills on their own, may help address this failure. But any policy discussion on training and an ageing workforce will be limited by the availability of data on training. For example, a key issue for an ageing workforce is the rate of depreciation of skills and specifically whether different types of investment (schooling versus employer training versus government training) depreciate at different rates. Does the depreciation rate vary for different types of worker? More generally, what is the relative effectiveness of alternative types of human capital investment for different groups of workers – youth, long-term unemployed, recently displaced workers, welfare entrants, women re-entrants, immigrants, and older incumbent workers? Knowing the answers to questions like these can help prioritize public spending, yet comparable data necessary to examine these issues are hard to find in any of the OECD countries (see the OECD (1999) for a detailed discussion of comparative data on training).

In sum, an ageing workforce employed in an economy that is characterized by rapid technological change suggests that a more detailed examination is merited of our educational and training institutions and how they provide for skills upgrading for incumbent workers. Even in countries such as Germany, the apprenticeship system which has served it so well in the past may need some retuning to better serve older workers in need of skills upgrading. In the United States, educational institutions such as community colleges may be an increasingly important source of skills upgrading for incumbent workers. No single institutional model will serve all countries, but the sooner countries examine the ability of their education and training institutions to meet the needs of an increasingly mature workforce the better. But how accurately countries will be able to assess this will be very much a function of their ability to measure investments in human capital that occur outside the formal educational system. If we fail accurately to capture the varied investments in human capital (both formal and informal) that are made over the course of a worker's lifetime, we run the risk of generating policy on the basis of what is easy to measure rather than what is necessary to measure.

Note

1. The research on which this chapter is based was funded by the OECD's Ageing Society project, and the author would like to thank Paul Swaim and Norman Bowers for their earlier comments. The conclusions expressed in this chapter remain the author's own and do not necessarily reflect the position of the OECD.

References

Ashenfelter, O. and Rouse, C.E. (1998) Income, schooling and ability: evidence from a new sample of identical twins, *Quarterly Journal of Economics*, 113(1): 253–84.
Barron, J., Berger, M. and Black, D. (1987) Employer size: the implications for search, training, capital investments, starting wages and wage growth, *Journal of Labor Economics*, January: 77–89.

Bartel, A. and Sicherman, N. (1993) Technological change and retirement decisions of older workers, *Journal of Labor Economics*, 11(1), pt 1: 162–83.

Bishop, J. (1994) The impact of previous training on productivity and wages, in L.M. Lynch (ed.) *Training and the Private Sector: International Comparisons.* Chicago: University of Chicago Press.

Black, S.E. and Lynch, L.M. (1996) Human capital investments and productivity, *American Economic Review*, 86(2): 263–7.

Brown, J. (1989) Why do wages increase with tenure?, *American Economic Review*, 79: 971–99.

Bureau of Labor Statistics (1995) International Labor Comparisons among G7 Countries: A Chartbook. Internal document, Bureau of Labor Statistics.

Fullerton, H. (1999) Labor force projections to 2008: steady growth and changing composition, *Monthly Labor Review*, November: 19–32.

Jacobson, L., Lalonde, R.J. and Sullivan, D. (1994) The Returns from Classroom Training for Displaced Workers. Rockville, MD: WESTAT.

Kane, T.J. and Rouse, C.E. (1995) Labor market returns to two and four year colleges: is a credit a credit and do degrees matter?, *American Economic Review*, 85(3): 600–14.

Leigh, D. (1995) *Assisting Workers Displaced by Structural Change: An International Perspective.* Kalamazoo: Upjohn Institute.

Lillard, L. and Tan, H. (1986) Private sector training: who gets it and what are its effects? Rand monograph R-3331-DOL/RC.

Lindbeck, A. and Snower, D. (1996) Reorganization of firms and labor market inequality, *American Economic Review*, May: 315–21.

Lynch, L.M. (1991) The role of off-the-job vs. on-the-job training for the mobility of women workers, *American Economic Review*, 81(May): 151–6.

Lynch, L.M. (1992) Private sector training and the earnings of young workers, *American Economic Review*, March: 299–312.

Lynch, L.M. (1993) Entry level jobs: first rung on the employment ladder or economic dead end?, *Journal of Labor Research*, 14(Summer): 249–63.

Lynch, L.M. (ed.) (1994) *Training and the Private Sector: International Comparisons.* Chicago: University of Chicago Press.

Mincer, J. (1988) *Job Training, Wage Growth and Labor Turnover*, working paper no. 2690. Cambridge, MA: National Bureau of Economic Research.

Mincer, J. and Higuchi, Y. (1988) Wage structure and labor turnover in the United States and Japan, *Journal of the Japanese and International Economics*, 2: 97–133.

OECD and Human Resources Development Canada (1997) *Literacy Skills for the Knowledge Society: Further Results from the International Adult Literacy Survey.* Paris and Ottawa: OECD/HRDC.

OECD, Centre for Educational Research and Innovation (1998) *Human Capital Investment: An International Comparison.* Paris: OECD.

OECD (1999) Training of adult workers in OECD countries: measurement and analysis, *Employment Outlook.* Paris: OECD.

US Bureau of the Census (1993) *An Aging World II.* Washington, DC: US Bureau of the Census.

US Department of Labor (1995) *What's Working (and What's Not): A Summary of Research on the Economic Impacts of Employment and Training Programs.* Washington, DC: Office of the Chief Economist.

7

From Human Capital to Social Capital

Tom Healy

Introduction

In the latter half of the 1990s the OECD's Centre for Educational Research and Innovation (CERI) was to the fore in developing analyses of human capital investment, describing the impact not only of education but also of learning throughout life on a wide range of outcomes. Conceptually and in policy terms the analyses went beyond the traditional human capital focus on individual skills and qualifications. The social, community and organizational context of learning assumed prominence, reflecting the cross-disciplinary and policy perspectives of work at CERI. Social capital embodied in communities, schools and organizations emerged as important for better learning outcomes. Learning in different environments was recognized as important for sustaining the shared values, norms and networks associated with the notion of social capital.

Although the term 'social capital' is still the subject of some controversy among academics (Schuller *et al.* 2000), the ideas and policy issues associated with it have attracted the increasing attention of politicians across the political spectrum as well as a diverse audience of policy interests ranging from international agencies, environmentalists, development economists, health promotion agencies, educationalists and voluntary groups. This chapter discusses the significant broadening of focus which this represents. It reviews some of the key conceptual and theoretical considerations in using human and social capital, and explores the concept of well-being. Some recent empirical evidence for the impact of human and social capital on social and economic well-being is then assessed. The final section raises some issues for future research and policy response.

The origin of the term 'human capital' and the rise of 'social capital'

Contemporary interest in the contribution of learning and knowledge to economic and social development dates back to the early 1960s when OECD sponsored an international conference on investment in education. Economists such as Gary Becker and Theodore Schultz established global reputations by recognizing the importance of including human knowledge and skills in models to explain economic development. However, not everyone took to this term initially. Some questioned the wisdom of encompassing human attributes and skills in an economic metaphor. Others questioned whether it would ever be possible to arrive at meaningful and operational measures of human capital alongside those of physical capital.

Over time, the notion came to be accepted, not just on the merits of its role as 'capital' in contributing to economic development but also as a vital set of resources, representing a combination of natural endowment as well as conscious investments of time and money in producing a stream of personal, social and economic benefits. The investment and benefit metaphor won out because human skills and knowledge were seen as too important to be relegated to a secondary role in mainstream economic and social analysis on supposed grounds of vagueness or lack of measurability. Spending on education and training is an investment, and many commentators have pointed to the need for it to be integrated into a better accounting framework covering key social, personal and economic costs and benefits.

Early work by economists in the field of human capital analysis recognized the importance of a variety of human attributes, including health, to the understanding of human capital, and not just skills and knowledge acquired through formal education or on-the-job experience (Becker 1993: 54–5). Moreover, they acknowledged the important contribution of education and human capital more generally to various aspects of human well-being – difficult as these are to measure and incorporate in a comprehensive cost–benefit analysis.

Decades later, the concept of human capital is firmly established, although its operational definition remains a matter of debate and contestation. A broad definition of human capital is used in the OECD report *The Well-being of Nations: The Role of Human and Social Capital*: 'The knowledge, skills, competencies and attributes embodied in individuals that facilitate the creation of personal, social and economic well-being' (OECD 2001a: 18). This emphasizes both the diverse contexts in which learning takes place and the combination of outcomes and goals for which learning takes place.

A limitation of most standard analyses of human capital was that they tended to focus on aspects of formal education or the relationship between initial education experience and individual income streams over a lifetime in the labour market. Different tracks of work increasingly emerged in the course of the 1980s and 1990s:

- A renewed emphasis was placed on the role of knowledge as a key factor in the economic growth process (following, especially, the work of the 'new growth economists' such as Lucas (1988), Romer (1990) and Barro (1991).
- The role of knowledge – both collective and individual – in organizations emerged as a key area in analysis of company performance and capacity.
- Various types of 'non-market' or 'social' benefits of education and learning were increasingly emphasized (Haveman and Wolfe 1984).
- The social, ethical and non-cognitive dimension of learning in schools received renewed attention.
- Finally, the social context in which learning takes place has received greater attention. This is especially marked by the rise of social capital and cultural capital as concepts complementing human capital, stemming from the work of James Coleman and others regarding the powerful influence of social networks and norms on the quality of learning outcomes (Coleman 1988).

The emergence of social capital

Alongside natural, physical and human capital, the notion of social capital was waiting in the wings where human capital had been waiting previously in the early 1960s. As in the case of human capital, the roots of the idea could be traced back into the work of sociologists and economists of the past two centuries. However, resurrecting a notion of capital which was relational and which brought civic and social norms into the picture would not be a smooth task. Many remain sceptical about the coherence of the notion of social capital and still more the feasibility of measuring it or applying its analysis to practical policy debate (for example, Solow 1999).

OECD met the challenge of setting out a framework for advancing the measurement and application of social capital through the publication of the *Well-being of Nations* report (WBN). The definition of social capital used in WBN is: 'networks together with shared norms, values and understandings that facilitate cooperation within or among groups' (p. 41). This particular definition is sufficiently narrow to exclude confusing social capital with anything and everything from institutions to outcomes such as social cohesion. At the same time, it is sufficiently broad to encompass the specific, complex cultural and relational features of various types of groups and organizations. Reference to 'shared values' gives explicit recognition to the importance of culture in an understanding of behaviour as expressed through networks. Close to this understanding of social capital is the role of trust as a crucial mediating factor in assisting social cooperation whether at the level of an organization, school or family. While social capital resides in social relations, human capital resides in individuals but is potentially a close complement of social capital.

An important three-way distinction introduced by many researchers of social capital (notably Woolcock 2001) is between bonding, bridging and linking. *Bonding* social capital describes social ties within relatively homogeneous groups such as families or closely knit ethnic groups (similar, but not identical, to the notion of strong ties). *Bridging* social capital typically describes ties between different types of individuals and groups. The latter ties tend to be weaker and more widely spread. Finally, *linking* social capital describes the relationships between individuals and groups in vertical, hierarchical or power-based relationships. A key dimension needed in further research on social capital and its link to education and lifelong learning is likely to be the extent to which individuals and groups interact in various learning environments with others who are dissimilar.

One of the objections raised to the use of the term 'social capital' is that its application does not distinguish between potentially destructive effects of particular networks and norms in some cases and positive manifestations in others. The latter provide a basis for wider levels of social cohesion across diverse groups and cultures, whereas the former, particularly those which reside in tightly knit groups that exclude or mistrust outsiders, tend to block cohesion and engender the exclusive pursuit of narrow, sectional interest. Although the terms 'positive' and 'negative' social capital are frequently used, strictly speaking these terms may mislead. Rather, social capital (people doing things together in networks on the basis of shared norms) can be used for positive or negative purposes depending on the judgement of the observer. It should be recalled that physical and human capital can also be employed for socially destructive purposes. This fact does not rob them of their potential as 'capital' to be used to produce a flow of benefits or results for those investing in them.

The complementarity between social and human capital is a key issue in any analysis of knowledge societies. This puts a premium on assessing overall levels of social capital, and trends in its growth or decline. In his analysis of trends in the United States, Robert Putnam, possibly the foremost exponent of social capital as a central concept in social science, documents the decline of social capital in the United States and identifies some likely causes and possible remedies (Putnam 2000a). He also analyses the available research evidence on the positive impact of social capital on economic, social and personal well-being. The evidence for declining social capital elsewhere – especially in Europe – is less clear, partly because of lack of good quality data to measure trends over a long period of time (Putnam 2000b). However, the evidence in most studies suggests a robust correlation between community and civic participation on the one side and educational attainment on the other, thus providing empirical evidence for positive complementarity.

The relationship to well-being

The starting point of the WBN report was not human and social capital but consideration of a broad range of economic, social and environmental concerns. The notion of well-being, which had been used in OECD work on social indicators in the 1970s, was already in vogue in policy discussions on sustainable development as well as measurement work on progress in quality of life. Measures of progress based exclusively or mainly on GDP or employment earnings are increasingly viewed as inadequate (see, for example, Eckersley 1998). The net had to be cast wider in discussions of the contribution of human capital to human well-being. WBN identified four key dimensions to well-being:

• sustainable consumption flows;
• sustainable capital stock – physical, natural, human and social;
• access to wealth, resources and income by different groups;
• subjective well-being and life satisfaction.

The notion of well-being is difficult to pin down. Some approach the concept at the level of individual or subjective life satisfaction. Still broader notions of well-being refer to societal values and preferences in relation to distribution of opportunities and 'weightings' between different dimensions of well-being (trading higher consumption against natural environment erosion or leisure time against lower income). However well-being is defined or measured, it is clear that a flow of income or economic output is only one contributor to well-being. Changes in the capital stock of society also impact on the future well-being of individuals as do changes in health, education, social status, social ties and relationships and the quality of public governance.

WBN develops a model in which changes in GDP according to the national accounts framework are a subset of what is referred to as economic well-being. Economic well-being relates not only to paid market or non-market activities but also to various forms of unpaid work (for example volunteering or caring for the young and old) which do not enter into the national accounts. Moreover, inequality and subjective perceptions of economic risk are also relevant to a wider notion of economic well-being. A further consideration is that some activities or expenditures counted in GDP may not directly contribute to economic or total human well-being. Examples of what are termed 'social regrettables' include expenditure relating to pollution or various forms of social dysfunction, including higher security or litigation costs associated with lower trust and greater anti-social behaviour.

The interrelationship between different forms of capital and their potential (joint) contribution to well-being is described in Figure 7.1. Total well-being refers to the entire circle incorporating economic well-being. Social regrettables lie outside total well-being. Well-being is certainly influenced by the quality of the natural environment. Beyond natural capital, resources in the form of machines, tools, buildings as well as the disembodied knowledge and information residing in organizations can contribute to economic output and well-being. The range of human and social capabilities encompassing the skills, values, relationships and institutions of a community at

Figure 7.1

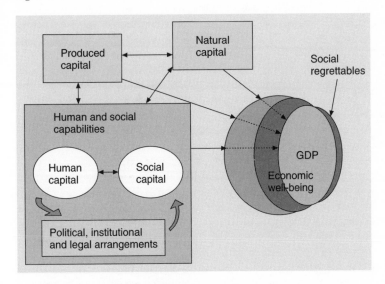

a given time and in a given cultural setting all potentially contribute to well-being.

A careful distinction needs to be drawn between the broad political, institutional and legal environments on the one hand, and social capital on the other, although the dividing line between networks – formal or informal – and various types of institution remains fuzzy. The institutional and legal environment is a vital component of human and social capability along with human and social capital. Effective institutions and laws provide a framework in which human and social capital can contribute to well-being.

Accounting for the impact of human and social capital

The positive correlation, at the level of individuals, between completed formal education and subsequent lifetime earnings and employment is well documented (OECD 1998). The evidence for macroeconomic impacts is less clear, but recent OECD work on the determinants of growth in GDP suggest statistically significant and large potential increases in GDP arising from investments in education. For example, one study found that for OECD countries as a whole, each extra year of full-time education (corresponding to a rise in human capital by about 10 per cent), is associated with an increase in output per capita of about 6 per cent (Bassanini and Scarpetta 2001). However, these results are at a very aggregate level of analysis and average out over different cultures, institutional arrangements and levels of quality of learning outcomes. They also focus on the measurable impact of initial or formal education on one aspect of economic well-being. Still, the evidence is highly suggestive and important for establishing the importance of knowledge and skills in sustaining economic growth and social development.

The impact of social capital on growth in GDP is also the subject of recent analysis. Cross-country analyses suggest a link between levels of trust and growth in productivity as well as between levels of trust and investment in physical capital (Knack and Keefer 1997; Knack 2001). The level of general interpersonal trust was measured by using data from the World Values Survey in which individuals were asked: 'Generally speaking, would you say that most people can be trusted, or that you can't be too careful in dealing with people?' The authors estimated that, on average, a level of trust that is ten percentage points higher in a country is associated with an annual growth rate that is 0.8 percentage points higher. But we need to be cautious: the meaning and interpretation of trust, behaviour and expressions of attitudes and values are open to question in any cross-cultural or cross-country study of aggregate trends and levels.

Some of the most striking evidence on the impact of human and social capital is in relation to personal and social benefits which extend beyond measurable improvements in productivity and employment (for example, see OECD 1998; Helliwell 2001; Schuller *et al.* 2001). Veenstra (2001) notes that the relationship between social status and health is a common theme of research on population health. This is founded on purchasing power (from income), knowledge power (from education) and employment power (from prestige and control). Alongside this more traditional approach, insights from psycho-social research have refocused attention on the role of social ties and norms as important mediating factors in influencing the impact of income, education and employment on physical health and mental well-being. Using US evidence, Putnam (2000a) cites the results of numerous new studies which indicate a link between social connectedness on the one hand and health and personal well-being on the other (after controlling for social, racial and demographic characteristics of individuals).

Underlying the impact of learning on health status is access to information, behaviour, attitudes as well as social status and employment. Learning can encompass a wide range of cognitive and non-cognitive skills, including the development of norms, attitudes and values conducive to the application of a sense of responsibility to oneself and others. The development of self-esteem, self-efficacy and interpersonal trust, together with a more active engagement in community activities, can impact positively on health as well as on personal well-being.

Measures of subjective well-being or life satisfaction provide a summary view of outcomes of investment of time and effort. By treating money, health, time spent in learning, working or caring and general ecological factors as inputs or investments, it is possible to construct a picture of what are the key determinants of personal happiness and well-being. The research evidence suggests diminishing returns to more income in terms of happiness (Blanchflower and Oswald 2000). Moreover, greater income inequality and higher levels of income generally can impair the life satisfaction of those who are marginalized. The opposite seems to hold in the case of human, and especially, social capital. More is generally better, and the impact of higher levels of social capital at the broad community level has a positive impact on individuals over and above any direct impact for individuals who trust more or who are engaged more in voluntary or civic activity. Various studies suggest that, beyond a certain level of income, diminishing returns apply such that given increases in income have less effect on well-being compared with what would hold at lower income levels. The higher the level of human, and especially social, capital in the locality, region or country where individuals live, the more likely they are to be happier than in another area (all other things constant), whereas higher average income in the region or locality relative to own income generally does not enhance personal well-being (Putnam 2001). Work by economists such as Blanchflower and Oswald (2000) also confirms the hypothesis that, beyond a certain threshold, income matters less for life satisfaction and the quality of interpersonal relations and that social ties together with important life events or experiences such as unemployment, education, divorce and health status become critical.

The social ozone layer

We have begun to assemble a body of knowledge to guide decisions in relation to education and training provision. However, large gaps exist with respect to knowledge about choices and strategies across different cultures, institutional settings and circumstances. When it comes to questions about how to invest in trust, stronger civic and local community networks and more public-spirited norms of behaviour, the answers become more difficult. If the very notion of investment was disputed in relation to formal education and training, still more the term is applied with difficulty to describe what most people do informally, spontaneously and frequently for reasons not consciously directed at social cohesion or the public good. Informal learning and social networks belong to a domain which is difficult for policy-makers to work on or grow. An important consideration is that benefits take time, and a range of enabling factors working in conjunction with human and social capital provide the basis for longer-term development. Providing the right context and conditions for lifelong learning and the effective management of knowledge for the benefit of all may produce long-term benefits in terms of stronger communities of practice. Certainly, public policy has a role – if only 'to do no harm'. However, the real success of policies to promote human and social capital depends on the essential ingredients of partnerships, shared understandings and a culture of openness to learning and change. All concerned can act to build commitment and trust through policies of inclusion, accountability and support for the weakest.

Calls for more lifelong learning, volunteering and civic responsibility are not enough. Individuals, communities and organizations need clearer signals and stronger incentives to continue to invest in high-quality learning experience. Part of an effective policy response is to provide more information about learning opportunities and the benefits of learning experience. Another key consideration is the creation of more flexible and responsive systems of learning adapted to the needs of individuals as learners. Enhancing both the means and the outcomes of learning opportunities requires the right kind of social capital to provide access to information and support. Knowledge and learning do not hold the key to the solution of all social problems. Neither does social connectedness provide a magic wand for raising well-being or economic performance. Human and social capital can be wasted or badly utilized. They can be put to destructive uses or be undermined by the existence of other factors which inhibit social and economic progress. However, investing in social and human capital can make good sense for families, communities, businesses and government – provided that it is possible to identify how best to invest time and money.

A key role for public, private and voluntary actors is to help the weakest to access learning opportunities through 'knowledge-friendly' networks that encourage the learning habit and learning experience. Creating learning-rich environments, not only in places designed for formal instruction and accredited learning, but also in workplaces, local communities and places where people meet and interact is a major challenge. Not everyone has equal access to information, learning, social networks or power. Giving poorer communities and disadvantaged groups a greater say and sense of responsibility is an important part of redressing social imbalance. In some cases, they may have the wrong kind of social capital or they may have plenty of social capital but not enough real access to financial or human capital to break out of cycles of poverty or exclusion.

If human and social capital are as important as physical or natural capital, then a key concern must be their maintenance and renewal – just like the other forms of capital. It took decades to identify important changes in the ozone layer and realize that they presented a problem. If it can be demonstrated that the 'social ozone layer' in the form of the networks, values and norms that underpin community life and cooperation at levels in our society is under threat, then there is a serious challenge to adjust responses and foresee what is needed for the future. It is easier to measure material resource flows, forest depletion and changes in global temperature. It is not as easy to measure possible subtle but vital changes taking place in the way that human beings interact with each other. If individuals have less time, or are less willing, to volunteer for local community sports, parental support for extracurricular activity or community organizations caring for the elderly and sick, then the social capital residing in the networks and associated norms of mutual obligation is weakened. Likewise, if employees and employers feel increasingly obliged to rely on recourse to legal and other formal control mechanisms to enforce contracts or avoid opportunism, then an economic cost is incurred.

Conclusions

A wide range of issues from flexibility in working time to provision of education, transport and residential care have been mentioned as potential areas for cooperative response to improve social capital. However, social capital can never become the Trojan horse to deliver economic and social progress. Likewise, the promotion of higher skills, knowledge and learning in schools, organizations and communities alone cannot deliver sustainable economic and social progress.

We need to rethink the implicit assumptions, underlying values and patterns of public, private and voluntary provision appropriate to another phase in our development. We need to acknowledge and enlarge concerns about measurable wealth and income to encompass quality of life and well-being, notoriously difficult as these are to account for. Getting the balance right calls for farsightedness, for example in making new and imaginative arrangements that are put in place to provide funds for individuals to draw upon for learning in the course of their lives; 'joined-up' thinking, for instance in recognizing that achieving higher levels of literacy and skill is a matter for all the social partners as well as all public agencies; and 'joined-up' action so that the right types of network and trust – social capital – are fostered in support of lifelong learning.

In the foreword to *Education Policy Analysis* (OECD 2001b), the Secretary-General of OECD, Don Johnston, has the following to say:

> At the same time, new and old skills demanded in the labour market must be complemented by skills that help foster the social networks, norms and values ('social capital') that are essential for well-functioning democracies, with active participation by citizens. They can provide the basic resources of leadership and strong social networks that contribute to better government. Schools and institutions of learning can help create values for social cooperation, and so nurture social capital along with families, local communities and firms.
>
> (p. 7)

Alongside human capital, social capital is now a welcome member of the family of 'capitals' used in discussions of the determinants of economic growth or well-being more generally. It remains to develop our understanding and use of the term in mainstream policy analysis by paying attention to its strong potential for playing a complementary role with human capital in improving well-being. The close fit between levels of social capital and human capital suggests that policies to promote widespread lifelong learning and inclusion of disadvantaged groups in learning activity may provide one of the most effective ways for public policy to renew social capital in the future.

References

Barro, R.G. (1991) Economic growth in a cross-section of countries, *Quarterly Journal of Economics*, CVI, May.

Bassanini, A. and Scarpetta, S. (2001) *Links between Policy and Growth: Evidence from OECD Countries*. OECD Economics Department working papers.

Becker, G. (1993) *Human Capital: A Theoretical and Empirical Analysis, with Special Reference to Education*, 3rd edn. Chicago: University of Chicago Press.

Blanchflower, R.D.G. and Oswald, A.J. (2000) *Well-being over Time in Britain and the USA*, working paper no. 7487. Cambridge, MA: National Bureau of Economic Research.

Coleman, J. (1988) Social capital in the creation of human capital, *American Journal of Sociology*, 94 (Supplement): S95–S120.

Eckersley, R. (1998) *Measuring Progress: Is Life Getting Better?* Victoria, Australia: Commonwealth Scientific and Industrial Research Organisation Publishing.

Haveman, R.H. and Wolfe, B. (1984) Schooling and economic well-being: the role of non-market effects, *Journal of Human Resources*, 19 (Summer): 378–407.

Helliwell, J.F. (ed.) (2001) *The Contribution of Human and Social Capital to Sustained Economic Growth and Well-being*: International Symposium Report, Human Resources Development Canada and OECD.

Knack, S. (2001) Trust, associational life and economic performance, in J.F. Helliwell (ed.) *The Contribution of Human and Social Capital to Sustained Economic Growth and Well-being*, pp. 172–202. International Symposium Report, Human Resources Development Canada and OECD.

Knack, S. and Keefer, P. (1997) Does social capital have an economic payoff? A cross-country investigation, *Quarterly Journal of Economics*, 112(4): 1251–88.

Lucas, R.E. (1988) On the mechanisms of economic development, *Journal of Monetary Economics*, 22.

OECD (1998) *Human Capital Investment, an International Comparison*. Paris: OECD.

OECD (2001a) *The Well-being of Nations: The Role of Human and Social Capital*. Paris: OECD.

OECD (2001b) *Education Policy Analysis*. Paris: OECD.

Putnam, R. (2000a) *Bowling Alone: The Collapse and Revival of American Community*. New York: Simon & Schuster.

Putnam, R. (2000b) *Gesellschaft und Gemeinsinn*. Gütersloh: Bertelsmann Foundation.

Putnam, R. (2001) Social capital: measurement and consequences, in J.F. Helliwell (ed.), *The Contribution of Human and Social Capital to Sustained Economic Growth and Well-being*, pp. 117–35. International Symposium Report, Human Resources Development Canada and OECD.

Romer, P. (1990) Human capital and growth: theory and evidence, *Carnegie–Rochester Series on Public Policy*, 32: 251–86.

Schuller, T., Baron, S. and Field, J. (2000) Social capital: an overview and synthesis, in S. Baron, J. Field and T. Schuller (eds) *Social Capital: Critical Perspectives*. Oxford: Oxford University Press.

Schuller, T., Bynner, J, Green, A. *et al.* (2001) *Modelling and Measuring the Wider Benefits of Learning: A Synthesis.* London: Centre for Research on the Wider Benefits of Learning, Institute of Education/Birkbeck College.

Solow, R.M. (1999) Notes on social capital and economic performance, in P. Dasgupta and I. Serageldin (eds) *Social Capital: A Multifaceted Perspective.* Washington, DC: World Bank.

Veenstra, G. (2001) Social capital and health, *ISUMA, Canadian Journal of Policy Research,* 2(1): 72–81.

Woolcock, M. (2001) The place of social capital in understanding social and economic outcomes, in J.F. Helliwell (ed.) *The Contribution of Human and Social Capital to Sustained Economic Growth and Well-being,* pp. 65–88. International Symposium Report, Human Resources Development Canada and OECD.

Part 3

On Organizing Learning

8

The Seventh Sector:
Social Enterprise for Learning
in the United States

David Stern[1]

Through several years of collaborative action research, Deborah McKoy and I have developed the concept of 'social enterprise for learning' (SEfL). This denotes activity that aims simultaneously to: (i) produce goods or services for clients or customers; (ii) provide benefits to a larger community or general public; and (iii) enable participants to develop specified kinds of knowledge or skill. The concept of SEfL extends the idea of school-based enterprise (van Rensburg 1977, 2001; Stern *et al.* 1994; McKoy 2000). By adding the dimension of social benefit, we have sought to capture an important aspect of certain activities that we have observed in the United States and other countries.

This chapter explains why SEfL is a unique setting in which to develop the practices of a 'learning society'. As depicted in Figure 8.1, it engages participants simultaneously in all three primary spheres of activity that occupy the usual weekday lives of people in industrialized societies: commercial enterprise, social-purpose work and education. Each of these primary spheres, alone, is bound by limitations that restrict the opportunities to integrate learning with daily life. By contrast, SEfL enables people of various ages to join work, service and learning. In so doing, it works towards the vision underpinning proposals for recurrent education that emerged around three decades ago and are expressed more recently in the broader concept of lifelong learning.

The concept of social enterprise for learning

- In physics and economics projects, students each year analyse energy use in some part of the school or in other local public facilities, and write proposals that include the estimated financial rate of return on proposed energy-saving measures.

- Students in a health sciences department run a snack bar offering blended fruit drinks and other healthy foods for sale, along with free brochures explaining the nutritional advantages.
- As part of a class in government and economics, students construct a plan for submission to a city planning department and the developer who is building a new commercial centre around a subway station. The students' plan, based on a survey of community priorities, describes both physical and financial dimensions.
- Students in environmental science issue periodic reports on the levels of pollutants in local water, air and soil.
- Construction students design and build a playground in a vacant city site.
- Students in a computer science department produce web pages for local non-profit community groups.

Each of these activities is an SEfL because it involves students and teachers in providing services that not only benefit the people who receive those services directly, but also benefit other people indirectly. These and many other examples of SEfLs can be found in schools (for example, see Wigginton 1986) and post-secondary education. Other examples may be found outside of schools, as discussed later.

We use the word 'enterprise' in 'social enterprise for learning', to denote the fact that SEfLs use resources to provide valuable goods and services for clients or customers. As in a commercial enterprise, participants should be mindful of expenses as well as revenues, if any. The costs of producing a service include: time of students, teachers and anyone else involved;[2] materials and utilities; use of space and equipment. In a school context, the SEfL may not actually be charged for any or all of these. Nevertheless, a complete account of the benefits of SEfL must also include an estimate of costs, whether paid by the SEfL or not.

The word 'enterprise' also signals that the services provided by SEfLs have a market value, whether or not the recipients actually pay any or all of it. In the example of the healthy foods snack bar, customers pay for fruit drinks, and this payment is a reasonable measure of the value to the consumers. In a commercial enterprise that sells ordinary goods and services, payments by clients or customers are generally a measure of what the goods or services are worth to them. However, some SEfLs do not charge anything for the services they provide, as in the example of students writing proposals for reducing energy costs. A first approximation of the market value of the service in this case would be what a consulting company would charge for this analysis. Similarly, the value of services provided by other SEfLs could be approximated by the cost of buying such services commercially. This would be an estimate of benefits to direct recipients of the service, our first category of SEfL benefits.

In addition to being enterprises that use resources to provide direct benefits to customers or clients, SEfLs also have a social impact. The word 'social', in 'social enterprise for learning', denotes our second category

Figure 8.1 The seven sectors

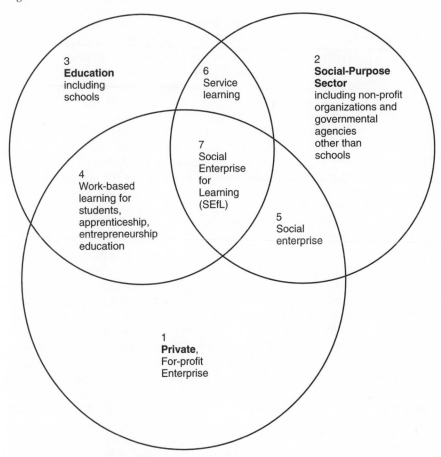

of benefits, which go indirectly to a larger community beyond the direct recipients of the service. (This idea is explained more fully in the discussion of the social-purpose sector below.) For example, if reports issued by the environmental science class result in actions that reduce pollution, everyone affected by the clean-up is better off. Estimating the value of environmental clean-up in monetary terms is a little complicated, but regulatory agencies and the courts have devised estimation procedures.

The social dimension of SEfL distinguishes it from other kinds of school-based enterprise or entrepreneurship programmes that have become increasingly prevalent in the United States. SEfLs espouse social purposes as do non-profit organizations. For instance, SEfLs that conduct purely charitable activities like feeding the homeless would be providing direct benefits to the people receiving food, and indirect benefits to other people for whom this matters.

An example may help to clarify the difference between SEfLs and other school enterprises that do not provide indirect social benefits. One common form of school-based enterprise is a shop, staffed by students and selling primarily to other students. It buys merchandise – sweets, snacks, T-shirts, key chains, and the like – to sell at a marked-up price. Suppose that gross sales are US$1,000 a month. In contrast, consider an SEfL that collects rubbish from the school – paper, plastic, aluminum, glass – and sorts and sells it to a dealer in recycled materials, with gross sales also US$1,000 a month. Does this mean that the two activities provide the same total benefit? No, the social benefit from the recycling service is greater because reusing materials reduces the need for cutting down forests, digging up minerals, and other activities that cause damage to the environment. The environmental damage is not reflected in the market price of new or recycled metal, paper, glass or plastic. The prevailing market prices for materials sold by the recycling centre are lower than they would be if buyers of materials had to pay the cost of environmental restoration in addition to the cost of extraction. Because the prices of materials are lower than they should be, profit-seeking enterprises will not find it financially worthwhile to do as much recycling as they would if the price of materials reflected the true social cost.

Because they address social purposes, SEfLs create a niche for school-sponsored enterprises that is not filled by for-profit businesses outside the school. An ordinary school shop, on the other hand, competes directly with profit-seeking retailers outside the school. If the school shop does not provide any other social or community benefits, its potential scope of operation is apt to be limited by local retailers who oppose school-subsidized competition. Sadly, many thriving school enterprises in the United States have been curtailed or shut down because they took customers away from local businesses.

The 'learning' in 'social enterprise for learning' is intentional and explicit, not merely incidental and implicit. The examples listed at the beginning use SEfL to motivate and contextualize learning that is part of the explicit curriculum in a particular academic discipline or occupational cluster. Teachers' evaluations of students' performance would normally include a written test, paper or other independent measure of what students have learned. The reason why many SEfLs are located in formal educational institutions is that these are the only institutions where such intentional learning of specified knowledge or skill is the primary purpose.

SEfL as a uniquely advantageous sector for development of a learning society

SEfL has unique advantages for the development of practices conducive to a learning society, and for the preparation of people who can participate in it. The rapid proliferation of new technologies, products and market arrangements requires individuals and enterprises to continue learning and adapting at a pace that is fast by historical standards. This requirement also represents an opportunity for more rapid and widespread development of human capabilities. Economic necessities and humanistic possibilities converge in the optimistic vision of a learning society.

However, rigidities in existing institutions pose obstacles to the full realization of this vision. To appreciate the potential of SEfL, we must contrast it with the institutions that occupy the most time for people between the ages when schooling and retirement begin. Workplaces and schools are the two main institutions, with workplaces divided into two primary sectors: (i) profit-seeking enterprises and (ii) social-purpose organizations (see Figure 8.1).

Private, for-profit enterprise is the engine that drives economic growth through the accumulation of financial capital. A fundamental characteristic is that the firm itself can be bought and sold. A business name or brand, and the goodwill attached to it, is a form of private property, separate from the tangible or intangible assets owned by the company. The equity may be owned by shareholders, partners or sole proprietors, and its value depends on current and expected profits. Maximizing the financial value of the enterprise is a dominant motivation.

A major limitation of private, for-profit firms for the development of a learning society is their limited incentive to invest in the human capital of their employees. Although every company provides training of some kind, it is usually restricted to knowledge and skills needed on the job. Firms are continually seeking more efficient means to enable employees to learn on the job and reduce the cost of training – so-called electronic performance support systems (EPSS) are an example (for example, Banerji 1999). But training for incumbent employees tends to be concerned with know-how rather than know-why (OECD 2000: 14).

The amount of training provided by enterprises is further limited by the fact that employees take their skills and knowledge with them when they leave the company. Enterprises cannot claim legal ownership of employees' human capital, so they must regard training as a cost rather than an investment for the firm, despite the continuing efforts of the OECD (1999) to have training outlays included with the other intangible assets in companies' balance sheets.[3] Although the success and growth of commercial enterprise depend on investments in human capital, companies themselves on average limit their own training expenditures to around just 1 per cent of total payroll cost (see Lynch 1994).

The social-purpose sector includes non-profit, non-governmental agencies, as well as governmental agencies other than schools (which are classified here as a separate sphere). Organizations in this second sector cannot be bought and sold. They can be liquidated through sale of the tangible and intangible assets they own, but beyond that they have no capitalized value.[4] This means that managers, directors or employees cannot add to their personal wealth by creating equity capital in the organization. Instead, motives other than wealth acquisition draw individuals to work in this sector, maintaining physical, institutional and social infrastructure or providing cultural or humane services not offered by the for-profit sector. These public and social purposes appeal to communitarian and altruistic motivations.

The meaning of public or social purpose

Although a full discussion of public or social purpose is well beyond the scope of this chapter, we need to address definitions in order to distinguish clearly between the social-purpose and profit-seeking spheres. The concept of public or social purpose used here is rooted in Samuelson's (1954, 1955) classic definition of a 'pure public good', which still serves as a starting point in contemporary texts on economics of the public sector (for example, Mueller 1989; Rosen 1999; Stiglitz 2000). A pure public good provides a benefit that is 'non-rival', in that availability of the benefit for one person does not reduce its availability to anyone else.

The paradigmatic example of a pure public good is a lighthouse shining its light for any and all vessels in the vicinity. Reduction of greenhouse gases is another example: if global warming is abated for one person, it is also reduced for everyone else. Anything that prevents or reduces pollution or other environmental degradation would yield a non-rival benefit. Other examples of pure public goods include reduction of the factors that spread communicable diseases, national defence, laws that establish ground rules for commercial transactions, and improvement of the prospects for world peace. Alleviation of poverty and human suffering can also be considered pure public goods if such charitable activity provides ethical satisfaction for the public at large.

In Samuelson's theory, the value of a public good for any individual is a matter of personal preference – keeping dioxins out of the ocean, for instance, is very important for some people, but not others. Given the distribution of preferences, Samuelson showed that the optimal level of spending to provide a public good depends on the sum of all individuals' willingness to pay for the non-rival benefit. For any particular public good, there may be many individuals who do not want to pay for it. But aggregating willingness to pay for very large numbers of people can result in a substantial demand.

In practice, it is extremely difficult to measure individuals' true willingness to pay for public goods. Individual payment for certain non-rival benefits can be arranged if some people can be excluded from enjoying them. An uncongested road provides a non-rival benefit, but it is possible to get people to pay for it by erecting a toll gate; a television broadcast is non-rival, but it is possible to charge for it by scrambling the signal and selling the unscrambling device. In many cases it is not feasible to exclude people from a non-rival benefit, and actual expenditure for these pure public goods may then depend on voluntary donations. Numerous non-profit organizations in the fields of environmental protection, public health, fine arts and social justice depend on such donations from individuals who value the benefit they provide. Relying on donations, however, creates the well-known 'free-rider' problem: some people who value the benefit do not contribute because they count on other people to provide the needed support, leading to sub-optimal expenditure. To prevent this, public goods are often financed by compulsory contributions in the form of taxes.[5]

This discussion clarifies the difference of purpose between sectors 1 and 2. The goods and services produced and sold in the for-profit sector mainly benefit the people who buy them. Their economic value is determined by the price at which they are sold; competitive markets can be efficient in producing such private goods. By contrast, goods and services in the social-purpose sector yield direct and indirect benefits for a diffuse set of people, including some who do not pay anything for them. The economic value of these services is difficult to measure, and competitive markets cannot allocate them efficiently.

Social-purpose organizations may have stronger intrinsic reasons to promote learning by their employees than commercial enterprises, if training is seen as a means to propagate the agency's mission. A non-profit organization charged with protecting the environment may want to instil knowledge about environmental issues in all its employees, so that they will continue to work for the cause even after they leave the organization. To the extent that social-purpose organizations have a greater interest than profit-seeking firms in giving employees lasting knowledge and skills, they are more inclined to encourage the integration of learning and work that is a hallmark of the learning society. Social-purpose organizations do have the major limitation, however, that their functioning depends on taxation and philanthropic contributions because they do not produce financial wealth. Many of them lack the discretionary resources, therefore, to invest in extensive employee training or education, even if they would like to.

Education (sector 3) is the third primary sphere of activity for most people in contemporary societies. Although learning certainly occurs in sectors 1 and 2, it is not the primary purpose. The unique importance of learning as a separate purpose is underlined by the fact that participation in school-based, organized learning is universally compulsory for children.

The justification for compulsion rests on the belief by a majority of the electorate that schooling accomplishes certain social goals, including preparation of young people to exercise their responsibilities as citizens and members of civil society. But it would not be accurate to classify schools in the social-purpose sector because much of the benefit from schooling is purely private. Education enables students to improve the quality of their individual lives, in part by earning higher wages and salaries for their own private use. Even if a school is operated by a public or non-profit organization, much of the benefit it confers on students does not satisfy the Samuelsonian definition of a public good.

The education sector is instead best understood historically as the result of industrialization, which removed production from households to firms.

Households retained responsibility for raising children but, without control of production, parents were not in a position to pass on their means of livelihood. With work and home no longer located in the same place, caring for children came to compete for parents' time with work. Schooling became universal, free and compulsory as a result of political struggles to reconcile parents' child-raising responsibilities with these new realities.

The contemporary education sector includes not only schools for children and adolescents, but also a growing array of institutions enrolling students well beyond compulsory schooling age. From pre-school to post-retirement, the mix of educational institutions includes profit-seeking enterprises in addition to public and non-profit organizations.[6] The Internet offers a growing number of educational options for individuals to engage in deliberate learning any time, any place. The growing presence of for-profit businesses among the organizations that sponsor schools is another reason for classifying education separately from the social-purpose sector.

Although learning is its primary purpose, the education sector is limited in its ability to enact the vision of a learning society because its very separation from the production sphere means that much of what goes on in educational institutions is decontextualized and unrelated to the world outside. Learning for its own sake is held in high esteem within academia. Keeping education aloof from the world of production makes it much more difficult to achieve the integration of learning and life envisioned in the learning society.

The limitations of decontextualized schooling have prompted the creation of various forms of work-based learning (sector 4), a hybrid activity located in the intersection of sectors 1 and 3, involving students in the acquisition of knowledge and skills through school-supervised work experience.[7] In the United States, this sector includes millions of secondary or post-secondary students enrolled in 'cooperative education', paid or unpaid internships, so-called youth apprenticeships, and diffuse forms of 'job shadowing' (Stasz and Stern 1998; Hershey *et al.* 1999). The traditional purpose of such arrangements has been for students to acquire work-related skills and knowledge that they can use in paid employment. School-supervised work experience also may be intended to advance broader kinds of learning such as development of personal and social skills, becoming acquainted with various aspects of an industry, or exploring different career possibilities. Traditional apprenticeship, in which participants are employees rather than students, also continues to enrol small numbers of people in the United States.

School-based enterprise is a particular form of work-based learning that engages students in the production of goods or services under the auspices of the school itself (Von Borstel 1982; Stern *et al.* 1994). Typical activities are student-run retail shops, restaurants or food services, child-care centres, house-building projects, automobile repair shops, and various kinds of media services. Most of these are outgrowths of vocational and technical classes, providing opportunities for students to practise their skills by serving real clients. Typically, school-based enterprises are owned by the school, though a few schools have created separate non-profit entities that own the enterprises and handle some of the financial management.

Entrepreneurship education also has flourished in US schools. Organizations that create and promote curricula engaging students in diverse simulations, business planning, and sometimes creation of actual enterprises include REAL Enterprise, the National Foundation for Teaching Entrepreneurship, Junior Achievement, and the Kauffman Center for Entrepreneurial Leadership. These enterprises are usually short-lived, designed to lead students through the process of planning, starting, operating and selling a business. In some instances, notably the REAL programme, students can create businesses that they may continue to operate after they graduate.

Work-based learning may increase the relevance of the school curriculum for some students. It may help to prepare students for participation in the learning society by giving them the experience of work and learning that are explicitly intertwined. But work-based learning in the intersection of sectors 1 and 3 does not address the well-being of the community or public at large. It may therefore fail to attract or inspire students for whom these purposes are important, and it does not acquaint students with the kinds of career options available in sector 2.

Social enterprise (sector 5) is another kind of hybrid activity. It occurs at the intersection of sectors 1 and 2, and does not involve educational institutions. It includes enterprises operated by social-purpose organizations that generate revenues or profits to help sustain the parent organizations. For example, Emerson and Twersky (1996) describe how 22 non-profit organizations created business enterprises to help defray the costs of providing food, clothing, shelter and social services to clients who included disabled individuals, disadvantaged youth, homeless people and ex-prisoners. Food services, retailing, construction, bicycle repair, cleaning services, vegetable gardens and recycling were among the business ventures. These usually yielded revenues that more than covered their own operating cost, and thus helped to defray the costs of their parent organizations. Participation in these enterprises also enabled clients to develop skills and work habits that improved their chances of succeeding in regular, paid employment. Similarly, Heath (2001) describes youth-based community organizations that operate after-school programmes, some of which generate revenues.[8]

Some leading US business schools have recently started programmes in 'social entrepreneurship'. In terms of the seven sectors in Figure 8.1, these aim to prepare managers for sectors 2 and 5. For instance, in 1997 the Stanford Business School launched a social entrepreneurship initiative, whose web page gives the following definition:

> Social entrepreneurs take innovative approaches to solving social issues, using traditional business skills to create social rather than private value. Included within this definition are:

- For-profit organizations that use their resources to creatively address social issues
- Non-profit organizations that assist individuals in launching their own small, for-profit businesses, referred to as micro-enterprise or self-employment
- Non-profit ventures that create economic value to fund their own programs or to create employment and training opportunities for their client population.
  http://www.gsb.stanford.edu/ces/social%5Fentrepreneurship.html

Similarly, the Harvard Business School has an initiative on social enterprise 'focusing on non-profit organizations and other private social-purpose enterprises. It was created to respond to the growing social and economic importance of the non-profit sector, and its ever-increasing interrelationship with business' (http://www.hbs.edu/dept/socialenterprise).

Social enterprise *per se* does not address the vision of a learning society. It is of interest here because, in harnessing wealth-creating enterprise to achieve social purposes, it embodies a core idea of SEfL. Unlike SEfL, however, social enterprise alone is not primarily concerned with learning, and therefore does not contain the means to replicate itself.

Service learning (sector 6) is the overlap of sectors 2 and 3. It involves the education sector, but not profit-seeking enterprise. In the United States, service learning includes millions of students participating in various school-supervised service projects as volunteers in non-profit or governmental agencies. Unlike work-based learning, which aims primarily to develop students' work-related skills and knowledge, the principal purpose of service learning is to acquire a better understanding of oneself and society by participating in altruistic endeavours.

Logically, if surprisingly, the training of military personnel would also belong in this sector. As a defensive or deterrent force, the military is properly classified as a social-purpose organization, since it satisfies Samuelson's definition of a pure public good for the inhabitants of a particular country. When it is not actually fighting, it spends much time in highly structured classroom instruction and training exercises. Military training therefore combines learning and public service, and logically parallels service learning by students.[9]

From the viewpoint of the learning society, the main limitation of service learning is its separation from wealth-creating enterprises in sector 1. This means it can expand only along the fringes of sectors 2 and 3, which are largely dependent on taxes and philanthropy.

Social enterprise for learning, SEfL (sector 7) overlaps all three of the primary sectors, and therefore has greater potential than any of the primary or other hybrid sectors to enact the full vision of a learning society. Unlike other forms of work-based learning for students, SEfL explicitly seeks to provide benefits that are public goods in the Samuelsonian sense, and therefore affirms that social purposes are important. SEfL also differs from other kinds of service learning because it engages participants in acquiring work-related skills and knowledge by operating productive enterprises that have a commercial aspect, and which therefore may have greater potential to expand. And SEfL is unlike other social enterprises because learning by participants is a primary purpose that receives explicit and sustained attention, so individuals who gain experience in one SEfL may be able to go and create other SEfLs on their own.

An example of an entire school designed as an SEfL is the Bay Area School of Enterprise (BASE), in the city of Alameda across the bay from San Francisco. BASE is an outgrowth of a project called HOME, which has offered an elective class in 'effective citizenry' and related after-school activities for high school students in Alameda. With the advice and encouragement of older adult staff, HOME students have created a number of successful youth-run ventures including a youth employment agency, a licensed child-care centre, a 15,000 square foot (0.14 hectare) outdoor skate park, a café and a recording studio. The plan for BASE also was developed by a design team composed of students, with support from adult staff. Students drafted the BASE mission statement, which reads:

> We are intelligent and committed youth who want to see change in our world and are assertive about achieving it. We see that traditional high schools do not meet the needs of all teenagers. We are providing an innovative alternative learning environment that will better serve today's youth. At the Bay Area School of Enterprise, each youth will create an individual plan incorporating enterprise, project-based learning, internships, small group instruction, and independent study, as appropriate to the way each individual best learns. Because learning occurs everywhere in the real world, our school will seek learning opportunities throughout our neighbourhood, community, region, nation and world. Our school will graduate powerful new citizens who are ready to take responsibility for the future. It will be a model of what is possible in education when youth are empowered to take charge of their own learning.
>
> (BASE 2001: 3)

This statement captures the integration of enterprise, public purpose and learning that a complete vision of a learning society must include. As perhaps the first entire school that is conceived and organized as an SEfL, BASE is a learning society in microcosm, and a model for bringing that vision to life.

Synergies and possibilities for expansion of SEfLs

The three purposes embodied in an SEfL can enhance one another, as suggested in Figure 8.2. Revenues from the enterprise help finance the

Figure 8.2 Synergies in SEfLs

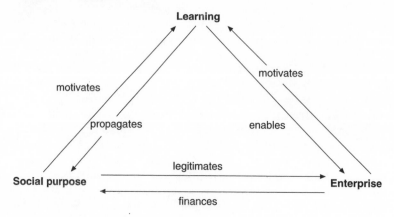

SEfL. The public purpose confers social legitimacy and may make the SEfL eligible for support from public and philanthropic sources. Commitment to social purposes, and the exigencies of operating real enterprises, can both motivate learning. The learning, in turn, enables participants to operate the enterprise, and may inspire them to propagate additional SEfLs in the future. On the other hand, pursuing several distinct purposes all at the same time may create problems of maintaining balance among them.

The existence of real SEfLs suggests that the model is a viable one. This chapter has concentrated on the United States but many examples can be found elsewhere. For instance, the Ashoka organization, which has as its mission 'to develop the profession of social entrepreneurship around the world', has, since 1982, selected more than 1100 social entrepreneurs in 41 countries to work in the six broad fields of education, environment, health, human rights, civic participation, and economic development (http://ashoka.org/home/index.cfm). Arenas (2000) has documented ecological enterprises run by rural schools in Colombia. Among the OECD countries, examples of SEfLs can be found in the production high schools in Denmark (Danish Ministry of Education 1994), and in environmental education programmes run by schools in several countries (OECD 1991).

The concept of SEfL has a clear affinity with the vision of a learning society, and the two may develop together. The ideal of a learning society is appealing in part because it suggests that human development becomes the goal of economic activity, rather than vice versa. Organizations in which human curiosity drives economic growth would be enterprises for learning. If such institutions are to do more than enrich their members financially and intellectually, they must also embrace the public interest and become social enterprises for learning. SEfLs are unlikely to become a dominant economic force in the near future, but they are already offering practical examples of what a learning society might be.

Notes

1. I would like to thank the editors and Alberto Arenas for helpful comments. I am indebted to many conversations with Deborah McKoy for helping to think through the issues in this chapter.
2. Normally, students are not paid for work done during school hours, but students or teachers may be paid for time spent working in a school enterprise after school, on weekends or during summer holidays. Part of the salary of teachers who sponsor SEfLs in their classes during school hours should be counted as a cost of their operation, even though it is absorbed by the school district or local education authority. If students or teachers spend non-school time but are not paid, the time is still an opportunity cost because it could have been used in other ways.
3. For instance, a company can obtain outside financing for new plant and equipment by offering it as collateral for the loan. But expenditures for training cannot be collateralized in this way.
4. A state-owned oil company, utility, railway or other enterprise with its own brand name may have a capitalized value greater than the assets it owns. This is evident when such enterprises have been privatized. For the purposes of this chapter, such enterprises are more appropriately classified in the first sector unless their policies with regard to pricing, environmental impacts or other practices are clearly designed to serve a public purpose as defined below.
5. The amount of tax paid by any individual, however, is determined by a political process, and does not correspond directly to the taxpayer's willingness to pay for particular public goods.
6. A recent US development since the 1990s has been the growing presence of profit-seeking businesses, such as the Edison Corporation, in the provision of primary and secondary education, with special charters or under contract to local educational authorities.
7. Some work-based learning also occurs in the intersection of sectors 2 and 3, but to the extent that this is focused on social purposes rather than individual skill formation it should be classified as service learning (see below).
8. If learning or training is an important purpose of a social enterprise, it would belong in sector 7 as an SEfL. One indication of the importance of learning or training is the extent to which it is deliberately planned and monitored, not just incidental and unstructured. Some of the social enterprises described by Heath and by Emerson and Twersky could qualify as SEfLs even though they are not sponsored by schools.
9. Would educational activities in prisons also be classified in this sector? Protecting the public against dangerous criminals is a Samuelsonian public good, but it would distort usual meanings to say that people serving time in prison are providing a public service.

References

Arenas, A. (2000) Ecological education: schooling, economics, and sustainability. PhD thesis, University of California, Graduate School of Education, Berkeley, California.

Banerji, A. (1999) Performance support in perspective, *Performance Improvement*, 38(7): 6–9.

BASE (Bay Area School of Enterprise) (2001) Charter petition submitted to the HOME project, 2750 Todd Street, Alameda Unified School District, Alameda, CA.

Danish Ministry of Education (1994) *Report to OECD: Danish Youth Education, Problems and Achievements*. Copenhagen: Danish Ministry of Education.

Emerson, J. and Twersky, F. (1996) *New Social Entrepreneurs: The Success, Challenge, and Lessons of Non-profit Enterprise Creation*. San Francisco: The Roberts Foundation.

Heath, S.B. (2001) *Making Learning Work*. Stanford, CA: Stanford University. http://www.shirleybriceheath.com/SocialEnt/makinglearningwork.html (accessed July 2001).

Hershey, A.M., Silverberg, M.K., Haimson, J., Hudis, P. and Jackson, R. (1999) *Expanding Options for Students: Report to Congress on the National Evaluation of School-to-Work Implementation*. Princeton, NJ: Mathematica Policy Research, Inc.

Lynch, L.M. (ed.) (1994) *Training and the Private Sector: International Comparisons*. Chicago: University of Chicago Press.

McKoy, D. (2000) Inside school-based enterprise: productive environments and enterprising minds. PhD thesis, University of California, Graduate School of Education, Berkeley, California.

Mueller, D.C. (1989) *Public Choice II*. Cambridge: Cambridge University Press.

OECD (1991) *Environment, Schools, and Active Learning*. Paris: OECD.

OECD (1999) International Symposium on Measuring and Reporting Intellectual Capital: Experience, Issues, and Prospects, Amsterdam, 9–11 June. http://www.oecd.org/dsti/sti/industry/indcomp/prod/intang.htm (accessed July 2001).

OECD (2000) *Knowledge Management in the Learning Society: Education and Skills*. Paris: OECD.

Rosen, H.S. (1999) *Public Finance*, 5th edn. Boston: Irwin/McGraw-Hill.

Samuelson, P.E. (1954) The pure theory of public expenditure, *Review of Economics and Statistics*, 36: 386–9.

Samuelson, P.E. (1955) Diagrammatic exposition of a theory of public expenditure, *Review of Economics and Statistics*, 37: 350–6.

Stasz, C. and Stern, D. (1998) *Work-based learning for students in high schools and community colleges*, Berkeley, CA: National Center for Research in Vocational Education, University of California. http://ncrve.berkeley.edu/CenterPoint/CP1/CP1.html (accessed July 2001).

Stern, D., Stone, J. III, Hopkins, C., McMillion, M. and Crain, R. (1994) *School-based Enterprise: Productive Learning in American High Schools*. San Francisco: Jossey-Bass.

Stiglitz, J.E. (2000) *Economics of the Public Sector*, 3rd edn. New York: W.W. Norton.

Van Rensburg, P. (1977) Combining education with production: situating the problem, *Prospects*, No. 3.

Van Rensburg, P. (2001) *Making Education Work: The What, Why and How of Education with Production*. Gaborone, Botswana: Foundation for Education with Production.

Von Borstel, F. (1982) Productive education. A comparative study of the present day experience in developing nations. PhD thesis, Department of Educational Theory, University of Toronto, Canada.

Wigginton, E. (1986) *Sometimes a Shining Moment: The Foxfire Experience*. New York: Doubleday.

9

Training Networks and the Changing Organization of Professional Learning

Pierre Caspar

Introduction[1]

Those who have lived through the past decades among the flurry of reports exchanged on the subjects of education, adult training and the evolution of societies have been extremely fortunate. They have been in a position to observe a number of changes that have taken place with unprecedented speed and scope, especially those working in an international context. Information processing and telecommunications technologies have had a major role to play in these changes, but are far from the only factors. The hardest problems to solve are not technical but human, through the changes that these technologies bring both in the skills needed of individuals and in the operation of institutions themselves.

Today, everyone is in agreement about the importance of genuine life-long learning. The education and training of adults goes far beyond any simple notion of just going back to school ('reschooling'). Education and training themselves are changing considerably: because of transformations in our world; because of radically changing relationships between work, employment, training and integration; and because relationships and identity at work are being thoroughly questioned. Entry into a 'knowledge-based society' (which operates in a predominantly global financial environment), is accompanied by an accentuated tendency toward individualization, conferring responsibility on individuals to manage their own skills. The accelerated development of scientific and technical knowledge and their applications directly quickens the rate of renewal of skills required by the professional sectors and the need for innovation and flexible learning facilities. This defines the environment in which the 'knowledge-based professions' will now operate, in a completely new way. We can hypothesize far-reaching changes in the design and implementation of adult professional education, with a considerable growth of informal training.

First, *training is designed in a different way*. The questions being asked of those responsible for training are posed less and less in terms of training itself; they refer instead to stability, modernization, internationalization, competitiveness and quality, social or spatial development – and also to return on capital investments. The initiatives and arrangements for training need to be reconceived, based much more on the resolution of problems than on the constraints of the various disciplines. The burgeoning focus on competences has taken away education's former monopoly. Many other activities are now competing for the production of competences, such as recruitment, out-sourcing, the management and mobility of careers, or the appropriate use of consultants. Professional training is much more focused on predetermined results or performances, and tends to be increasingly a part of work itself. Beyond strategic forms of training, the devolution of training decisions much closer to operational activities has added considerably to the demand for experts and consultants in the field. And the entry of training into the market economy has earned an irrevocable place for sales, marketing and managerial activities within the training professions.

Secondly, *training is implemented in a different way, and in new spaces*. The threefold division of time, place and action, which has traditionally characterized the training process, is no longer adequate to match the pace of work and its constraints. The trend is towards much more complex arrangements: project work, face-to-face teaching, open access and remote facilities (teleconferencing, virtual groups, remote tutorials), periods of self-documentation and independent learning (Internet, intranet, resource centres) and accreditation of experience. The barriers between training, information, communication and documentation are being blurred in favour of networks of expertise and knowledge, giving a key role to those who mediate the information with which the networks function.

It follows that *training needs to be implemented and managed differently*. First, this is because all the above demand an increasingly high level of training in the relevant professional sectors. It is also because the entry of training into the service economy, which is just as competitive as other sectors, requires the development of sophisticated managerial and technical tools, largely software-based. In addition, whether the mode of service provision falls within a client/supplier relationship, or more elaborate partnerships for joint design and implementation of training projects, the concept of product and service quality assumes a dominant role. This being so, training serves many different masters, involves many actors, and covers many different issues. Tools provide reassurance. They confer transparency upon the educational process. Their development is not, however, without risk, in particular the danger of ignoring anything that is not measurable, or that involves skills other than those directly 'useful, usable and used' in professional life. Finally, budgetary constraints have an impact on training as they do in other sectors of the economy. 'Doing more with less', 'doing exactly what is needed, when it is needed' and so on becomes the rule. The more we depend on training, the more it becomes standard to expect to see the accounts.

In short, this is a panorama of contrasts. There has never been so much need for professional training, there have never been so many resources available to it, nor so much of it organized. But it has never before experienced such a range of tensions and constraints.

The future of training is already upon us. To illustrate this more precisely, this chapter examines two fields that are especially characteristic of the future: the 'mutualization of competences' on the one hand, and the transformation of 'the knowledge professions' on the other.

The mutualization of competences

The new technologies hold a fascination, inspiring dreams (as in the 1970s) of the possibilities and utopias offered by programmed and computer-assisted learning. There followed a mastery of the tools. Then we discovered that the technologies fulfil a dual role for education and training. They contribute to the success of training in conditions of risk, of wide dispersions of staff, and of the fragmentation or scarcity of available time, in which traditional training methods are impractical or excessively costly. They also contribute to developing new professional skills that are acquired almost independently of their content and format. But we also discovered that this dual role was not a technical matter that could be carried out separately from the human factor and the involvement of individuals, because the attitudes of trainers and students predetermine the nature and the quality of the training.

It is possible that we are now experiencing a new stage in the relationships between employment, training and new information processing and telecommunications technologies. There may even be a veritable hiatus in the relationships between people and knowledge, whether this is within the context of an emerging learning society, or, more modestly, in organizations which are seeking skills. The notion of sharing, or the 'mutualization', of knowledge is central to this. The World Wide Web is opening up immediate access to very remote sources of expertise, to networks for the exchange of knowledge and to ad hoc virtual meetings on a unprecedented scale. These exchanges are based on a rationale of shared information which is considered to be mutually profitable, personalized access to knowledge, and the tailored construction of expertise and behaviours adapted to specific situations. The specification of expertise, especially when it brings together both sound and images, means a complete departure from traditional forms of information research, the design of teaching aids, illustrations and the testing of competences.

This development is, however, not all positive. While all those involved could theoretically access all knowledge, that knowledge has also become a commodity on the world markets. Strategic information can already command a high price. It can also be misappropriated and plundered. Are we heading inexorably towards an international trade in knowledge? That said, it should also be recognized as a great advance. The relaxation of the boundaries between training and how knowledge is documented, referred to earlier, will not just be to the benefit of 'key competences', or for immediate professional applications. It can enable access to public debates held anywhere in the world in a given discipline, and the gathering in real time of the bases for a report or communication, so that no one need be confined to a specialist field of operations or fall behind on up-to-date knowledge. In other words, it means being able to access the latest advances in science as well as the most basic or eclectic types of knowledge, at will or as required. It also means being able to archive and mobilize useful information, updating information and enriching it using databases, resource centres or experts that would hitherto have been inaccessible. This too may help to inject learning into most professional situations.

Further key resources for true lifelong learning are to be found in regular skills audits, assessing what we know and do not know. The information and documentation professions in particular will find this revitalizing and value-enhancing. Many are already prepared for this and offer new services focused on the management of stored knowledge and intangible assets. Ultimately, internal frameworks for professional training may evaporate as the growing decentralization of training activities brings flatter forms of organization and allows recourse in the short term to a less sophisticated educational professionalism – in a sense, 'barefoot trainers'.

Above all, it will come about through the resurgence of less formal, less visible and less structured types of training which are collectively easily targeted and controlled. Future training will combine self-taught material in its various forms: mentoring and remote tuition; in situ or distance learning; courses run via face-to-face teaching, actual professional scenarios, the use of simulation techniques, or even the analysis of the dysfunctions of production systems. All these will run in variable time and space, not forgetting the multiple forms of 'informal' training, which are more or less 'invisible'. These range from mentoring, training 'on the fly' and spontaneous networks of exchanges of knowledge to specifically educational instructions, including the sharing of everything that arises from ingenuity, innovation and organized experimentation at work. Actual work is often different from specified work: it is often more effective and it always leads to unexpected learning situations, because it requires the application of its own intelligence to working practice.

Finally, this mutualization of competences will probably lead to a new redistribution of locations and resources for training. The 'traditional' *training bodies* still have a healthy future ahead of them, especially if they can get beyond a simple client/supplier rationale and establish with their sponsors a shared design, and sometimes also a shared investment relationship in respect of training. Corporate *training centres and services*, which have become highly professional, are even more essential given that training is now increasingly decentralized and with the greater communication of knowledge. These all require specific engineering and maintenance to permit the fine 'engineering' of competences they allow for. Moreover, all these actors will increasingly find themselves in *resource networks*. The expression 'being sent on training' becomes 'being on training', here and now, depending on what is needed and when. *Resource centres* will become the nodes in this kind of network. Having been distributed geographically around foci of employment that economically justify their activity, they accommodate people within a travelling time radius of about half an hour, who are thus able to follow training courses compatible with their workloads and constraints of their jobs. Finally, what some companies call *training points* may well see an increase. This involves a set of 'course delivery stations', linked to a corporate remote training network, located at a fixed work site and accessible to all staff at that given site. Close to the workplace and freely accessible, the training point thus enables the learning of whatever needs to be learned, when needed, in the right place and for those who call for it.

All of this constitutes a veritable knowledge network – a set of human and technical learning resources, made up of different levels of professional training interconnected and shared by a mobile population of students. Our hypothesis is that these network architectures of human, documentary and educational resources will increasingly constitute the bases of true learning organizations. They will have meaning only if there is a positive managerial stance on access to learning for everyone, with the right to set aside time for acquiring professional experience at an individual level and for taking advantage of that of others.

The development of the knowledge-based professions

Such a major set of changes has far-reaching implications. It calls for more rigorous 'engineering' and management of training arrangements and their resources. It suggests greater attention be given to educational choices as well as to the upstream and downstream of these choice points. And, it requires an increased professionalism on the part of those who design, conduct and evaluate these activities, integrated into the widest field of competences and human resources. What is referred to as the 'knowledge-based professions' cover both activities directly linked to the development and operation of training structures, and functions of mediation on behalf of students, in terms of their access to professional skills development and their validation by employers.

At the first level, we see many different complementary professional categories. The *management of training systems* requires very specific competence. This is the role of training managers and directors, assisted by colleagues specializing in the management of people and skills. 'Engineering' a partnership is an important aspect of such management, and is essential wherever justified by the volume of investments to be brought together, the need for a training body to enlarge its professional development capacity, quality requirements or the intention to achieve profitability by selling products and educational services in a wider market. Proffering advice to decision-makers at all levels of the hierarchy of production systems is also part of this management process. All these activities refer to a key responsibility, called by Lévy (1997) the 'administration of collective intelligence'.

The *'engineering' of training systems and management of projects* represent essential functions for the nurturing of knowledge-based networks. These activities are becoming increasingly professionalized. Direct 'engineering' is the work of an architect who constructs the networks, assisted by specialists in professional education who supply appropriate educational resources and accompanying tools. When 'engineering' is 'convergent' or 'back office', it offers the whole set of skills essential to the proper working of educational systems, for example logistics administration, finance and fiscal engineering where appropriate. The management of projects, their negotiation and their financing are fundamental to this function.

To enter into these systems brings changes of scale. On the one hand, there is a whole range of *technical professional disciplines* linked to IT, publishing, graphics, telecommunications, multimedia, 'client service', the maintenance of service quality and the management of costs. On the other hand, there are all the *educational and teaching functions* that contribute to the design and production of educational resources. The 'tail may wag the dog', thereby further raising the stakes – changing the technical medium of a piece of knowledge means changing the message being transmitted, perhaps even the way of thinking that it induces. Focusing too much on the technical quality of an image risks detracting from the educational message it is intended to convey. New generations of educators will need to create design tools for teaching aids, and methodologies for the management of the quality and evaluation of initiatives and training facilities. They will also need to know all the techniques available or emerging for the construction of editorial resources and for the creation of technical specifications in the production of teaching materials. They need to be able on appropriate occasions to launch or restart complex remote tutorials and interactive learning stations: currently one or two simultaneously, soon five or six, and in future many more. Finally, they need to be able to work in challenging intercultural environments.

We can broaden the focus further and consider a number of key responsibilities directly linked to the operation of the new educational relationships, in which the act of teaching comes after the fact of learning itself and being able to apply what one has learnt.

Administrators of resource centres accommodate trainees, evaluate their training needs, sometimes in collaboration with the local managers, help them to use multimedia resources and draw up their personal, professional learning strategies. However, not usually being expert in all the fields covered by the centre, the administrator cannot help learners with the basics. Someone else is thus essential: the trainer-tutor, who will sometimes be a tutor and sometimes a learner in turn. Whether through face-to-face teaching or distance learning, the tutor's role is to intervene on request from the learner and to answer their questions on the content of the training given, in their capacity as a specialist. The tutor may intervene in real time in an exchange with the learner at their place of work or over the telephone, or when 'leading them by the hand' at a distance on the multimedia training station in order to help that person apply the knowledge and learn what is needed, physically or mentally, for that particular work situation. The trainer may also intervene with a time difference using an oral or written messaging system. Experts in the field being studied provide back-office support. All trainer-tutors in a given field or work organization may be formed into a network.

What was understood not so long ago by the traditional title of 'trainer' has thus now been considerably extended and diversified. Learning is becoming in one sense much easier, as one can access so much available knowledge, via resource centres, databases, portals and different kinds of network. In another sense, it is becoming much more complex, due to the tools, networks and technological prerequisites involved in the learning process. Each of the activities summarized above is not in itself new. It is their combination that is leading to a profound change in the forms and functions of education, in the form of a systematic networking of the various actors. Teaching functions have experienced both a dilution in their traditional professional scope, given that the task has become less a transmission of content and more a learning support role, but also a reinforcement of their contribution, given the proximity of this form of learning support to the professional contexts for which training is needed. The links between the different actors involved and the quality of their exchanges has now become more important than the operation of technical platforms and places of learning.

Conclusion

The establishment of lifelong learning is leading to a new form of society, described in the EU White Paper as 'cognitive' (in French, or 'learning society' in English). This is a society where initial and continuing education are designed so that content is fully integrated and interlinked (especially the core knowledge that is much prized by UNESCO as well as key competences), for access or return to the world of work and for the exercise of citizenship. It is a changing society, within which each individual can also develop, and anticipate the changes so as to be better placed to deal with them. It is a society where learning is a natural process, where everyone is potentially teaching and learning. And, it is a society where stringent efforts are made to avoid a deep gulf opening up between those continually enhancing their access to knowledge and its application, and the others who are losing it.

This represents an irreversible transformation of traditional educational and training relationships, in which the 'programme' determined the route through education, in which there was imbalance of power and relationship with truth in the 'master/pupil' relationship, and in which the division into disciplines skewed any approach to dealing with the problems we confront in our professional and personal lives. To educate and train is no longer reduced to applying intelligence and sensitivity to the transmission of knowledge. It is no longer just technical or educational but social. A first consideration is the need to respond to each learner who needs assistance, who must have their learning facilitated, the nature and scope of their problems diagnosed, and be given the tools to get over these difficulties at the time they arise. This already represents a considerable transformation for trainers in their relationship with knowledge and the authority of 'the one who knows'. It leaves behind the comfort zone provided by the mastery of a specific learning discipline, and is based on problem-solving rather than the given truths of established science. It also means being more vulnerable as it requires an intervention in the content, teaching arrangements and everything that justifies, prepares, supports and validates training – nothing less than the whole gamut of the personal and professional life of everyone, and in its implementation. An onerous responsibility.

A second consideration is that it then falls to educators and trainers to help learners to change their attitude given that learning support materials are changing so radically. There is still very firm attachment to 'paper knowledge', but we are entering an era that is technically and philosophically revolutionary: the era of the virtual. Using the digital networks referred to above means taking a deliberate step towards a mutualization or sharing of knowledge, something we have often been badly prepared for in such a hypercompetitive society. It involves learning to research widely dispersed knowledge, contained in electronic, audio-visual, digital and multimedia formats. It involves using software and teaching applications. It involves 'hyperspaces' – where everyone maps their own course, and follows their own path, not always going where they would like to go, thereby finding themselves either hindered or enriched – and it means learning to live in a 'VDU culture' where speed, transience and rigour go hand in hand. The younger generations have always had a screen in front of them and a keyboard under their fingers. They already exist in a 'cyberculture'. But the older generations are not there yet, and in some cases do not feel able to face it. It is true that a lot is being asked, as our very intelligence is being changed, not just our physical capacities and skills.

A third consideration is therefore required, which is located in the interface between the learner and the social group to which they belong – family, city, company, professional organization, country, etc. There needs to be a mediation between the personal identity that the learner creates and recognizes and the identity the learner seeks to have in the eyes of others via their own personal and professional mobility. Learning? Yes. But for what purpose, for whom and why? Such questions involve the learner in first identifying what they need to take possession of (or not) in these multiple worlds of knowledge to which they have access, to a greater or lesser degree. The emphasis on competences means that learners should have access to the resources and monitoring abilities they need to be able to assemble a relevant project for themselves. The learner needs landmarks in order to understand what needs to be acquired and how best to go about doing so. This often presupposes that the learner has the means to survey knowledge already acquired, and what is at an appropriate level for them, in order to optimize the learning path. Skills audits, validation of experience, support in the compilation of a project are thus an important element of this third social consideration. In future we may well spend less time in training and more analysing our needs, comparing the skills we need to acquire and those we already have, and preparing for their professional validation within the social context. We have a better grasp when we have a picture of what we already know. Teaching will have a greater return when it concentrates on what is important, avoiding needless repetition and demotivation. The return on the investment from training is all the greater when the individual chooses it for themself. The training provision assumes its full impact only when it is complemented by the commitment of the individual.

All this is easy to state, but an extraordinary form of learning is needed by all of us to take advantage of these opportunities. This is a final key question to which we need some answers, which confronts educators and trainers directly. Learners are sometimes considered to be autonomous within these new educational environments, and capable of allocating themselves a project, responsible for their own learning and updating their skills themselves. For UNESCO (1998), the learner is deemed to have acquired self-determination, to know how to make decisions, how to 'learn how to be' and live alongside others. The learner knows that there is a lifelong learning imperative. Some companies even regard individual learners as joint managers of their human resources who are thus legitimately jointly responsible for any loss in their own employability. This is a major responsibility that usually assumes the availability of both support, in order for it to be fulfilled with discernment, and consideration of how to achieve recognition of its true worth.

The implementation of collective intelligence requires the acceptance at all levels of the existence of a shared intelligence. Otherwise, how can young people assume a fully autonomous role in society? How can staff combine effectiveness at work and quality of life? How can the unemployed be reintegrated into work or an activity that does justice to their competences and background? How can the retired continue to play a role in society using the intangible assets they continue to sustain? And, how can we make the transition from an information society, already in place at least in the OECD countries, to a 'knowledge-based society', where we access information and knowledge while being able to give it meaning?

Note

1. An initial version of part of this text formed the conclusion of *Nouvelles technologies éducatives et réseaux de formation; des entreprises parlent de leurs expériences*, edited by Pierre Caspar (Editions d'organisation, Paris, 1998). This present text is a significantly revised and updated version.

References

Lévy, P. (1997) *La cyberculture*. Paris: Editions Odile Jacob.
UNESCO (1998) *L'éducation: un trésor est caché dedans*. Rapport de la commission présidée par J. Delors. Paris: UNESCO.

10

Learning in Post-industrial Organizations: Experiences of a Reflective Practitioner in Australia[1]

Bill Ford

This chapter draws on the reflections of my work over the 1990s as a player/coach involved in the transformation of a number of leading Australian enterprises as they undertook their journeys to becoming learning enterprises. The organizations were: a chemical refinery, a brewery, construction sites, insurance and banking, and a world famous centre for performing arts.

In discussion with a senior executive involved in transforming a leading organization in Australia, I handed him a book which I thought might be useful for his work. He flipped through it, put it to one side and said, 'another boring book with no diagrams or blueprints to show what it is about'. My experience in organizations is that most writers fail to communicate with the majority of people who are involved or affected by organizational change. The core of the communication culture of many occupations and organizations is visual rather than literary. We live in an environment where media, marketing and entertainment are dominated by visuals. Presentations, which comprise someone reading bullet points on a screen, do little to excite or interest an audience who want to know 'what will it look like?'

This overwhelming dominance of printed words over illustrative visuals ignores the multifaceted nature of human and organizational learning and is an affront to the action learning of key groups in economic organizations. In short, in a knowledge society, knowledge is not best derived from text but from visualization.

To support the learning of people who are endeavouring to rethink and reframe their organizations in dynamic environments, I have worked with them to develop 'visual tools'. These visuals are not pretty pictures taken from a PowerPoint collection, which often tend to distract rather than facilitate a discussion. Developing visual tools requires design skills to highlight shifting structures, barriers, boundaries and blurring of boundaries, complexity, connections, discontinuities, linkages, dynamics, directions, gaps, integration, interdependencies, networks and spatial relations. Such diagrams facilitate informed dialogue, which is often very robust, about the nature and direction of organizational journeys and the requirement for conceptual shifts and continuous learning.

I have developed hundreds of visual tools with people who are engaged in transforming their organizations, to be used in organizational learning activities involving staff, customers, suppliers, partners and alliances. I have chosen the following few examples which have helped people in organizations to rethink and reframe their understanding and involvement in organizational dynamics and learning.

Transformation of organizational life

The visual in Figure 10.1 allows people to see connections and relate their experiences to broader organizational transformations. People often use the visual to illustrate diverse philosophies. For example, outsourcing in industrial economies is driven predominantly by cost considerations whereas in a knowledge economy it is an important method of acquiring proprietary knowledge and skills. The visual invariably involves discussion on values and the need for trust and shared learning in a world of relational space. It also

Figure 10.1   Transforming the nature of organizational life

The 21st Century
Odyssey
an eventful journey

JVs, alliances,
partnering,
M&As, buy-ins
& spin-offs

flattening

**knowledge
& mobile** economy

industrial economy

**Integrating
and outsourcing**

**global
networking**

**hierarchical/
divisional**

breaking-out

Rigid Structures   Transforming the World-Class Enterprise   Relational Space

a spatial
b business
c cost

© Bill Ford/Cliff Shaffran 8th edition Jan '01

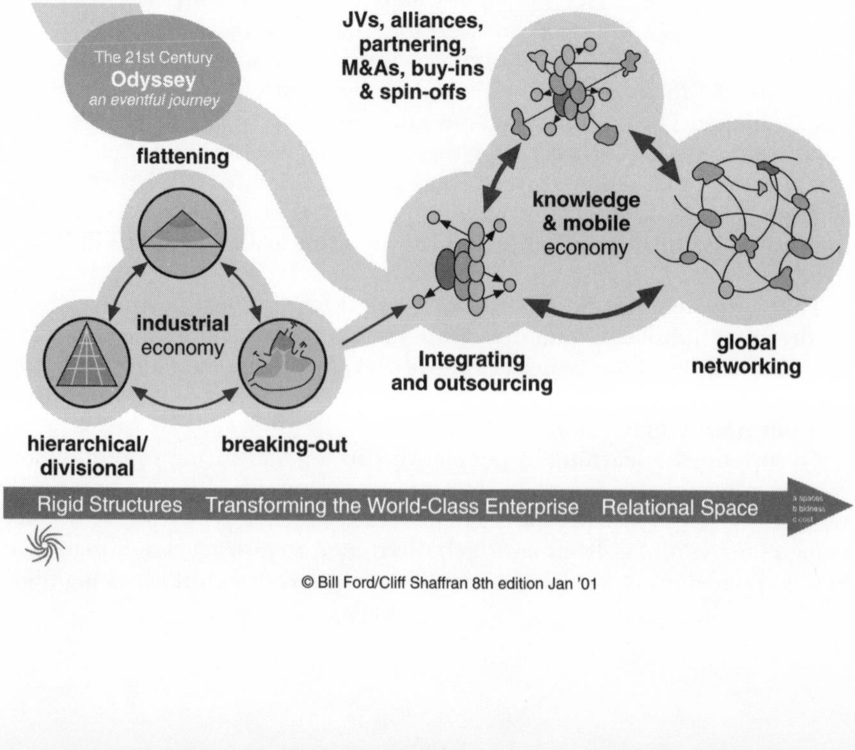

provokes dialogue about the nature and importance of conceptual changes in transforming organizations and a recognition that language may need to change to express new meanings.

The visual highlighting of innovations in organizational design helps break down the one-dimensional focus on technological innovation that dominates many organizations. In the increasingly dynamic global economies, new business models and organizational strategies are continually emerging. To deliver these strategies, new organizational systems have developed. Often these are made possible or inspired by innovative and disruptive technologies. The traditional industrial model organization of hierarchy and division has too many limitations to deliver the new business strategies in dynamic, predominantly knowledge-based, learning societies. These limitations include: too many internal organizational interfaces; demarcated and restricted mindsets; barriers to communication, knowledge and skills; long and variable lead times; and command and control philosophies.

For many older established organizations, the flattening of their structures was the first stage of their transformation. Unfortunately, this re-engineering and restructuring was driven predominantly by cost-saving priorities rather than by the creation of dynamic learning and adaptive organizations. The old dinosaurs were merely replaced by young dinosaurs. The new strategy-focused organizations are shifting to integrating, outsourcing and networking, and the creation of joint ventures, alliances, partnerships, mergers and acquisitions, buy-ins and spin-offs. These transformations create new shared learning needs for individuals, teams, organizations and networks, and reinforce the importance of establishing cross-cultural, continuous learning. This requires a significant conceptual and organizational shift from the industrial economy concepts which still underlie much of training and development in traditional organizations.

Appropriate workplaces for today and tomorrow

In the transformation of organizational life, leaders of learning organizations will play an important role in influencing the concepts and design of the appropriate workplaces for today and tomorrow. The leaders of such organizations recognize that they are on an odyssey of continuous discovery and creation (Figure 10.2). This will not be a clear, linear journey, nor one that passes along clear, logical routes. Disruptive technologies, shifting markets and strategies will ensure an eventful journey. The competitive advantage, even survival, of enterprises will be their ability to learn faster than their competitors. This requires an ability to reflect and learn from organizational activity. Thus, action learning is becoming a central focus of the emerging work organizations and workplaces.

In increasingly knowledge-based economies, such as Australia, action learning, team learning, organizational learning and cross-cultural learning

Figure 10.2   Shifting mindsets

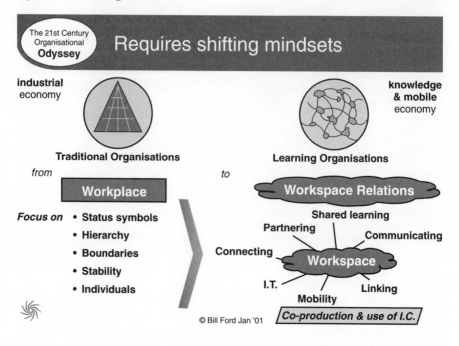

The 21st Century Organisational Odyssey

Requires shifting mindsets

industrial economy

Traditional Organisations

from

knowledge & mobile economy

Learning Organisations

to

Workplace

Focus on • **Status symbols**
• **Hierarchy**
• **Boundaries**
• **Stability**
• **Individuals**

Workspace Relations

Shared learning

Partnering

Communicating

Connecting

Workspace

I.T.   Linking

Mobility

© Bill Ford Jan '01

Co-production & use of I.C.

are becoming critical concepts in the design of appropriate workplaces. One-dimensional technocratic visions of the workplace of the future ignore human and organizational needs. Simplistic notions of the availability of new and exciting technologies fuel such technocratic dreams, and then often result in organizational nightmares.

Data and information flow freely in cyberspace but knowledge needs to be produced, mediated and used in workplaces. Knowledge needs to be mediated across the cultural boundaries of occupations, professions, organizational functions, industries and nations. Factory and office workplaces, designed for traditional industrial economies, are inappropriate to the spatial relations and the learning needs of team, network, and global and mobile economies. The emerging workplaces of today and tomorrow must integrate people, process, partners and place. Too often, decisions on each of these are made in isolation. The people issues are seen as the domain of human resource staff; the processes are increasingly determined, often tactically, by information technology specialists; the partnerships are dominated by legal and financial specialists; and the place is seen as the sole responsibility of the dealmakers in the property department and their designers.

In increasingly interconnected workplaces, such divisional autonomy is a recipe for organizational and financial disaster. The emerging innovative, learning-based workplaces develop spatial relations that support the diverse organizational needs of:

- work and learning;
- communication and reflection;
- individuals and teams;
- collaboration and competition.

Such learning-based workplaces also support conceptual and mindset shifts from:

- information hoarding to information sharing;
- off-the-job training to real-time learning (coaching, mentoring);
- property refurbishment to business refurbishment.

Developing these exciting new workplaces is a broad process of engagement and learning, not the application of a product or property design.

Cross-cultural learning

Australia is often viewed as a multicultural society. However, we tend to limit our interests and concerns in cultural diversity to ethnic and national cultures. The multicultural nature of organizational life is much more complex and deserves more attention, particularly by people concerned with organizational learning.

Figure 10.3 illustrates how intellectual capital that is constructed conceptually and culturally needs to be mediated into other cultures if it is to be

Figure 10.3 Mediating knowledge and know-how between diverse cultures

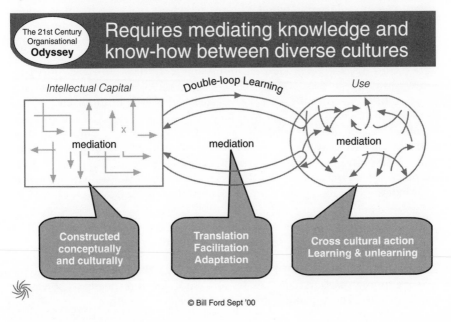

© Bill Ford Sept '00

used effectively. The process of double-loop learning requires the developers and users to share experiences and knowledge and be willing to unlearn as well as to learn. Industries, organizations, occupations, professions and organizational functions develop distinct cultures, and as the women's movement has shown us, we have diversity and changing gender cultures in our organizational life.

Why is it important that we develop a clear and deeper understanding of the cultural complexity of our organizational life? Occupational, professional and organizational cultures often have developed strong barriers to the transfer and integration of external knowledge. On joining a new enterprise or industry, I have often been attacked for bringing ideas from another enterprise or industry. In emerging knowledge-based economies, such as Australia, organizational sustainability requires the ability to mediate knowledge across cultural boundaries to develop cross-cultural learning organizations and networks.

It is the ability to adapt and use new technologies across industrial, organizational and occupational cultural barriers that has created some of the most important innovations in contemporary economic life. The concept of just-in-time manufacturing emerged from Toyota's ability to adapt the knowledge it gained from the observations of a Toyota engineer on the operation of American supermarkets. The port of Rotterdam authorities subsequently sponsored two scholars to study the Toyota system so that it could be translated into port activities. Clearly, the ability to move knowledge across national and industry cultural boundaries was important in both cases. Australia is often an early adapter of new technologies. However, our ability to use effectively such technologies depends on organizational investment in adaptive learning-based cultures, which reward dismantling barriers to learning and knowledge sharing, rather than knowledge hoarding.

The organizational investment must also include an understanding of the implications of the cultural origins of new technologies. For instance, designers and developers of German industrial technology work within structures, knowledge and skills formation systems, and work organization systems that are different from those into which the technology is imported, such as those in Australia. When importing such technologies, processes need to be developed to ensure that an adequate level of cross-cultural knowledge and skill is mediated between the developers in Germany and the users in Australia. I have worked in plants where the imported technologies were never adequately used because the local users did not understand the operational knowledge and skills assumed by the German designers.

Culture of continuous learning

The fourth visual (Figure 10.4) allows people to see the magnitude and range of learning that is often necessary to build strategic and speedy responses to dynamic and often turbulent environments.

Figure 10.4 Cross cultural learning

© Bill Ford Nov '98

In my experience in transforming traditional organizations into robust learning organizations, the following processes were critical:

- Developing an agreed understanding of the need for continuous learning. This means openly sharing knowledge, particularly of the dynamics of markets, technologies, strategies, skills and organizations.
- The design and organization of work needs to be influenced by the needs of coaching, mentoring and action learning.
- Developing enterprise activities as learning opportunities. For instance, project management must not only adhere to the disciplines of cost, time and quality but also deliver in terms of action learning, innovation and integration.
- The introduction of new technologies and systems provides excellent opportunities for organizational learning. The inclusion of operators of new processes in teams that specify, install and commission new systems has significantly improved individual, team and organizational learning.
- The design of workplaces needs to shift from being based on linear production, hierarchy and status to design criteria which include knowledge and skill sharing, adaptability, flexibility, engagement and enjoyment.
- Customer and supplier relationships are becoming essential to enhancing value exchange for people and organizations. Large investments in such relationships often fail because of the lack of continuous shared learning.

- Teams are developing as critical learning communities as organizations conceptually shift from values of knowledge hoarding to knowledge sharing. The nature and variety of teams and their learning needs, opportunities and processes change, as organizations move from structured hierarchies to the relational space of knowledge and mobile economies.

Early industrial teams developed around divisions, hierarchy and occupations. With the flattening of organizations, multifunctional and work area teams emerged. These required the sharing of knowledge and learning across previously strong occupational and divisional boundaries. As the pace of change increased, project and self-organizing teams became more prevalent. Project management knowledge and skills were required to deliver on-time, on-budget and on-quality. As integration and networking became more important, aligned and cross-cultural teams developed. More recently, global and multi-time-zone teams have emerged. This changing nature of teams and their learning needs is a good illustration of the dynamics of organizational learning. Traditional concepts are often powerful barriers to change; new concepts are often necessary to express new knowledge and learning. The concept teams search internally and externally for new ideas and knowledge. This is a critical role but finding new ideas is not enough. Appropriate ideas need to be culturally translated, absorbed, adapted and integrated to support sustainable learning and transformation.

Concept teams design the transformation strategy in alignment with the business strategy. They provide leadership and demonstrate involvement and share responsibility in implementing change. They are not traditional, isolated planning groups. Change is a risky business. Concept teams manage these risks by integrating theory and practice, and thinking and doing; by sharing knowledge and experience; by linking learning and change; by providing leadership and mentoring; by demonstrating commitment and involvement.

Experience has shown that there are critical competences needed for concept teams. These include strong conceptual skills, cross-cultural learning and communication skills, a willingness to question the way things have been done in the past, confidence to transgress traditional corporate custom and practice, willingness to research, listen and evaluate and integrate internal and external information and knowledge, and an ability and desire to continually learn and translate knowledge across different cultures between and within their organizations.

Barriers to continuous organizational learning

The fifth visual (Figure 10.5) highlights powerful conceptual shifts. It shows where we are coming from and where we are aiming to be. The success of any journey towards the development of a learning organization depends on the willingness to recognize and dismantle the many barriers to learning

Figure 10.5 Shifting organizations

© Bill Ford Jan '01

in traditional organizations. It is not unusual to find organizations which have large budgets for learning programmes but which ignore the barriers to the effectiveness of these programmes. What are some of these barriers?

First, traditional social, physical and organizational architecture reflect hierarchy and division, status and power, demarcation and restrictions, not openness and learning. In organizations that I have worked with, I ask people to redraw their organization charts to show how their organization really operates. Some executives find this extraordinarily difficult. They often freeze in front of a whiteboard. Then I ask people to draw an organizational chart that would support their organization's learning and effectiveness. This invariably proves to be a very positive learning process, as it requires considerable mediation between conflicting views of the organization's operations, communications and learning.

Another major barrier to creating learning organizations is the separation of work and learning in the allocation of organizational time. This is seen in such concepts as learning leave. Adults learn best through action research and learning. Therefore, the creation of learning-based work organizations such as 'communities of practice' is essential to the development of a learning organization. This of course requires moving away conceptually from the conflict-based ideas inherent in traditional industrial relations.

A further barrier is the restricted mobility within and between organizations. Individuals and teams with dynamic knowledge and skill sets are essential to building an organization's intellectual capital. Yet, many organizations still have resource allocation policies which allocate people to jobs without any consideration of the learning needs of the individual, team or organization.

Next comes the restricted notion of an organization's bottom line. There is an urgent need to establish concepts of a balanced scorecard for projects to ensure a sustainable future for any organization. In Stage I of Lend Lease's large Darling Park construction project in Sydney, a big sign was erected over the first hut at the entrance to the site. It read 'Lend Lease Learning'. This was a visual reminder to all on site that there was a place to discuss the integration of work and learning that was critical to the agreed workplace reform agenda. Agreed innovation in learning and workplace relations became one of the key deliverables on that site. I have often been asked how can I justify the cost. My answer is that the continually multiskilled workers operating in new work area teams topped off the building fourteen weeks ahead of a very tight schedule. The resultant gains allowed for additional expenditure on the development of civic art and space around the building, which enhanced the long-term value of the building to its owners, tenants and the city of Sydney. The innovations also provided a highly multiskilled, adaptive and motivated workforce to deliver the new Olympic swimming pool ahead of schedule. This was a very tangible contribution to Sydney's winning bid for the 2000 Olympic Games. The more appropriate question is, how can you afford *not* to create a learning worksite?

Finally, perhaps the most crucial concern is lack of leadership in removing the organizational barriers to learning. Too often, this is the assumed role of human resource staff. Instead, it is the role of everyone concerned with establishing a viable future for their organization and the people in it.

The composition of intellectual capital and the need to answer some new questions

The visual shown in Figure 10.6 emphasizes the broad composition of intellectual capital. Organizational leaders need to understand the nature and dynamics of intellectual capital. While there is not an agreed definition of intellectual capital, it is generally viewed as including human capital, systems capital and relational capital. Human capital includes both formal knowledge and tacit knowledge. The latter is often ignored because it is difficult to measure and transfer. Systems capital includes organizational software and work organization. The ability to work in diverse teams is a valuable organizational asset, particularly as it increases the pace of organizational learning. Relational capital includes the ability to capture and use customer and supplier knowledge. This may be enhanced by information technology, but tacit knowledge is elusive.

There is an increasing demand, particularly from accountants, lawyers, investors and governments, for ways of measuring intellectual capital.

Figure 10.6 Building and using intellectual capital

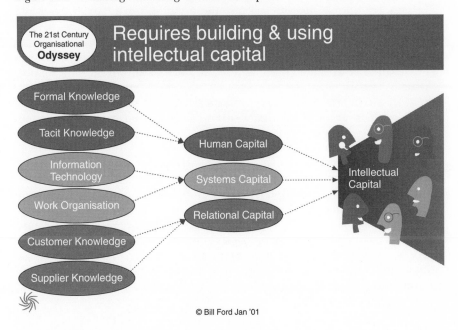

© Bill Ford Jan '01

However, much of the discussion is based on traditional static concepts such as intellectual property, rather than on concepts more applicable to the dynamics of the emerging information, knowledge and internet economies. Understanding the potential of organizational learning will require developing performance measures to evaluate an organization's capabilities to build, mediate and effectively use intellectual capital. It will also require the effective integration of intellectual capital, social capital and financial capital.

To do this, we need to ask new questions:

- *How effective is an organization in acquiring, adapting and using intellectual capital?* That is, how fast can an organization effectively learn to apply new knowledge and know-how? Traditional static notions of organizational learning curves are often major barriers to answering such questions. This is particularly important for assessing the speed with which an organization can learn to get value from new technologies.
- *How effective is an organization's stock of intellectual capital?* For instance, what are the different densities and integration of knowledge and know-how across an organization? Intellectual capital protected in traditional organizational silos can be a barrier to integrated innovation and learning.
- *How fast does intellectual capital flow in an organization and its key networks?* Speed to market has become critical. What type of work organization will facilitate learning and the flow of knowledge?

- *What are the barriers to internally mediating, building and using intellectual capital?* Traditional measures ignore the organizational barriers to effectively utilizing people's knowledge and know-how. These barriers include traditional organizational cultures, structures and concepts such as jobs and workforce classifications. For example, such nonsensical concepts as semi-skilled or unskilled often ignore the stock of know-how built up over years of experience.
- *How effective is shared learning in relation to alliances, joint ventures and partnerships?* The accounting, financial and legal models of these relationships ignore the very elements which make such relationships successful.
- *How effective is an organization's cross-cultural learning in mediating (i.e. culturally translating, facilitating and adapting) intellectual capital across increasingly diverse organizational and network cultures?* For instance, how effective are an organization's cross-functional and/or global teams in the co-production and use of intellectual capital?
- *How effective is the organization learning to support the development of communities of practice and value-creating communities, to leverage value from diversity?* These are critical questions for organizational leadership and for the systemic development of enterprises in dynamic knowledge-based learning economies.

Note

1. In recognition of D.E. Schön (1983) *The Reflective Practitioner.* New York: Basic Books.

Part 4

Globalization and
Higher Education

11

Globalization, Development and the International Knowledge Economy

Martin Carnoy

Historic changes are transforming the lives of people in the developed countries and most developing ones. National economies and even national cultures are globalizing. Globalization means more competition, not just with other companies in the same city or the same region, but with companies worldwide. Globalization also means that a nation's investment, production and innovation are not limited by national borders. Everything, including relations among family and friends, is rapidly becoming organized around a much more compressed view of space and time. Companies in Europe, the United States and Japan can produce chips in Singapore, keypunch data in India or the People's Republic of China, outsource clerical work to Ireland or Mexico and sell worldwide, barely concerned about the long distances or the variety of cultures involved. Even children watching television or listening to radio are reconceptualizing their 'world' in terms of the meanings that they attach to music, the environment, sports, or race and ethnicity.

A global economy is not a world economy – that has existed since at least the sixteenth century (Braudel 1979). Rather, a global economy is one whose strategic, core activities, including innovation, finance and corporate management, function on a planetary scale in real time (Carnoy *et al.* 1993; Castells 1996; Carnoy 2000).[1] And this globality became possible only recently because of the technological infrastructure provided by telecommunications, information systems, microelectronics machinery and computer-based transportation. Today, as distinct from even a generation ago, capital, technology, management, information and core markets are globalized.

Globalization together with new information technology and the innovative processes they foment is driving a revolution in the organization of work, the production of goods and services, relations among nations, and even local culture. No community is immune from the effects of this revolution. It is changing the very fundamentals of human relations and social life.

Two of the main bases of globalization are information and innovation, and they in turn are highly knowledge-intensive. Internationalized and fast-growing information industries produce knowledge goods and services. Today's massive movements of capital depend on information, communication and knowledge in global markets. And because knowledge is highly portable, it lends itself easily to globalization.

If knowledge is fundamental to globalization, globalization should also have a profound impact on the transmission of knowledge. I suggest that it does, and that its effects are particularly great on higher levels of education. Why is this the case? The answer lies in three parts. Rising pay-offs to higher levels of training in a global, science-based, knowledge-intensive economy make secondary and higher education more of a necessity to get 'good' jobs even in developing countries. This explains, in part, the exploding demand for higher education even in low-income countries. Demographics and democratic ideals increase pressure on upper secondary schools and universities to provide access to groups that traditionally have not attended these levels. The growing power of 'externally defined' global market values (in which universities themselves play an important role) increases pressure on upper secondary/post-secondary vocational schools and universities to reinvent local communities and culture.

Globalized markets and the globalization of skills

Governments in a global economy need to attract foreign capital and, increasingly, knowledge-intensive capital. This means providing a ready supply of skilled labour, and translates into pressure to increase the average level of education in the labour force. The pay-off to higher levels of education is rising worldwide as a result of the shifts of economic production to knowledge-intensive products and processes, as well as because governments implement policies that increase income inequality. Rising relative incomes for more highly educated labour increases the demand for university education, pushing governments to expand their higher education, and, correspondingly, to increase the number of secondary school graduates ready to attend post-secondary education. In countries that were previously resistant to providing equal access to education for young women, the need for more highly educated low-cost labour tends to expand women's educational opportunities.

In the past 50 years, most countries have undergone rapid expansion of their primary and secondary education systems. Thanks to a widespread view that basic education should be available to children as a right, even financial constraints in many debt-ridden countries such as those in Latin America did not prevent them from increasing access to basic and even secondary education (Castro and Carnoy 1997).

University education has also expanded, but this has not prevented rates of return on investment in higher education from rising relative to primary and lower secondary schooling. Rates of return to higher levels of education are also pushed up by structural adjustment policies. These tend to favour those with higher skill levels hooked into the export sector and the multinational companies.[2] By increasing the *relative* demand for higher-level graduates more rapidly than upper secondary schools and universities can expand their supply, globalization puts continuous pressure on the educational system to expand.

Higher rates of return (both private and social) to higher education have important effects on the rest of the educational system and on income inequality. They imply that those who get that education benefit more from their investment in education than those who stop at lower levels of schooling. In most countries, those who get to higher levels of schooling are those from a higher social class background. So not only do those families with higher social class background have more capital to start with, but under these circumstances they get a higher return on their investments. This is a sure formula for increased inequality in already highly unequal societies. In addition, higher socio-economic status (SES) students are those who get access to 'better' schools, in regions that are more likely to spend more per pupil on education, particularly in those schools attended by higher socio-economic class pupils. Competition for such higher-pay-off education also increases as the pay-off to higher levels of education increases, because the stakes get higher. Higher SES parents become increasingly conscious of where their children attend school, what those schools are like, and whether they provide access to higher levels of education. Schooling becomes more stratified at lower levels rather than less so, especially under conditions of scarce public resources. National economic competition on a global scale gets translated into sub-national competition in social class access to educational resources.

In addition to raising the pay-off to higher levels of education, globalization appears to have raised the rate of return to women's education. In many countries, rates of return to education for women are higher than for men (Psacharopoulos 1989; Ryoo *et al.* 1993). The reasons for the increased participation of women in labour markets are complex, but two main factors have been the spread of feminist ideas and values and the increased demand for low-cost semi-skilled labour in developing countries' electronics manufacturing and other assembly industries. The worldwide movement for women's rights has had the effect of legitimizing equal education for women, women's control over their fertility rates, women's increased participation in wage labour markets and women's right to vote (Castells 1997; Ramirez *et al.* 1997; Carnoy 2000). The increased demand for low-cost labour and greater sense by women that they have the same rights as men has brought enormous numbers of married women into waged employment worldwide. This in turn has created increased demand for education by women at higher and higher education levels. So globalization is accentuating an already growing trend by women to take as much or more education than men.

The demographics of higher-level education expansion

In the past 20 years, 'new' demand for higher levels of education in both developed and developing countries has come mainly from two groups that traditionally did not attend these levels: a 'rising' lower-middle social class, and women. These sources will continue to fuel higher-level educational expansion and will be fighting for more places in elite institutions. As basic secondary education becomes increasingly less valuable in labour markets, the next wave of potential higher secondary and college graduates may be the growing lower social class population that is for the first time completing mass basic schooling. Yet, in the traditional sense, this next wave may not be prepared for higher-level education.[3]

Greater fertility among less-educated, lower-income families affects societies, especially in the current global environment. It means that most children may be growing up in families that cannot prepare them adequately for the ever higher educational requirements needed to succeed in labour markets. This is not to say that higher-educated men and women make better parents than those with less education. But being a parent in the global economy requires much more information than in the past, and the stakes in children's educational success are much higher. *On average*, less-educated parents are increasingly at a disadvantage in supplying what it takes for young children to be prepared to do well in school.

This potential problem is accentuated by three other factors. The first is that in many countries, income distribution has become more unequal in the past generation, with the real incomes of less-educated families stagnating or even declining. The second is that a high fraction of females heading households are not only poor because they are women, but doubly poor because they have low levels of schooling. The third factor is that public investment in the early care and education of children worldwide is low. Under these three conditions, the ability of children of less-educated families to escape poverty is the exception rather than the rule. Even in a rich country such as the United States, in the mid-1990s, 15 per cent of children were growing up in poverty, the highest level in the OECD (Smeeding *et al.* 2000: table 2). In most developing countries the level of child poverty is far higher. Since the family is still the entity responsible for child-rearing, differences in access to information and networks extant among social groups are likely to be reproduced from this generation into the next.

Globalization and the struggle for community

Education does much more than impart skills needed for work. Schools are transmitters of modern culture. The meaning of modern culture as interpreted by the state is a crucial issue for educators and is contested in every society. Globalization redefines culture because it stretches boundaries of time and space and individuals' relationship to them. It reduces the legitimacy of national political institutions to define modernity.

So globalization necessarily changes the conditions of identity formation. Individuals in any society have multiple identities. Today, their globalized identity is defined in terms of the way that global markets value individuals' traits and behaviour. It is knowledge-centred, but global markets value certain kinds of knowledge much more than others. Global markets place high value on scientific and technical knowledge and less on the kinds of local, artisan skills that serve more basic needs. The global market does not work well as a source of identity for everyone.

Cultural identity, whether religious, ethnic, racial or gender, and whether local, regional or more global, is an antidote to the complexity and harshness of the global market as the judge of a person's worth. For nationalists, it is also an antidote to the globalized bureaucratic state. But such a trend could mean increased social conflict. If some localities/ethnicities/religious groupings feel increasingly excluded from the high end of the market, a weakened nation state incapable of reincorporating them socially could mean less stability. Even though the political positions of various nationalist movements may differ considerably, they all tend to play to the sense for many of exclusion from participating in the fruits of globalizing national economies.

The market in itself has never been sufficiently inclusive. Strong, undemocratic, non-egalitarian nation states existed before the free market dominated economic systems, so many analysts believe that states are no guarantee of inclusion. But the modern capitalist state developed into a successful market 'softener'. The decline of that role in the face of powerful global marketization of national economies pushes the 'dispossessed' to seek refuge in new and more exclusive collectives. These collectives generally do not have the power or the funds to help the dispossessed financially or to develop the skills and knowledge valued by global markets. They can help develop self-knowledge and therefore self-confidence. They can provide community and therefore a sense of belonging. They often do so by defining others as 'outsiders' without the 'true' self-knowledge or the 'right' ancestors. At the extreme end, the communities are often highly undemocratic. If the nation state does not have the financial capability or the political legitimacy to dissipate such movements by incorporating its members into much broader notions of community and values, societies unable to maintain market success may face serious, unresolvable divisions.

The conflicts in identity formation necessarily affect education. The distribution of access to schools and universities, as well as educational reforms aimed at improving its quality, are all headed towards forming labour for a market conditioned by globalization. But education can become more inequitable rather then more inclusive. Thus, in any strategy, central governments must still assume responsibility for levelling the playing field for all groups. This is particularly true because excluded groups see the educational system as both crucial to knowledge acquisition yet not serving the needs of their 'community'. Schools and the educational system become primary targets for social movements organized around 'self-knowledge', such as religious or ethnic identity. The educational system has enormous resources devoted to knowledge formation for dominant groups. Why should not education in a democratic society serve all groups, even those that differ markedly from the ideal of the new, competitive, globally sensitive worker? It is no accident that much of the struggle, for example, between religious fundamentalists and the secular, rational state, is over state education. The public sector has the funds to place children in an educational institution, but not the commitment to create a moral community. Instead, the state has succumbed to crass materialism on a global scale. Fundamentalists want to attract those who are not happy with their value in a world economy, and to educate them and their children in a way that will strengthen religious affili-ation, not economic productivity. The more they succeed, the less the educa-tional system will be able to develop global economy workers. Yet, at the same time that schools and universities are the sites of intense struggles over the definition of culture, they represent to those who are not included in the global economy the single most important route to access global culture. Minority groups may try to control the cultural norms purveyed by schools and universities, but they often engage in such battles believing that their children should have a chance to learn skills valued by the global economy.

In addition, proactive movements, such as feminism and environmental-ism, postmodern in their outlook and in direct conflict with globalization, are attempting to redefine the conception of 'global' in the education system. For example, feminism is gradually shaping global culture to include gender equality and equity, first in education, then in labour markets. Envir-onmentalism has had an enormous impact on global culture through envir-onmental programmes in schools worldwide. These proactive movements are having a major impact on how schools define new global culture, and in that sense are most closely associated with challenges to the techno-economic definition of globalized culture.

Education plays and will continue to play a fundamental role in this struggle. The inroads that the women's movement has made into the edu-cational system even in traditional Muslim countries reflects its power over the past generation to shape knowledge institutions at the heart of the globalization process. Even so, as the continued subordination of women in societies such as Pakistan and Afghanistan suggests, other anti-global move-ments rooted in male-dominated traditional culture see women's equality as a global notion, and oppose it as part of their resistance to globalization.

Implications for higher levels of education

Globalization is bringing new kinds of people into upper secondary and tertiary education. They want higher-level schooling to make them valuable in the global economic system. At the same time, universities as sites of cultural formation are under new kinds of pressures because global market culture is highly exclusive and destructive of local culture. These new and contradictory pressures will be played out in expanding higher education systems over the next generation.

A new accountability

Basic secondary education, once itself seen as relatively elite, is rapidly being accepted in many developing countries as part of public 'mass education'. But upper secondary and tertiary education maintain their status as education reserved only for those who can qualify. In many countries, this means a highly elite education. Drop-out rates at these higher schooling levels continue to be very high. Viewing upper secondary and post-secondary education as a privilege rather than a right implies that disadvantaged young people will begin to graduate from higher levels of education in large numbers only when their primary and basic secondary education improves sufficiently to prepare them for higher levels. It puts pressure on primary and secondary schools to get better at teaching children that increasingly come from low-income, less-educated families. The standards movement worldwide has pushed many countries to make schools account for and improve their performance with low-income students. Yet, the view of higher levels of education as a privilege helps upper secondary and post-secondary institutions avoid this same kind of accountability. The traditional message to higher-level institutions is that they need not worry about good teaching or diagnosing the reasons for high drop-outs – their role is to bring together the most capable students from high school so that they become more capable.

If lower-scoring groups of students are systematically excluded from higher levels until such time as the primary and basic secondary schools learn how to raise student scores, an entire generation of disadvantaged minorities may be increasingly distanced from better-paying jobs. The drive to increase standards at the upper secondary level also faces the danger of actually increasing drop-out rates at that level. If low-scoring students perceive their chances of post-secondary education as dimmer than the high-scoring students, they may leave education earlier. In effect, there may be an increased separation between those who respond positively to the standard-raising and those who turn away even more.

The alternative to emphasizing accountability only at the primary and basic secondary levels is to place similar demands on upper secondary schools and universities. The drop-out rate from upper secondary schools and universities in developing countries is high. Yet, some higher-level institutions in every country have consistently above-average success rates and some have below-average rates. Today, the tendency is to place blame for this situation on individual students, particularly their capacity to handle an upper secondary or university curriculum. But more and more attention should and will be paid to higher-level education institutions themselves, particularly their capacity to teach successfully an increasingly diverse student body.

Multicultural universities in a global environment

Universities and other higher-level institutions do not just serve to add market worth to students hoping for a place in the globalized economy. These higher-level educational institutions are definers of culture in national and diverse regional and local communities. In many ways, universities are also community centres as such. For example, the university may represent for a community a centre of particular culture in a multicultural society, or may represent new definitions of multiculturalism. Thus, the university becomes an important site of conflict between global culture, in its role of preparing students to be economically successful in a global economic environment (scientific, global, economically valued knowledge), and local cultural forms that build self-identity (self-knowledge). Often, this self-identity is an antidote to a global identity that fails to include even many university graduates in the developing countries.

Today's more globalized notion of national identity in a period of declining state power makes it less logical to impose a narrow sense of national, regional or local culture. Since markets are increasingly global, an individual's economic value is determined by broader criteria than his or her local 'acceptability'. Further, declining state capacity to impose norms creates political space for counter-dominant concepts of self-knowledge. In practice, groups that do not assimilate well into the global market knowledge culture have greater political options today than even a generation ago of forming relatively autonomous cultural groups with their own knowledge institutions. This is true for fundamentalist religious groups as well as for particular immigrant groups wanting to preserve language and native culture.

In terms of how upper secondary schools and universities may react to globalization, this suggests approaches to self-knowledge community very different from those of the past. Two models come to mind. The first is one where the state allows any community group to create a knowledge institution with public funds as long as it meets minimum legal criteria. Each community in society could therefore socialize its children and transmit knowledge in the way it chooses. This implies a vision of society where groups with widely different beliefs are held together by market relations but not necessarily other common bonds. Those who support educational vouchers for privately run schools, charter schools, and ethnic or religious upper secondary schools and universities catering for very different groups tend towards this approach. The second model is one where the state uses a multicultural self-knowledge approach to socialize all young people in the public system. This multicultural approach differs from totally autonomous definitions of self-knowledge by each group.[4] It also abandons the imposition of a single, dominant culture, but does make all children attending publicly funded institutions learn about the variety of cultures in the community (and their points of view). In that sense, the state (national, regional or local community) continues to impose an ideological perspective, but one that reflects the diversity of today's post-industrial societies.

The first model assumes that market relations (the profit motive) are enough to keep increasingly diverse societies working together successfully. I have my doubts. To build social capital, diverse communities need to share *common* social experiences. In knowledge-based society, a common school, upper secondary school and university experience with young people having at least some diversity in background and values serves this function. A multicultural approach to socialization does more: it not only allows children of various groups to gain an understanding of their own history and culture but also allows them to think critically about it. This makes it consistent with the higher-order problem-solving skills needed for an innovative, democratic society. It is also consistent with a positive, constructive vision of what post-industrial societies are becoming – a vision distinctly opposed to the parochial, defensive, anti-globalism of the nationalist right.

Elitism versus lifelong education in a globalized economy

The most salient feature of the globalized economy in the information age is that it requires nations, regions and local communities to focus on the enhancement of their human resources. As I have argued, some communities may choose to develop the kinds of skills most valued in global markets; others may end up emphasizing ethnic identity and culture-centric education in the hope of preserving community against the individualistic, materialistic values of the global economy.

Whatever course nations, regions and communities choose to follow, they will need to be inclusive rather than exclusive in their educational strategy. This means that women and girls will have to be a major part of their educational strategy, particularly bringing them into fields long dominated by men, such as science and engineering. It also means that concepts of age-specific education need to be reconsidered. Obviously, education in the early years of a child's life is fundamental, because it is developmentally appropriate, because children are economically 'cheaper' to educate, and because they have many more years to garner returns on their learning. However, new conditions in the global economy have tended to reduce the economic value of less-educated youth and adult workers. This makes adult education not only more relevant (increasing skills for new kinds of work), but also more economical, since the earnings that less skilled workers forego when they attend adult education have declined in the past two decades and for more skilled have risen.

The main obstacle to a greater emphasis on adult education and greater flexibility in the age that youth take their regular upper secondary and higher education is institutional custom. Just as fields such as science and engineering are seen as male occupations, anyone not 15–19 years old does not fit into upper secondary schools, and students older than their mid-twenties are out of place in post-secondary institutions. These narrow definitions of educational appropriateness are particularly harmful to those of lower socio-economic background, who may have been pushed to work early or started school late, or repeated grades, hence were already 'out of place' as youth in school. For social reasons, it may indeed not be appropriate for adults to attend school with young people, but communities can develop educational institutions that grant regular degrees to older students. As educational technology develops further, the possibilities increase.

Post-secondary institutions, with their already older youth clientele, could most easily accommodate adult students. US public universities, which have always been more flexible in allowing adult students to enter even in their thirties and forties, are a good model for developing countries. In the 1970s and 1980s, most enrolment growth in US universities came from women in their late twenties and thirties enrolling after beginning families and then deciding to return to school to 'upgrade' to a university degree. That type of 'lifetime learning' flexibility gave the US economy millions of university graduates it would not have had were the educational system less flexible. The most famous case of educational flexibility is the GI Bill, which produced a major increase of college graduates in the United States in the 1950s and 1960s by subsidizing returning veterans of World War II and the Korean War to attend university at government expense.

Developing countries need to follow such examples of making their upper secondary and post-secondary systems more flexible to accommodate older students who are capable of higher-level education degrees but for various reasons could not attain those degrees in their youth.

Notes

1. Real time is, in entertainment parlance, 'live', meaning that information is exchanged or communicated as it is produced.
2. Estimated rates of return in countries such as Hong Kong (Chung 1990), the Republic of Korea (Ryoo *et al.* 1993), and Argentina (Razquin 1999), as well as in a number of the OECD countries (OECD 1998), show that rates of return to higher secondary and university education are as high or higher than to either basic secondary or primary. Furthermore, some of these same studies measured rates of return for several different years in the 1970s, 1980s and 1990s, showing that rates of return to higher levels of education have risen faster than primary and secondary rates.

3. In many parts of Africa, the AIDS virus could drastically reduce the number of children from lower-income families who reach secondary and university age, as well as drastically reduce population growth over the next generation. In these countries, population growth rates may approach developed-country levels not because of lower fertility rates, but because of higher death rates. Even so, the pressure for higher-level schooling expansion will be great and the students entering secondary schooling and university will increasingly come from low-income, low-education families.

4. Critiques of multicultural approaches to self-knowledge focus on their flight from the classics of western civilization and the new 'fascism' of political correctness. It is ironic that neo-conservatives critique multiculturalism in the form that could certainly occur under a voucher system or charter schools – educational alternatives pushed by neo-conservatives. I agree that there is some validity in these criticisms. They are primarily aimed at minorities' and women's attempt to define culture in new ways, but to be consistent, would also have to critique Christian or Muslim fundamentalists who want to use public funds to socialize their children into values and norms inconsistent with tolerance and enlightenment. It is also ironic that in their fear of the multicultural future, neo-conservatives push for the alternative implicit in these critiques – namely using the state to impose an assimilationist view of language, history and culture on groups that seek their own interpretation of history and culture – at the same time as they want highly localized autonomy over school curriculum, teacher hiring and modes of socialization.

References

Braudel, F. (1979) *Civilization and Capitalism*, Volume II, *The Wheels of Commerce*. New York: Harper & Row.

Carnoy, M. (2000) *Sustaining the New Economy: Work, Family, and Community in the Information Age*. Cambridge, MA: Harvard University Press, and New York: Russell Sage.

Carnoy, M., Castells, M., Cohen, S. and Cardoso, F.H. (1993) *The New Global Economy in the Information Age*. University Park, PA: Pennsylvania State University Press.

Castells, M. (1996) *The Rise of the Network Society*. London: Blackwell.

Castells, M. (1997) *The Power of Identity*. London: Blackwell.

Castro, C.M. and Carnoy, M. (1997) *La Reforma Educativa en America Latina*. Washington, DC: Inter-American Development Bank, Department of Social Programs and Sustainable Development.

Chung, Y.P. (1990) Changes in rates of return over time: the case study of Hong Kong. Mimeo, paper presented at the Comparative and International Education Society Annual Meeting, Atlanta, Georgia.

OECD (1998) *Human Capital Indicators*. Paris: OECD.

Psacharopoulos, G. (1989) Time trends of the returns to education: cross-national evidence, *Economics of Education Review*, 8(3): 225–39.

Ramirez, F., Saysal, Y. and Shanahan, S. (1997) The changing logic of political citizenship: cross national acquisition of women's suffrage rights, 1890 to 1990, *American Sociological Review*, 62(October): 735–45.

Razquin, P. (1999) Changes in rates of return to education in Argentina, 1980–1996. Mimeo, Economics of Education Workshop, Stanford School of Education.

Rifkin, J. (1994) *The End of Work.* New York: Putnam.

Ryoo, J., Carnoy, M. and Nam, Y.S. (1993) Rates of return to education in Korea, *Economics of Education Review,* 12(1): 71–80.

Smeeding, T., Rainwater, L. and Burtless, G. (2000) *US Poverty on a Cross National Context,* Luxembourg Income Study, working paper no. 244. Maxwell School, Syracuse University.

12

Globalization, Universities and 'Knowledge as Control': New Possibilities for New Colonialisms?

Terri Kim

With the rise of network society, the ways in which knowledge is created, transmitted, managed and used are undergoing dramatic change. This chapter analyses global developments in the creation of new forms of universities, including virtual universities and global alliances between universities and various corporations, to explain the changing boundaries of learning and provision and the emergence of new forms of colonialism. These are visible in the context of South East Asia, and are closely linked to language issues in the worldwide transmission of knowledge and provision of global-scale online education. The conclusion questions the legitimacy of neo-liberal market-principled educational discourse in the new global age.

Educational space has become more and more unified globally. The direction of the global economy is towards a further liberalization of markets, including trading in education and professional services regulated by GATT/WTO (http://www.wto.org). Most countries are now faced with a challenge to develop internationally competent and globally competitive domestic institutions of higher education, as a pool for new human resources in nations fit for new knowledge-based high-technology industries.

East Asian countries have responded to these new economic and educational challenges. For instance, the proclaimed policy goals of South Korea in the Five-Year Economic Plan for 1993 to 1997 included deregulation, technology development, human resource development, and the promotion of foreign direct investment. The South Korean government has confirmed that it will invest – along with the private sector – 1.37 trillion won (almost £5.5 billion) in the nation's nanotechnology (NT) industry, the most cutting-edge of all industries which is expected to grow rapidly in the years to 2010. Along with this investment, the government plans to have three to four universities in the country launch NT-related departments, as part of the strategic development of the nation. The ultimate target for the government is to increase NT research staff to 13,000 from the current 1000 by 2010 (*Chosun Ilbo*, 20 May 2001; www.chosun.com).

Similarly, Malaysia has devised policy goals with a strong export orientation. Twelve, mainly capital-intensive industries have been targeted through the Industrialization Master Plan (1986–95). Inter-industry links have been strengthened for automobiles and electronics (industry clustering), and the intention is to improve the information infrastructure in the New Industrialization Master Plan (1996–2005) (Anderson 1999: 9). Singapore's vision for meeting the challenges of globalization is expressed in the catchphrase: 'Thinking schools, learning nation'. According to a Singaporean government statement: 'It is a vision for a total learning environment, including students, teachers, parents, workers, companies, community organisations, and government'.

Especially after the Asian economic crisis of 1997–99, South Korea and other East Asian countries felt it necessary to reform, quite urgently, their universities and human resource development (HRD) programmes. In 1999, the South Korean government launched a grand higher education project, Brain Korea 21 (BK21), to internationalize both the higher education system and the academic manpower working in research and development. The BK21 project was aimed at getting the higher education system to meet the global challenges posed by the advanced knowledge-based economies. The South Korean government also inaugurated a new presidential commission, the Human Resource Commission. The job of the Commission is to formulate policies on higher education and HRD for the 'Internet knowledge-based economy' (http://www.moe.go.kr). Thus economic globalization has already affected what we used to know as 'the university', including the idea of the university in East Asia.

In East Asia, ideas about universities share a common heritage in academic models which originated in Europe. The first university academics recruited to teach in the modern higher education systems were western colonial expatriates. The idea of the modern university was thus an imported one. Even the Japanese colonial higher educational institutions in Korea and Taiwan were based on the Japanese adaptation and interpretation of European models (Kim 2001). The other main foreign influence (for example in China and in Korea) was from American missionaries. Thus German and American university traditions were strong in forming the modern university academic culture in East Asia and in Korea. These inherited imported models were affected by three processes of 'domestication' (in both colonialist and nationalist periods): (i) the insistence that universities increasingly serve national economic purposes; in many cases, one university (e.g. the University of Tokyo or, later, Seoul National) was seen as a crucial agent of modernization of the nation; (ii) especially from the 1950s, the 'social' demand by national populations for access to expanded higher education systems; and (iii) the consequent rapid expansion of both the number of students and the number of institutions in higher education systems – the 'massification of higher education', a dramatic process especially since the 1960s in East Asia. For example, South Korea retains the second highest rate of enrolment in colleges and universities in the world, next to the United States.

However, economic globalization is altering some of these traditional assumptions. Even the 'best' national universities – Tokyo, Seoul National, or for that matter Oxford and Cambridge – can grow rigid when they become overconfident in their local prestige. Mass university education, well suited perhaps to an industrial age with its demands for a generally high level of reasonably competent labour, may be less well suited for the creative and cutting-edge research needed by knowledge economies. Examination-oriented schooling systems in East Asia, based on severe and standardized tests of school knowledge for university entry, may be less well suited to the creation of flexible and confident symbolic analysts for this century. What is excellent and outstanding when judged on national criteria, may be less than marvellous when judged on international criteria of excellence.

Economic globalization is disturbing other assumptions. The earlier massification of higher education is now becoming a global business, often beyond the control of national governments. Likewise, the knowledge-based global market economy now brings into question the idea of the university as a fixed site. In the era of globalization, the asynchronous e-learning networks of universities and the corporate sector make cyberspace a new academic locus, transforming the traditions of higher education.

Similarly, academic mobility has continued to increase across the globe (Blumenthal *et al.* 1996), and academics are becoming internationally mobile knowledge workers. Universities are less and less seen as national institutions of higher education in which mainly the 'locals' work, and there is a new, extensive development of university academic forums across the conventional borders – often via the Internet – and beyond intellectual disciplines. Through the use of information and communication techno-logies (ICTs), we are already seeing university institutions that exist only in cyberspace, such as Cardean University (www.unext.com), Jones International University (www.jonesinternational.edu) and Western Governors University (www.wgu.edu) in the United States.

The question of the *site* of the university is thus an important part of the contemporary change of universities. Even though, throughout the history of the university, an international academic forum outside specific territorial boundaries has always existed in a form of 'the college invisible' (Rothblatt 1997), we are probably in a new situation. The historical change is in the balance between the visible and invisible sites of university academic com-munities. Of course, national higher education systems are still different in each country, in terms of structures, curriculum, funding, and student and academic populations. Nevertheless we are now witnessing a global con-vergence around market-oriented higher education systems driven by neo-liberal, knowledge-based economies. In this trend, the traditional forms of national institutions of higher education do not seem, to governments, to be meeting the new imperatives of the globalizing world economy.

The challenges are massive. For example, given regional and global integration, intellectual capital and research increasingly cross the territorial boundaries of nation states. There has been a growth in transnational enterprises, international firms and global learning organizations (World Bank 1998). There are sharper versions of older problems, such as intellectual property rights or changing definitions of university staff roles and relationships and new issues, such as the commodification of university teaching, courses and qualifications, as if these were export industries.

Overall, the challenge flows from three new models of the university: the entrepreneurial research university, the virtual university and the corporate university.

The entrepreneurial research university

The rapid growth in the number of university-based research centres with close ties to industry shows an increasing permeability of boundaries between the two sectors. The new type of university/industry collaboration, at both national and international levels, has become a global pattern. The ownership of the world's knowledge resources is now increasingly exercised by commercially motivated private-sector corporations. In accordance with the rise of private-sector ownership of knowledge, research universities are becoming corporatized; and university academics are encouraged to participate in knowledge-based economic production. Consequently, the imperatives of economic globalization have already generated a new model for research universities, namely 'the entrepreneurial research university'. In the currently market-oriented university sector, the new entrepreneurial research university expects faculty members to bring in money not only through conventional types of research grants and contracts, but also through patents, licensing agreements and other innovative intellectual-economic activities, worldwide (Slaughter and Leslie 1997; Clark 1998).

In response to the imperatives of economic globalization, some major research universities have formed a new global academic alliance to develop commercial capital in pursuing academic excellence and quality assurance beyond national boundaries. For instance, the London School of Economics (LSE) in the UK established a new Internet education company, called UNext.com in collaboration with four major research universities in the United States: the University of Chicago, Columbia University, Stanford University and Carnegie Mellon. UNext operates Cardean University, an accredited online university which sells MBAs and other business courses to the corporate sector, targeting managers in transnational global organisations (www.unext.com). UNext is currently working with more than 40 businesses worldwide. As the UNext's first joint venture in the Asia-Pacific region, UNext Korea serves corporate clients in Korea, Singapore, Japan and India. The company expects Asia to be an explosive long-term market for its online education programmes.

Universitas 21 (U21) is another example of a new global academic alliance among major research universities. Formed in 1997, U21 is a company incorporated in the UK with a network of 18 universities in ten countries. U21 member universities span the globe throughout Europe, North America, Australia, New Zealand and East Asia. There are three Asian universities which are members of the U21: the National University of Singapore, the University of Hong Kong, and Peking University. Collectively, U21 enrols about 500,000 students each year, employs some 44,000 academics and researchers, and has a combined operating budget of almost US$9 billion as of 2001 (www.universitas21.com). Thomson Learning, one of the world's largest providers of lifelong learning information, joined the online venture, called U21 Global, to develop and deliver online learning materials for the growing global e-education market with U21 in 2001. The U21 Global project focuses on marketing postgraduate courses, including MBAs in e-commerce and information systems. The courses will target South East Asia and Latin America and be delivered in English, Mandarin and Spanish.

Since the 1980s, with the growth of a neo-liberal market ideology led by Anglo-American countries, the traditional research function of many universities has become geared to market principles. With the systematic conversion of intellectual activity into intellectual capital and hence intellectual property, university research activities have become commercialized. Learning becomes a product to be bought and sold, to be packaged, advertised and marketed on a global scale.

The networking process of educational globalization has arrived faster than expected. By the end of the twentieth century, higher education had already become a highly profitable sector of the global market. In the United States, the education sector is ranked fifth in terms of services export revenue, accounting for 4 per cent of total services revenue in 1999 and over US$14 billion of export receipts in 2000 (http://www.tradeineducation.org). That makes the amount that the United States spends on lifelong learning more than the total spent on national defence. Foreign scholars doing research or teaching in research universities in the United States increased by 5 per cent in 1998 (*Chronicle of Higher Education*, 11 December 1998: A69; http://www.iie.org/opendoors/). There were 74,571 foreign scholars at US academic institutions in 1999/2000. This reflected a continued increase in the flow of scholars, especially from China and India, for the fifth year in a row. Over 43 per cent of foreign scholars in the United States come from Asia. Estimates are for the US distance education academic market to grow from US$16 million in 1997 to US$1.57 billion in 2002 and the corporate market from US$217 million to US$7.6 billion in the same period (Oblinger and Kidwell 2000: 33).

The growth, then, of the 'entrepreneurial university' as a powerful model poses some severe challenges to the university systems of East Asia. Do the East Asian systems 'compete' – and if so how, and on what criteria? At least in the late nineteenth century or early twentieth century, as major 'local' universities were developed in East Asia, this could be done in a slow and measured way for the purposes of colonial or national development. Young scholars could be sent overseas; knowledge acquired; nationalism and status honour would bring them home; a 'national' system of universities or at least one major 'National' university could be constructed. One such example, from a different continent, is the United States borrowing the basic idea for the creation of a 'graduate school' from Germany, subsequently copied by many other nations in the world. How – and at what speed – in the twenty-first century is such borrowing to occur? Or, as importantly, how is international hegemony of 'the' research university over local higher education systems to be avoided? Thus, for example, the strategy of Brain Korea 21 is clear in South Korea, but it is important for South Korea that the time needed for the policy to work can be safeguarded. This general problem is compounded by the growth of yet more new forms of the university.

The virtual university

Unlike the conventional model of research universities, the virtual university puts relatively little emphasis on faculty research or scholarship. It employs relatively few full-time faculty members. In the case of the University of Phoenix in the United States, most faculty members – around 90 per cent – have full-time jobs elsewhere. Paid between US$950 and US$2000 per course as of 1999, they are discouraged from lecturing and are expected to play the role of 'facilitator', ensuring that the standardized curriculum delivered entirely via modem is followed precisely and that student discussion takes place in a managed academic culture (http://www.uophx.edu). The New School for Social Research in New York now routinely hires outside contractors, mostly unemployed PhDs, to design online courses. The course designers are not hired as employees but are simply paid a fee, and then the university has all rights to the course designed by them. In this way, the New School has been running the online courses without having to employ academic staff (Noble 1998).

In the virtual mode of higher education, basic lecturing might be the work of a handful of on-screen academic stars, and so universities are likely to need fewer lecturers. The major role of academics then shifts from lecturing to mentoring, advising students and guiding them in their educational pursuits. This seems to be a paradoxical turn in contemporary university development: despite the trend to massification, technology-aided higher education requires more tutorial-style teaching and learning, one early model of which was English collegiate education at Oxford and Cambridge – in the thirteenth century.

More importantly, perhaps, online education has become a global business, through transatlantic and transcontinental alliances. Worldwide, distance teaching universities have developed into mega-sized institutions of higher education. The term 'mega university', coined by Sir John Daniel, former vice-chancellor of Open University in the UK, is defined as a university in which more than 100,000 students are enrolled (ICDL 1995: foreword). On this definition, there are ten mega universities, located in China, France, India, Indonesia, South Korea, South Africa, Spain, Thailand, Turkey and the UK (Daniel 1996: 166–96). The double phenomenon of mega-size and bureaucratization has depersonalized the university dramatically. Or perhaps more fairly, the phenomenon clearly makes personalizing the university a bit of a problem. The development of distance education now challenges further the traditional mode of university education. With the rise of the Internet, online education looks like becoming an imperative for conventional universities as well.

The great advantage of such universities is that their unit costs are low. In one sense they are an attractive model in East Asia, since they can mop up the social demand for higher education at little public cost. They can produce an 'all-graduate' population. The historic question is whether East Asia can afford the routinization of training and intellect – already strong in the secondary schools of the region – implicit (at the moment at least) in the pedagogical models of such universities. How much intellectual homogenization is appropriate for the twenty-first century university? What is the balance between elite formation and egalitarian access to higher educational opportunity? Governments in East Asia are uncertain, but the tendency is towards recovery from brain drain, the training of new elites in new areas of knowledge and a sharp sense of the need for competitiveness in a world knowledge economy. Paradoxically, that makes new forms of the delivery of mass higher education attractive: the economic costs are low, and the social costs have not yet been thought about.

The corporate university

There has been, clearly, a convergence of organizational structures, management, and the technologies of computing and communications, which has had an effect on educational practices and the university itself. The new structure of virtual universities provides people with almost ubiquitous access to information and knowledge. Through the virtual institutions of higher education and the multi-site global business of higher learning, a global curriculum can be created across national borders. The establishment of international standards for accreditation, certification and transfer of credit has become an urgent task between educational actors involved in global higher education. The emergence of new developers and brokers of higher education content and delivery outside the academy adds more complexity to the challenges with which traditional higher education is faced now. But the challenge also includes the theme of money – large amounts of it.

As changes in the patent system in the 1980s enabled the universities to become major vendors of patent licences, the vendors of the network hardware, software and 'content' now think of higher education as 'the focus industry' for lucrative investment in the future. David F. Noble, in an article entitled 'Digital diploma mills', speculated that the higher education market would eventually become dominated by EMOs (education maintenance organizations) just like HMOs (health maintenance organizations) in the health care market (Noble 1998). His forecast soon became a reality. Publishing companies that supply students with textbooks and course materials now own colleges that supply the course, based entirely on the Internet. For instance, Harcourt General Inc., one of the largest publishers of academic textbooks in the United States, established a for-profit, online university, accredited to award BAs and MAs in liberal arts, business, information technology and health care (http://www.harcourthighered.com). In these new contexts there are major questions about control and benefit: who validates knowledge, and who benefits from online higher education? Corporate universities are business enterprises.

Thus one of the immediate challenges for East Asian higher education is whether it should be in a free market for the sale of educational services at all. Clearly there are major pressures, from GATT and the World Trade Organization (WTO), for this to happen. Equally clearly, this is an ideological position derived from the principles of neo-liberal economics. The East Asian countries need to begin to assess the social and political implications of a wide-open international trade in educational services. Behind the immediate and alleged benefits of a free trade in educational services, there are two strategic, long-term concerns for all nations. These are the ideology of lifelong learning and the practices of knowledge control on the one hand, and the changing partnerships of universities and nation states on the other. Both can be understood in terms of economic imperative; and both can be assessed in terms of anxieties about social costs and international inequalities.

Lifelong learning and knowledge control

In the process of economic globalization, employability is expected to depend on continually mastering new skills. Responsibility for constant learning is now increasingly taken by individuals and the private sector. Lifelong learning, it is often argued, is necessary for the individual and for nations to survive, and there are growing opportunities for individuals to achieve lifelong learning. It is less frequently argued that there are potentially increasing social chasms in this new world full of the warm rhetoric of lifelong learning. In fact, there is an emergence of a new international division of intellectual capital as a consequence of the fact that the actual benefits from the knowledge-based economy are unevenly distributed throughout the world (Tapscott 1995).

National governments need to deal with the growing inequalities in, and concentration of, global knowledge assets. Higher education reforms in many countries promote the private sector in educational and training services (Bennell and Pearce 1998). Courses are increasingly offered via the Internet, franchising, overseas campuses, twinning programmes and split-site PhDs. Foreign degrees and diplomas are exports for some, but they are imports for others. More than 1 million students study outside their home country.

According to the OECD report on international trade statistics in services, the four major 'exporters' of trade in educational services are Australia, Canada, the UK and the United States. The major import countries of educational services are often non-OECD countries. Among all foreign students studying in OECD countries, Greek, Japanese and Korean students comprise the largest proportion of students from other OECD countries. China (including Hong Kong) represents 8.6 per cent of all foreign students studying in OECD countries, followed by Malaysia (3.8 per cent) and India (2.8 per cent) (OECD 2001). In this global trade in educational services, however, national higher education qualifications, locally obtained without international academic recognition, are likely to be devalued.

Similarly, various ways to manage intellectual property have been sought as part of international trade agreements, for example the GATT/WTO, NAFTA (North American Free Trade Area), FTTA (Free Trade Area of the Americas), AFTA (the ASEAN Free Trade Agreement) and APEC (the Asia-Pacific Economic Cooperation). The growth of global business has meant the urgent need for specific efforts to develop global regulation of professional qualifications and higher degrees, even though an individual organisation may still operate in a national, regional or local setting (OECD 1995).

Such processes of educational globalization have brought widening inequality. Considerable inequalities persist in access and in the quality of educational provision and research. It is not merely a question of the extremes, where, for instance, in sub-Saharan Africa the number of students enrolled in higher education is one per 1000 inhabitants, in contrast to North America where it is one per 50 (Delors 1996: 130). Even in East Asia there are difficulties and new forms of international inequalities – and not merely in cutting-edge research.

In South Korea, the utilization of ICTs in education was based on the Education Reform Initiatives in 1995, followed by the Master Plan for the Information Infrastructure Project, launched in 1997. According to the Plan, every elementary and secondary school now has at least one computer laboratory. Every classroom is equipped with multimedia devices such as a PC or a projector. Every teacher is provided with a PC in order to prepare teaching and learning materials and class activities. Further to that, every school and every classroom is to be connected to the high-speed Internet (MoE 2001).

Despite the government's grand project, the use of ICT in education in South Korea tends to be limited to the domestic education networks, using only the Korean language as the medium of communication. For instance, Edunet, established as a total education information service in September 1996, is operated entirely in Korean and is being used by over 2 million people in South Korea (MoE 2001: 47; http://www.edunet4u.net). It is in that sense a big, but also a very local, service. On the other hand, Singapore, with a British colonial tradition, pragmatically uses English as the sole medium of university instruction, and is more actively participating in the global discourse of e-learning than other East Asian countries.

In the globalization of higher education, there are new possibilities for cross-cultural communication. However, the dominance of English as the global language in ICTs as well as conventional educational practice points to English as the global language of higher education. Increasingly, English is being adopted as the language of higher education in non-English-speaking sites for practical reasons: it is useful economically and even culturally at both national and international levels. To attract more foreign students to the countries where English is not in use officially, nor as the academic medium at the university, more national governments – for example in Sweden, Denmark, the Netherlands, France and Belgium in Europe, and Japan, South Korea and Malaysia in East Asia – are now trying to provide more university courses offered in English.

The case of France seems one of the most visible and successful in this trend (Kakouridis and Magnan 1998). France aims to play an important role in higher education and scientific exchange around the world, and thus intends to increase the number of foreign students it receives each year. The French government established the EduFrance Agency as Groupement d'Intérêt Public to internationalize higher education programmes. EduFrance is reportedly an integral part of the fulfilment of France's economic and cultural role in today's world. Two years after the establishment of Edufrance, the state agency succeeded in attracting more foreign students. This trend shows that the decline of French impact on international educational service since 1993 – the number of foreign students studying in France dropped from 162,000 to 150,000 – has been successfully reversed (www.edufrance.com).

Thus the decision for East Asian higher education systems is difficult. Will East Asian higher education systems merely 'plug into' international provision of educational services? Will they plug-in in English? Will they, in contrast, compete in the sense that they too will establish 'international' graduate schools, and if so on what terms? For instance, the South Korean government is now encouraging universities to establish international graduate schools and research centres and to use English as the medium of instruction (MoE 1998). In reality, however, it is the private sector of higher education that leads the way in South Korea, as with the development of e-learning courses at the international graduate schools of some major private universities such as Ewha and Yonsei University. Such differences in local adaptation to the pressures of educational globalization are important – and the role of states remains crucial.

National governments and universities

A paradox of the globalization of higher education is in the relationship between the national governments and the university. The process of economic globalization has altered the traditional concept of a national basis for learning. Like health care, education is now being seen less and less as a social service. Despite the widespread rhetoric about lifelong education and learning societies, the future locus of education is found in the global capital markets. According to research by Merrill Lynch, education has the potential to capture between 5 and 10 per cent of the capital market by 2010. The combined corporate learning and higher education market is expected to grow from US$2.3 billion today to nearly US$20 billion by 2003 (GATE E-Newsletter; www.edugate.org). With this in prospect, the Web-based Education Commission to the President and Congress of the United States released a 170-page report entitled *The Power of the Internet for Learning: Moving from Promise to Practice*, in 2001. The report calls upon the new congress and administration to embrace an e-learning agenda as the centrepiece of US federal education policy (GATE E-Newsletter, 13 March 2001; www.edugate.org).

Overall, the rapid development and expansion of the global e-learning market in particular suggests major changes in the traditional partnership of national governments and universities. Confronted by these challenges and by the new forms of entrepreneurial research, virtual and corporate universities which are developing so rapidly in 'the West', many governments find themselves in confusion. It is not too clear how to avoid the massive potential international hegemonies implicit in the idea that only a few 'nodes' will be centrally involved in the creation and transmission of knowledge, the certification of competence, and the possession of intellectual property. The implications for new forms of international inequality are considerable.

Conclusion

To solve these confusions, even the thinking of some of the most brilliant writers on comparative higher education of the twentieth century does not take us quite far enough. According to Eric Ashby, the central dilemma of a university is that it 'must be sufficiently stable to sustain the ideal which gave it birth and sufficiently responsive to remain relevant to the society which supports it' (Ashby 1966). The core problem is that nowadays 'the university' is not supported by 'a society'. Universities like so many other institutions exist within, but also *between* societies: they are interstitial, global, networked, even virtual. Of course, they are also of interest to particular national governments but the university is less and less nationally located as a working institution. The site of the university is again global. The globalization of the university does not simply mean a technological transformation. Beneath the change, and camouflaged by it, lies another: the commercialization of higher education and its worldwide expansion. Technology is just a vehicle here.

This automatically raises a number of crucial policy issues, for example:

- Issues of intellectual property in transnational education services.
- New hierarchies of academic quality – and new hierarchies of social and economic inequality at both national and international levels.
- Language issues related to global academic mobility and global accreditation of higher education.
- Changes in international academic mobility, staff recruitment and professional services in the context of globalizing higher education, and the governance of such changes.
- Issues of hybrid academic identities and the management of academic manpower at both national and international levels.
- Issues of academic freedom.

The potential international inequalities are so large that the old word 'colonialism' (with its fairly clear specification of space and linear lines of control) will probably block rather than assist fresh reflection on the political processes of globalization of higher education, within which new international hegemonic knowledge relations are being created. 'Knowledge' has indeed become control, in an unexpected way.

References

Anderson, T. (1999) *Policies for Knowledge-based Industries in the Asian Economies.* Paris: OECD.

Ashby, E. (1966) *Universities: British, Indian, African: A Study in the Ecology of Higher Education.* Cambridge, MA: Harvard University Press.

Bennell, P. and Pearce, T. (1998) *Internationalization of Higher Education: Exporting Education to Developing and Transitional Economies.* Brighton: Institute of Development Studies, University of Sussex.

Blumenthal, P., Goodwin, C., Smith, A. and Teichler, U. (eds.) (1996) *Academic Mobility in a Changing World: Regional and Global Trends.* London: Jessica Kingsley Publishers.

Clark, B.R. (1998) *Creating Entrepreneurial University: Organizational Pathways of Transformation.* Oxford: Pergamon/IAU Press.

Daniel, J.S. (1996) *Mega-universities and Knowledge Media: Technology Strategies for Higher Education.* London: Kogan Page.

Delors, J. (1996) *Learning: The Treasure Within. Report to UNESCO of the International Commission on Education for the Twenty-first Century.* Paris: UNESCO.

ICDL (International Centre for Distance Learning) (1995) *Mega Universities of the World: The Top Ten.* Milton Keynes: The Open University.

Kakouridis, T. and Magnan, M. (1998) Global English: A European perspective, *EAIE Forum,* June.

Kim, T. (2001) *Forming the Academic Profession in East Asia: A Comparative Perspective.* New York: Routledge.

MoE (Ministry of Education, ROK) (1998) *Education in Korea, 1997–1998.* Seoul: The Government Press.

MoE (Ministry of Education, ROK) (2001) *Education in Korea, 2000–2001.* Seoul: The Government Press.

Noble, D. (1998) Digital diploma mills. Part II: The coming battle over online instruction. http://communication.ucsd.edu/dl/ddm2.html

Oblinger, D. and Kidwell, J. (2000) Distance learning: are we being realistic, *Educause Review*, May/June: 31–9 http://www.educause.edu/pub/er/erm00/erm003.html

OECD (1995) *Knowledge Bases for Education Policies*. Proceedings of a Conference held in Maastricht, The Netherlands, 11–13 September 1995. Paris: OECD/CERI.

OECD (2001) E-learning in post-secondary education: trends, issues and policy challenges ahead. The 7th OECD/Japan Seminar, Tokyo, 5–6 June.

Rothblatt, S. (1997) *The Modern University and its Discontents: The fact of Newman's Legacies in Britain and America*. New York: Cambridge University Press.

Slaughter, S. and Leslie, L.L. (1997) *Academic Capitalism: Politics, Policies, and the Entrepreneurial University*. Baltimore: The Johns Hopkins University Press.

Tapscott, D. (1995) *The Digital Economy: Promise and Peril in the Age of Networked Intelligence*. New York: McGraw-Hill.

World Bank (1998) *World Development Report 1998*. Washington, DC: The World Bank.

13

Universities and the Knowledge Society

Chris Duke

Institutions and systems in an emergent knowledge economy

Late last century a galaxy of rectors, vice-chancellors and principals cele-
brating Bologna's nine hundredth anniversary reaffirmed the abiding significance of the university in contemporary society. Bologna since gave its
name to a plan to 'harmonize' European degree structures for mobility and
transferability within the European Union. It is a short step from harmonization to forms of standardization which limit diversity and the uniqueness
of different institutions. Is the future of the university found via standardization or – as here argued – via diversification anchored within clarification
of both old and new commonly valued purposes?

One key to the future of the university in the knowledge society is the
capacity to design diversity into emergent tertiary education systems. 'If the
natural world tended towards product standardization, why are there so
many ways of being a fish?' (McQueen 2001). Universities idealized as unique,
autonomous communities of scholars sit within higher or tertiary education
systems planned to meet the labour market needs of modern complex societies, variously characterized as post- or late industrial or postmodern. Here
we see them as emergent knowledge societies. In such systems each institution is a subsidiary part of a greater whole, its mission and contribution
prescribed from beyond its own level of governance. This chapter seeks to
identify a continuing valued role for the (learning) university in the (learning) knowledge society.

The relationship of the university to its society is depicted negatively as
an ivory tower, inaccessible dreaming Oxford spires, and more positively as
the nerve centre, powerhouse and critical conscience of society. Academic
autonomy, an excuse for irresponsible and non-accountable privilege as
portrayed by such novelists as Malcolm Bradbury and David Lodge, Andrew
Davies and Tom Sharpe, is also a necessary condition for universities to be

an essential estate of the democratic realm in an open society. In stark contrast is an ideal of the university as a 'lighthouse institution': if not a model community then at least an estate of the realm representing a distinct set of social and civic values and purposes extending beyond sectoral interest. New Zealand's universities are required by statute 'to accept a role as conscience and critic of society' (TEAC 2001). It is increasingly recognized that the older academic collegial tradition is also the work environment required, if not demanded, by a new wider breed of knowledge workers.

A common confusion assigns to universities two central responsibilities: the core businesses of teaching and research, creation and dissemination of knowledge. A third leg of *community service* is then added, essential to balance the stool in the tradition of American Land Grant colleges, and commonly now to help universities survive by income diversification in a more commercial world. This feeds a false perception that in some gentler time and more pristine condition universities were innocent of their supporting societies, with research as pure blue-skies enquiry, teaching as the nurturance of intellectual curiosity in institutions dedicated to the abstracted pursuit of knowledge as its own liberal end.

It was never thus. Such an idealized and historical portrayal makes it all the harder to look constructively for the role of the university in the knowledge economy – or society – and for the continuance of any unique, abiding contribution. It is better to start with the social context and see community service in one sense or another at the heart of both research and teaching. Studied as organizational forms and networks of influence within themselves and in their social contexts, we find a basis for looking for continuities in universities' role. We can also locate ourselves within the evolutionary and optimistic tradition of modernity and the 'enlightenment project' rather than unpredictable postmodernism which has made catastrophe theory a popular and powerful explanatory perspective. Recognized or not, community context and service has always been the third leg. Its informing relationship to research and teaching avoids one false dramatization of the crisis of the university. Partnership and social service are not the same as commercialization.

Less easy to think through is the evolution from a small set of institutions socializing the future leadership (and possibly intelligentsia) into mass higher education and now rapidly into a universal system of tertiary education. In a context of rapid socio-cultural, economic, technological and demographic change, university autonomy interferes with the need to allocate scarce public resources to meet diverse and complex objectives. Mostly the objectives are economic. The massification of higher education is accompanied by the twin forces of marketization and managerialism (Tapper and Palfreyman 2000). Higher education is seen as the engine of the economy, its task to produce and sustain competent knowledge workers, key to the knowledge economy. It becomes not so much a separate 'pillar of the society' as part of the economic pillar, measured by its contribution to higher levels of skills formation, and to maintaining the stock of human capital for the knowledge economy through lifelong learning.

As the tertiary system becomes ever larger, more complex and more costly, putting a lifelong learning paradigm into working order becomes central to the policy agenda. This is problematic for the individual university with its own cultural capital, social location, networks and institutional memory. Being planned as a bit within a complex national system where duplication is unaffordable mocks institutional self-governance. It infects with cynicism the mission statements and strategic plans which preoccupy managements. External accountabilities feed the dysfunctionalities of (negatively understood) managerialism. The pivotal question beyond the absolute level of public-sector funding is about diversity and hierarchy within the system. So far, system planning and accountability via standard indicators have favoured homogenization.

Is diversity best exercised within or between institutions? Can hierarchy secure diversity of outcomes to meet needs which are wider than any one institution can meet? Is some form of non-dominant hierarchy attainable? Can different contributions be duly valued and rewarded, creating diverse benevolent environments for diverse students and staff? The choice between diversity at system and institutional levels may be crucial to sustaining a healthy and valued self-governing university for a knowledge *society* as well as *economy*. If the system level is not resolved, confident institutional self-governance is arduous indeed.

So far, negotiation of differentiation within a mass system has been rudimentary and weak – aggressively hierarchical, win–lose, dog-eat-dog. The ivory league tradition of the United States is echoed with more or less subtlety in Britain's competitive clubs and groupings. In Australia the 'sandstone' Group of Eight (Go8)[1] oppose the other thirty universities for research funds and stature. Universitas 21 (U21), an international association of some 18[2] relatively prestigious universities in Asia and Australasia, Europe and North America, led initially by the University of Melbourne, claims stature and privilege and aspires to capitalize on these in business terms. However, it also applies universal benchmarks to hugely different socio-cultural, political and administrative traditions – China to the United States, Scotland to Singapore, Australasia to Sweden – reinforcing the globalizing process.

Globalization thus conflicts with nationally planned tertiary systems. It threatens to break the nexus between each university and its context. The new and untested world of virtual corporate university global markets may prove another dotcom bubble. The significance of globalization to this discussion does not depend on the ultimate business performance of the various ventures vying for profile and business such as Western Governors and Phoenix, UNext and Cardean, Jones International and U21 (see Chapter 12, this volume). More significant is its relevance to the place of universities in their respective societies, economies and planned tertiary systems. Will the classic collegium celebrated at Bologna revive by taking the road to global markets and stature (a rediscovery of Erasmus perhaps), or by rediscovering a vital role as a university of critical discourse back in each respective society? Is the university an open 'people's cathedral on the hill' in an open participatory society, or a successful business venture delivering knowledge, workers and skills to the knowledge economy (Inayatullah and Gidley 2000)? Most such dichotomies mislead. Let us ask instead how such roles may be compatible. First a word about language.

Discourse and the evaporation of meaning

The concept of half-life applied to renewal of curriculum and the professional updating of graduates has a hollow echo in the tools of discourse about education generally. Changing fashion and a desire to capture market attention come at a cost to comprehension. 'Adult education' (AE) gave way to 'continuing education' (CE) as the more modern term, as CE shook off a specific vocational updating connotation. Terms like extramural, extension and outreach remained in use in some places. T for 'training' was added to E, affronting the 'liberal tradition'. A wish to focus more on students and their needs than on providers favours 'learning' over 'education', confusing two different functions and perspectives.

'Recurrent education', a concept developed in Sweden and vigorously promoted by CERI in terms of a new way of conceiving and making educational policy, was explicitly a strategy for lifelong learning (OECD 1973). It is periodically misrepresented as just economic rather than also social. Like 'lifelong education' it went out of fashion, while the contemporary *education permanente* was seen as meaning permanent schooling, in a confusion between languages. 'Lifelong learning' has since become highly popular after a period of relative disuse. Its use is so wide and loose as to drain meaning. Every conceivable learning opportunity, not least those offered for financial gain and late night broadcasting, is described as lifelong learning but deeper and more radical implications are seldom absorbed. All too often it simply means educational opportunities for adults.

Still worse is the state of discourse concerning 'learning' applied to organizations, cities, regions and societies. The 'learning organization' is trivialized as a place where a lot of people are trained. It lost appeal as the 'knowledge economy' and 'knowledge management' won attention through the 1990s. High-profile areas of research and development such as biogenetics become equated with knowledge, overlooking the permeative character of new information technology which changes ever more areas of work and life. Reductionism is one problem, the ephemerality of changing fashion another.

As knowledge management has come to capture attention, the idea of the learning organization has been treated somewhat as last year's discarded fashion (Scarbrough *et al.* 1999; OECD 2000). This shows the problem of replacing one important insight with another when both are relevant and their synthesis is essential, as in the case of the learning organization and knowledge management. Not only is the learning organization in danger of slipping out of sight, but 'a third of the managers interviewed across Europe . . . already see "knowledge management" as a buzz-word, or fad, that will be replaced by something new in the next few years . . . If they are already dismissing the still-evolving concepts behind the term, that would be truly discouraging' (CSBS 1998: 4).

Further muddying the emergent relationship between education and the knowledge society, confusion surrounds 'flexible learning' and the virtual, as in 'virtual university'. Flexibility and responsiveness to the diverse needs and circumstances of lifelong learners take many forms. They cover different and extended uses of the campus and other learning sites; flexible design and accreditation of the curriculum, workplace and community partnerships, including the accreditation of workplace and other prior and experiential learning; and diverse modes of providing face-to-face and other learning support and feedback.

The loose notion of the virtual university sweeps aside this complex repertoire of possibilities in a simple dichotomy between a costly and dated campus approach and the high-tech hyperbolic virtual university dispensing entirely with community and other-than-electronic contact (compare Merrill Lynch 2000). The majority of established universities are already partly virtual, or rather mixed-mode. The weight of such evidence as exists favours mixed-mode and supported learning in which the virtual has a place (CVCP 2000). The trend towards the virtual makes the university all the more 'concrete' (Goddard and Cornford 1999).

As new terms become fashionable they also devalue and displace earlier terms, breaking the thread of understanding of historical development, weakening social and organizational learning. The recently known requires rediscovering. Extreme propositions put forward for effect need moderating. The death of the university in the face of trillion-dollar virtual business is an example. The histories of 'lifelong learning' and the 'learning organization' are problematic. Concepts of knowledge management, knowledge workers and the knowledge economy are too important to be trivialized, but they risk a similar fate.

The knowledge economy and the tertiary system

We live, work and think in a hurry. The 'knowledge economy', for example, suffers such short-circuiting carelessness. It is located in the same ideological space as globalization, free trade and liberal economic rationalism. It frequently shares with technological innovation a presupposition of inevitability. Along with lifelong learning it attracts hostility from adult educators who cleave to values deemed older, wider and more generous.[3] In a similar but subtler vein, Sennett (1998) suggests that people become plastic, moulded by the combined forces and values of global economies and lifelong learning. Human resources, malleably reshaped to meet changing economic needs, are renewable, replaceable and disposable bits in knowledge systems. The essentially humane values of the learning organization are corrupted by the language of human resources and their management. Janus-like, adaptability to change and flexibility become denatured, disassociated and disaffiliated vulnerability. The workplace ceases to be a convivial community with tacit knowledge and institutional memory. Knowledge management is a matter of software: hard systems and softened-up people.

Meanwhile the new management of knowledge becomes an indisputable basis of productivity and prosperity. Farmworkers disappear, 'knowledge workers' multiply. Investment in people, their skills and their adaptability is a key to global competitiveness. Its relative valuing and investment is an important OECD benchmark.

New information and communication technologies (ICTs), especially new forms of tacit knowledge and know-how, drive higher education towards mass tertiary systems. These equip ever larger numbers and deeper layers of knowledge workers as the technologies spread wider and penetrate deeper. The unmotivated and excluded who cannot function as productive workers (and so as active consumers) are drawn in with subtlety or directness, as through 'study for the dole' schemes.

The trend towards universal tertiary education is thus democratic, inclusive, and at the same time coercive. The education system, especially postschool, shifts from being free-standing to becoming essentially part of the economic system. This makes it a server, compliant to economic policy imperatives. This is not new, as merger or absorption of state education departments into departments of education and employment shows. OECD and CERI have walked this tightrope rather skilfully, re-igniting policy debate about tertiary system planning while holding to wider social objectives, problematizing rather than naively embracing lifelong learning (see, in particular, Papadopoulos (1994) for the story of that walk).

The knowledge society and the abiding university – rebuilding the ruins

A tertiary system providing a flow of skilled and continuously updated knowledge workers appears essential. It begs a question about the university as an institutional form. In a bleakly insightful analysis of loss of national rationale and universality of discourse, Bill Readings characterized it as being in ruins, believing that it had abandoned idealism and the guardianship of culture for a bureaucratic-administrative alternative, under the masquerade of the 'discourse of excellence' (Readings 1996: 150). This sits in disturbing juxtaposition with Sennett's portrayal of character-corrosion. It can take us beyond binary and oppositional analysis into the actual pluralities of meaning required for essential functional diversity among universities in complex higher education systems.

The knowledge economy is a subset of the knowledge society. The university is an element within a tertiary system for skill formation and upgrading, but also a wider notion. Within the ruins of the university there survived for Readings a community of discourse. Beyond the excesses of economic rationalization and such evasions of accountability as 'trickle-down' there survives a more innately optimistic view of the nature of people, their societies, communities and institutions. In the broader notion of a knowledge society, the economic is but one dimension.

The shift represents a rediscovery of the 'enlightenment project'. It nurtures a more generous social ethic, challenging widening inequalities within and between nations. An old discourse of equity of opportunity – access and participation in the context of education – is reborn in the language of social inclusion; the recognition of community, its strength, value and sheer utility, is rediscovered through various notions of social capital. Within the ruined university, collegiality, battered by corporate business imperatives (Marginson and Considine 2000), again becomes plausible since the organizational culture required to nurture and retain knowledge workers resembles the older *collegium* (EIU 1998).

We may therefore expect the learning organization to be seen as a means to enable effective knowledge management (Scarbrough and Carter 2000). Institutional memory, discarded along with disposable workers much as each new generation of software replaces that in use, will be seen as a valuable intangible asset. The university will remain a place or network of places, a community or set of communities, and a series of living experiences. It will be 'owned' by a growing army of knowledge workers who need such resource centres, whether as alumni or as a surrogate *alma mater* for life in a mobile society, throughout and beyond working life.

This implies a role as lifelong learning resource centre for many kinds of tertiary institutions, some of them called universities. *University* only makes sense as a unique institutional form and estate of the realm with diversity of mission, function and mode between institutions. The biggest threat to the reborn and historic college community is competitive homogenization. National system planning fed by standardized benchmarking damages national diversity; the damage is increased if the benchmarking contest is international.

Much depends on institutional leadership. Attributes required include courage and clear purposefulness to hold to agreed and fitting institutional aspirations; and the longer vision, transparency and adaptability which call for intelligence, an open mind and self-confidence. Not all are thus endowed. Diversity demands more than does conformity. The larger the tertiary system the more damaging become standard performance measures. All those involved get damaged, from the most prestigious to the newest and most indigent. All drive to embrace an unattainably wide span of tasks and roles. The most imaginative solution to this conundrum is at best sub-optimal. It is to become an entirely private corporation evading some of the constraints of conformity as well as penury.

Jennifer Gidley captures the dilemma of diversity well in analysing different scenarios for the future of universities. The most attractive and significant from our perspective here she characterizes as 'meaning-making' (Gidley 2000; see also Inayatullah and Gidley 2000: chapters 19 and 20). The socially purposive, ecologically oriented, meaning-making university of the twenty-first century (from Newman through Halsey in the British tradition) inherits high moral purpose as an idealized university dedicated to truth-making as well as knowledge, the creation and exercise of wisdom as well as information.

What this means for each unique institution varies with the context. Auckland, for example, is the premier university in a remote and distinctive country, where a generation of free-market economics has created a competitive army of tertiary providers. It has also become a unique society. As well as being strongly bicultural with its indigenous Maori tradition, Auckland is the largest city of diverse Pacific islander peoples in the world as well as an Asian city following high inward migration in the 1990s. There persists a national ethic of social and civic purpose, which in modern terms is referred to as social inclusion, equity and sustainability. The flagship University of Auckland is New Zealand's only member of Universitas 21, posing a latent identity crisis between global benchmarking for international stature and profit, and playing a historically conditioned leadership role in making New Zealand a knowledge society. Walking a tightrope between the global and the local, the university vice-chancellor joined the prime minister to co-chair a high-profile conference to examine how New Zealand might become not only a *knowledge economy* but more richly also a *knowledge society*. The university thus staked a claim to position itself as New Zealand's community development leader, while seeking also to ratchet up its research performance and lobbying for more state-funded research as a world-class university.

The predicament of many universities is well exemplified by a legal requirement on New Zealand universities to exercise open entry to all who complete upper secondary education, and to all irrespective of prior educational attainment once they are 20. This ill accords with the more elite pressure of U21 benchmarking. There is also the statutory requirement on New Zealand universities to serve as critic and conscience of society (TEAC 2001), referred to earlier. Bringing these elements together in a time of inexorable competitiveness and contracting public funding demonstrates the difficulty of taking an appropriate role as a valued institution embedded in its society. Success requires not just clear and confident direction and leadership but also national acceptance of real diversity and autonomy within each emerging universal tertiary education system.

Conundrum and choice – foxgloves and fractals

Within the knowledge society the university must be a learning organization to thrive and give meaning to the term 'university'. To learn, it must be strongly networked internally and externally. Otherwise learning and effective knowledge-production will be impoverished (Gibbons *et al.* 1994). Renewal of mission means reoccupying higher ground abandoned in fear and confusion in the 1970s, when the transition beyond elite higher education exploded universities in number, scale and function beyond older metaphors and roles. Not every society lays down New Zealand's statutory requirement to be a conscience and critic of society. It is an identity which the tabloid media can make distinctly uncomfortable, but without it the idea and unique function of the university will be incomplete.

The funding and operating environment of universal tertiary education systems is problematic for the historic public university. Its resolution requires a deeper grasp and exercise of diversity through planning than has hitherto been widely achieved.[4] Some universities are tempted to opt out entirely, others to discriminate in sharp hierarchic tongue between higher and non-higher, even between education and training. This is poor shelter. The knowledge society implies ever wider extension of social and economic participation, competence and the exercise of multiple kinds of skills, from manipulating information to exercising social wisdom.

A property of digitalis is, I understand, that its potency increases exponentially with dilution. Similarly for higher education and the role of the university. In fostering societal learning the future lies through complementarity of partnerships with other educational institutions, and with diverse public, private sector and community non-education bodies. Identity as a unique institutional form will be won through the integrative leadership of learning societies, and of their regions.

We polarize, as if mutually exclusive, choices such as between excellence and equity. The fractal offers a richer metaphor. It is holistic. It suggests that the same issues, properties and potential are replicated and can be found at different levels and places down through and within the total system. Seen thus, the university guides, informs and actualizes what is latent in and as a knowledge-based learning society, rather than just training and socializing a bigger governing class. This side-steps insoluble disputation about equities of opportunity and outcome, levelling down and meritocracy. It may still reproduce privilege, but its focus shifts: from privileging individuals to enabling social development in a more inclusive and anchored way.

The hyperbole, or rather 'cyberbole' (OECD 2001), of the virtual corporate university may sit alongside this, using the name but not capturing the soul of the older public university. Measured challenges to education and higher education by Salmi and others (for example, Carneiro 2000; Salmi

2000) can be accepted if some traps are avoided: traps of language and its trivializing obsolescence; of tidy-minded bureaucracy unable to stomach diversity; of short-term protectionism which blinds longer vision and masks even self-interest.

There is no easy road to Utopia, but universities can still look ahead with more purpose than fear. Nine hundred years into the past with Bologna may be too far to reach back and comprehend. Nine years forward is not far to look ahead. By 2010, collective ingenuity will have devised in at least some nation states a system of more openly tolerant and supportive non-hierarchical differentiation in which many kinds of university have a valued place – diversity with equity of valuing. Together they will provide wider and deeper permeation of the knowledge society, strongly networked bricks-and-mortar-based nerve centres of diverse learning regions within know-ledge societies. They will aspire to wisdom as well as skills formation for the widening compass of the socially included, since the alternatives to active, participative – and prosperous – social systems will be unbearably bereft of vision. Such a medium-term view shows a vigorous future for meaning-making universities in a knowledge society, within the aptly chosen subtitle of Inayatullah and Gidley's (2000) symposium: 'global perspective on *the futures* of universities'.

Notes

1. Adelaide, Melbourne, Queensland, Sydney and Western Australia, together with the more recently founded Australian National University, New South Wales University and Monash. They have their own lobbying office in the federal capital, are outside the universities' collective association for industrial relations negoti-ations, and press for greater research selectivity in particular.
2. It is difficult to state the exact number in mid-2001.
3. A worldwide community of adult educators, strong in this radical tradition and reinforced by the periodic gatherings of leading international and regional non-governmental adult educator associations, sustains civic and societal values in opposition to what is seen as the reductionism of a competence approach to training and to the scope and purpose of adult education. For a new fundamen-tal critique of contemporary economics itself, see Keen (2001).
4. Mark Latham, a persistent and intelligent analyst of Australian society and higher education, develops a 'new paradigm' for Australian higher education via a six-way typology of universities, funded in different ways to achieve different prin-cipal missions (Latham and Botsman 2001).

References

Carneiro, R. (2000) On knowledge and learning for the new millennium. Australian College of Education conference paper. Sydney: Australian College of Education.
CSBS (Centre for Strategic Business Studies) (1998) How do you value knowledge?, *The Antidote* 11: 4.

CVCP (Committee of Vice-Chancellors and Principals) (2000) *The Business of Borderless Education: UK Perspectives. Analysis and Recommendations.* London: CVCP.

EIU (Economic Intelligence Unit) (1998) *Knowledge Workers Revealed: New Challenges for Asia.* Hong Kong: EIU.

Gibbons, M., Limoges, C., Nowotny, H. *et al.* (1994) *The New Production of Knowledge.* London: Sage.

Gidley, J. (2000) Beyond the market model, *The Australian Higher Education,* 12 (July).

Goddard, J. and Cornford, J. (1999) *Space, Place and the Virtual University: The Virtual University is the University Made Concrete.* Newcastle: CURDS, University of Newcastle upon Tyne.

Inayatullah, S. and Gidley, J. (eds) (2000) *The University in Transformation: Global Perspectives on the Futures of the University.* Westport, CT: Bergin & Garvey.

Keen, S. (2001) *Debunking Economics. The Naked Emperor of the Social Sciences.* Sydney: Pluto Press, and London: Zed Books.

Latham, M. and Botsman, P. (2001) *The Enabling State.* Sydney: Pluto Press.

Marginson, S. and Considine, M. (2000) *The Enterprise University. Power, Governance and Reinvention in Australia.* Cambridge: Cambridge University Press.

McQueen, H. (2001) Capitalism – the real thing. *Sydney Morning Herald Spectrum,* 12–13 May.

Merrill Lynch (Moe, M. and Blodget, H.) (2000) *The Knowledge Web. People Power – Fuel for the New Economy.* Merrill Lynch: New York.

OECD (1973) *Recurrent Education: A Strategy for Lifelong Learning.* Paris: OECD.

OECD (2000) *Knowledge Management in the Learning Society.* Paris: OECD.

OECD (2001) *E-learning: The Partnership Challenge.* Paris: OECD.

Papadopoulos, G. (1994) *Education 1960–1990: The OECD Perspective.* Paris: OECD.

Readings, B. (1996) *The University in Ruins.* Cambridge, MA: Harvard University Press.

Salmi, J. (2000) Tertiary education in the twenty-first century: challenges and opportunities. Institutional Management in Higher Education conference paper. Paris: OECD.

Scarbrough, H., Swan, J. and Preston. J. (1999) *Knowledge Management: A Literature Review.* London: Institute of Personnel and Development.

Scarbrough, H. and Carter, C. (2000) *Investigating Knowledge Management.* London: Institute of Personnel and Development.

Sennett, R. (1998) *The Corrosion of Character.* New York: W.W. Norton.

Tapper, T. and Palfreyman, D. (2000) *Oxford and the Decline of the Collegiate Tradition.* London: Woburn Press.

TEAC (Tertiary Education Advisory Commission) (2001) *Shaping the System: Strategy, Quality, Access,* 2nd TEAC Report. Wellington: TEAC.

Part 5

Internationalizing Literacies
and Learning

14

Problems of Adult Literacy in the Knowledge Society: Lessons from International Surveys

Albert C. Tuijnman

Introduction and background

Several large-scale surveys of reading comprehension and literacy proficiency among the adult population have been undertaken in North America since the 1970s. The latest of these are the Literacy Skills Used in Daily Activities (LSUDA) survey conducted by Statistics Canada in 1990 and the National Adult Literacy Survey (NALS) conducted in the United States by the Educational Testing Service between 1989 and 1992. These surveys produced a wealth of data and new insights relevant to literacy policy and practice. Whereas early studies treated literacy as a condition that adults either had or did not have, the important innovation introduced in these recent surveys was to measure literacy proficiency along a continuum denoting how well adults used information to function in society. Thus, for the purposes of the LSUDA and NALS surveys, literacy was no longer defined in terms of an arbitrary standard of reading comprehension, distinguishing the few who completely failed the test (the 'illiterates') from the majority who reached a certain threshold (those who are 'literate').

The 1990 LSUDA and the 1992 NALS findings did not support the common belief that literacy difficulties beset only a tiny and marginal proportion of the population. Researchers associated with the survey discovered that, when tested with 'real-life' texts and stimuli, up to one-quarter of the adult population was found to have only rudimentary literacy skills, a level deemed insufficient for coping with the demands of everyday life and work in a complex, information-dependent society. This finding gradually led to a rethinking of the nature and magnitude of the literacy issues faced by North America. But critical questions were frequently asked. Among these were questions such as whether the applied definitions of literacy were appropriate, whether the proficiency levels and the 80 per cent probability threshold applied in the assessments were set too high, and whether the levels of literacy of North American citizens were any different from those of populations in other countries of the OECD. Action on the literacy policy front was seen as depending in part on answers to these questions.

The building of an international assessment

As part of its project 'Technological Changes and Human Resources Development', the Centre for Educational Research and Innovation (CERI) of the OECD launched a study on the theme of adult illiteracy and economic performance in the autumn of 1990. Jarl Bengtsson, a senior CERI staff member at that time, had taken the initiative and had obtained support for the study principally from the government of Canada. At about the same time, the UNESCO Institute for Education (UIE) in Hamburg organized, in cooperation with CERI, an experts' meeting on the theme of functional adult literacy in western and eastern European countries. The meeting was also attended by a number of American and European researchers interested in adult education and literacy, and persons who had played instrumental roles in the design and coordination of the large-scale surveys that had recently been conducted in North America.

Quite a few of the participants were soon to meet again, in several small-scale meetings. The report from the CERI study on the implications for human resources development of technological change was published in 1992 (OECD 1992a), and it became an instant bestseller and was reprinted several times. This was probably in large part because it was easy to read and also because it contained a summary of the empirical findings from the Canadian LSUDA survey (Montigny *et al.* 1991; Neice and Adsett 1992), references to the US Young Adult Literacy Survey (Kirsch and Jungeblut 1986) and a major survey that had been conducted in Australia by Rosie Wickert (1989). This publication marked the first time the OECD – a mainly economic think-tank – had shown an interest in issues concerning adult literacy.

Lack of attention to literacy issues arose in part because it was believed that since all adults had received a minimum of at least a few years of formal schooling they were assumed to be literate (Jones 1998). In contrast, the notion of illiteracy commonly applied at that time was defined, for the sake of measurement, as the percentage of people in the population without a minimum of four years of schooling. This approach proved unhelpful, not only because it employed a proxy measure that effectively assigned 'literacy' to the quasi-totality of many OECD countries (see UNESCO 1999), but also because it failed to recognize that people in OECD countries are literate to a certain degree, that literacy requirements are not static but evolve with social and economic change, that literacy is a multifaceted phenomenon, and hence, that no single standard of literacy can be applied. What is at issue is not whether adults can write their name or read a brief and simple sentence, but rather whether they have the ability to read with the increased levels of competence required in the knowledge society.

Also in 1992, CERI published the first edition of *Education at a Glance: OECD Indicators* (OECD 1992b). This was the result of a large-scale effort intended to improve the coverage, quality and comparability of international education statistics and indicators, known as the INES project. The first OECD report on education indicators was a milestone in certain respects, for example because it leveraged additional resources and energies to further expand the statistical portrait of education systems at the international level. But the report also had many gaps in coverage. Principal among these was the total absence of data on adult education participation and the actual skills profiles of the workforce. The INES project, which depended to a large extent on the voluntary financial contributions made by member countries, was structured around several networks of experts. It was in the background of the work undertaken by one such network that the possibility of undertaking an international survey of adult education participation gradually gained ground.

Meanwhile, in the United States, Archie Lapointe, who at that time was responsible for a large project called the International Assessment of Educational Progress (IAEP) based at the Educational Testing Service (ETS), had been exploring the possibility of organizing an international assessment of adult literacy skills, modelled on the NALS that had just been completed. Lapointe had succeeded in gaining support for this idea from persons in key government or academic positions in several countries. The problem for the ETS, however, was how to secure active participation by the United States.

The National Center for Education Statistics (NCES) of the US Department of Education had invested heavily in the NALS, but the final report on that survey had not been published at the time. This came a year later (Kirsch *et al.* 1993). Among policy-makers in the United States at that point there was little interest in undertaking a new data collection on adult literacy. This was due not only to its expected high costs but also to policy considerations. The release of the NALS results had led to major headlines in the media and created some controversy, politically as well as academically. In particular there were those who questioned the use of the RP-80 criterion. A substantially lower proportion of Americans would have scored at the lowest level of literacy had a lower threshold been applied, for example the 50 per cent criterion commonly used in the National Assessment of Educational Progress. Furthermore, Department officials opted for a more active US role in the international arena by providing substantial support for the IEA Third International Mathematics and Science Study (TIMSS) and also by investing in the INES networks. Consequently, the efforts of the ETS concerning the IAEP and the building of an international adult literacy assessment did not receive high priority.

In the spring of 1993, Paul Bélanger of UNESCO, Scott Murray of Statistics Canada, Norman Davies representing the Commission of the European Communities and Albert Tuijnman of CERI met informally in Paris. At this point some missing pieces in the strategy puzzle that was to lead to the launch of the first International Adult Literacy Survey (IALS) were put into place. Statistics Canada was ready to commit human resources and the expertise necessary for the establishment of a centre for international study coordination at the Special Surveys Division of Statistics Canada, with the ETS as a strategic but somewhat less visible partner responsible for assessment design and the scaling of the proficiency estimates. This development, and a promise of limited financial support for the initiative received from the Commission of the European Communities through Eurostat, the statistical office of the Commission, led officials in the United States to reconsider the possibility of participation.

Decisive for the US decision to join the survey were the roles played by Eugene Owen of the NCES, and Ronald Pugsley, director of the Division of Adult Education and Literacy, who in January 1994 had attended a meeting on the measurement of adult basic skills organized jointly between Jarl Bengtsson and Albert Tuijnman of CERI and Daniel Wagner of the National Center for Adult Literacy at the University of Pennsylvania (see Tuijnman *et al.* 1997). Paul Bélanger at UIE found financial support from UNESCO and World Bank sources that would allow for the participation of Poland, and Albert Tuijnman succeeded in convincing the Netherlands Ministry of Education and Science to join as well. Walo Hutmacher and Uri Peter Trier managed to obtain funds from the Swiss National Research Programme 33 to finance the participation of Switzerland. Finally, at a meeting in Washington, DC, in February 1994, Jarl Bengtsson secured the support of Ulf Lundgren, who at that time was the Director-General of the Swedish National Agency for Education. This concluded the line-up of countries that were to field the world's first comparative international assessment of adult basic skills.

For those not familiar with the history of international comparative surveys of student achievement, it may come as a surprise that it took close to five years of planning and negotiation to establish the project consortium and secure the line-up of countries participating in the first wave of the IALS. But there were some major obstacles that had to be overcome. Literacy surveys had been undertaken in North America but the Europeans were completely unfamiliar with them. In the early 1990s, low literacy was something of a non-issue in Europe. Money was another matter. The IALS design, because it required interviews and testing in respondents' homes, was much more expensive per completed case than the school-based student assessment surveys with which policy-makers were more familiar. Then there were numerous questions about validity and cultural appropriateness. Because it had never been done before, no one could guarantee at the outset that it would prove feasible to field the study as specified. The decision to commit a country to the study therefore required not only financial muscle but also the willingness to take the risk. Further, an international secretariat and a project consortium had to be established, and partnerships wrought among international organizations that often pursued different agendas. Finally, there were numerous technical and methodological challenges that had to be overcome.

The International Adult Literacy Survey

Thus it came about that national statistical and research agencies in nine countries, supported by three international organizations and financially backed by the US and Canadian federal governments, provided the framework and the means to develop and field the first International Adult Literacy Survey.

In 1994, nine countries – Canada (English- and French-speaking populations), France,[1] Germany, Ireland, the Netherlands, Poland, Sweden, Switzerland (German- and French-speaking regions) and the United States – fielded the world's first large-scale, comparative assessment of adult literacy (IALS). Data for seven of these countries were published in December 1995 (OECD and Statistics Canada 1995). While the report on the first wave of data collection was being written, an additional five countries or territories – Australia, the Flemish community in Belgium, Great Britain, New Zealand and Northern Ireland – decided to administer the IALS instruments. In these countries the main data collection took place in 1996 and their results were published in November 1997 (OECD and Human Resources Development Canada 1997). Finally, ten other countries or regions – Chile, Czech Republic, Denmark, Finland, Hungary, Italy, Norway, Portugal, Slovenia and the Italian-speaking region of Switzerland – participated in a new wave of collection in 1998. Results for these latter countries became first available in June 2000 (OECD and Statistics Canada 2000).

In all, over 75,000 adults from 22 countries were interviewed and tested in their homes in 15 languages between 1994 and 1998. Together these countries accounted for over 50 per cent of the world's entire GDP. As such, the literacy data produced contributed importantly to an understanding of the demand and supply of skills in the global, knowledge-based economy. The purpose of the study was to improve understanding of the nature and magnitude of the literacy issues faced by nations and to investigate the factors that influence the development of adult literacy skills in various settings – at home, at work and across countries.

Table 14.1 shows, for each of the countries included in the analysis, the test language used, the number of survey respondents and the number of persons in the corresponding target population. Detailed information about all aspects of survey design, data collection, data quality and comparability is presented in Murray *et al.* (1998), Carey (2000) and annexes A–C in OECD and Statistics Canada (2000).

The assessment methodology

In IALS, proficiency levels along a continuum denote how well adults use information to function in society. Thus, literacy is defined as *the ability to*

Table 14.1   Test language, target population and survey respondents, 1994–98

Country	Test language	Target population aged 16–65	Survey respondents aged 16–65
Australia	English	11,900,000	8,204
Belgium (Flanders)	Dutch	4,500,000	2,261
Canada	English	13,700,000	3,130
	French	4,800,000	1,370
Chile	Spanish	9,400,000	3,502
Czech Republic	Czech	7,100,000	3,132
Denmark	Danish	3,400,000	3,026
Finland	Finnish	3,200,000	2,928
Germany	German	53,800,000	2,062
Hungary	Hungarian	7,000,000	2,593
Ireland	English	2,200,000	2,423
Italy	Italian	38,700,000	2,974
Netherlands	Dutch	10,500,000	2,837
New Zealand	English	2,100,000	4,223
Norway	Norwegian	2,800,000	3,307
Poland	Polish	24,500,000	3,000
Portugal	Portuguese	6,700,000	1,239
Slovenia	Slovenian	1,400,000	2,972
Sweden	Swedish	5,400,000	2,645
Switzerland	French	1,000,000	1,435
	German	3,000,000	1,393
	Italian	200,000	1,302
UK	English	37,000,000	6,718
United States	English	161,100,000	3,053

Note: Readers are advised to consult annex B, *Literacy in the Information Age: Final Report of the International Literacy Study*, in OECD and Statistics Canada (2000), for further information about sampling and achieved response rates.
Source: IALS

understand and employ printed information in daily activities, at home, at work and in the community to achieve one's goals, and to develop one's knowledge and potential. In denoting a broad set of information-processing competences, this conceptual approach points to the multiplicity of skills that constitute literacy in the advanced industrialized countries.

The conceptual framework and the definitions of the literacy domains used for the assessment built on the seminal work of Kirsch and Mosenthal (1990) and Mosenthal (1998). In particular, the IALS assessment was based on the theoretical and methodological insights offered by four large-scale North American surveys: the Functional Reading Study conducted in the United States by the Educational Testing Service (ETS) in the early 1970s; the Young Adult Literacy Survey fielded in the United States by ETS in 1985; the Survey of Literacy Skills Used in Daily Activities, undertaken by

Statistics Canada in 1989; and the National Adult Literacy Survey conducted in the United States by ETS in 1990.

Literacy is measured operationally in terms of three domains, each encompassing a common set of skills relevant for diverse tasks:

- Prose literacy – the knowledge and skills needed to understand and use information from texts, including editorials, news stories, poems and fiction.
- Document literacy – the knowledge and skills required to locate and use information contained in various formats, including job applications, payroll forms, transportation schedules, maps, tables and charts.
- Quantitative literacy – the knowledge and skills required to apply arithmetic operations, either alone or sequentially, to numbers embedded in printed materials, such as balancing an account, figuring out a tip, completing an order form or determining the amount of interest on a loan from an advertisement.

The IALS employed a sophisticated methodology developed and applied by the ETS to measure literacy proficiency for each domain on a scale ranging from 0 to 500 points. Literacy ability in each domain is expressed by a score, defined as the point at which a person has an 80 per cent chance of successful performance from among the set of tasks of varying difficulty included in the assessment.

The data presented in this chapter were collected by the countries participating in successive cycles of data collection between 1994 and 1998, using nationally representative samples of the adult population aged 16–65. The fact that some countries collected data a few years earlier or later than others is thought not to affect the international comparability of the survey data because the literacy profiles of nations are quite stable and are normally expected to change only slowly.[2] The survey was conducted in people's homes by experienced interviewers. The design used for IALS combined educational assessment techniques with methods of household survey research. Multiple quality control measures were implemented throughout the course of the study in order to ensure that high-quality data would be obtained. (Annex B in OECD and Statistics Canada (2000) describes the measures that were taken to improve data quality and comparability.)

In brief, respondents were first asked a series of questions to obtain background and demographic information. The background questionnaire contained a range of questions, for example concerning the respondent's demographic characteristics, family background, labour force status, reading habits at work and at home, participation in adult education and training, and self-reports on literacy ability. Once this background questionnaire was completed, the interviewer presented a booklet containing six simple tasks. If a respondent failed to complete at least two of these correctly, the interview was adjourned. Respondents who completed two or more tasks correctly were then given a much larger variety of tasks, printed in a separate booklet. The assessment was not timed, and respondents were urged to try each exercise. Respondents were thus given maximum opportunity to demonstrate their skills.

During the development stage of the survey, countries were provided with a 'master' English-language version of the background questionnaire and task booklets. With respect to the background questionnaire, the master copy clearly indicated which questions were optional or mandatory and whether and how countries could adapt response categories to country-specific needs. Moreover, as a result of the pilot test, any items that failed the study's standards for psychometric equivalence were identified and countries requested to verify possible translation, adaptation or scoring problems. With this additional information in hand, the countries were able to further improve the adaptations and translations of their instruments, consisting of a background questionnaire and a literacy test.

Each respondent completed the questionnaire and took the test, of approximately one-hour duration, during a personal interview. These interviews and tests were conducted in people's homes in a neutral, non-pressuring manner. Interviewer training and supervision was provided, emphasizing the selection of one person per household (if applicable), the selection of one of the seven main task booklets (if applicable), the scoring of the core task booklet, and the assignment of status codes.

An overview of major findings

The international comparative results so far obtained in IALS have been reported in three main publications: *Literacy, Economy and Society* (OECD and Statistics Canada 1995), *Literacy Skills for the Knowledge Society* (OECD and Human Resources Development Canada 1997), and *Literacy in the Information Age* (OECD and Statistics Canada 2000). Results for France are published in *Measuring Adult Literacy* (Carey 2000) and results for Italy in *La Competenza Alfabetica in Italia* (CEDE 2000).

Table 14.2 presents summary results for the prose literacy scale. It shows the population mean scores for the different countries together with the associated standard errors. Table 14.3 presents the proportions of adults aged 16–65 scoring at each of four levels of proficiency, ranging from the most basic level (level 1) to the most advanced level (level 4/5). For both tables, the results refer to the prose literacy scale. This scale is chosen for this presentation because it conforms most closely to conventional notions of reading literacy. For a more complete picture of the results, including the average performance levels on the document and quantitative literacy scales, the reader is referred to the final IALS report (OECD and Statistics Canada 2000).

Adults in Sweden, Norway, Finland and the Netherlands score in the top group. Swedish adults have a statistically significant edge over those in the other countries. There is a number of alternative possibilities for explaining this outstanding result for Sweden. These include the historically important

Table 14.2 Mean scores and their standard errors, prose literacy scale, population aged 16–65, 1994–98

	Mean	Standard errors (s.e.)
Sweden	301.3	0.8
Finland	288.6	0.7
Norway	288.5	1.0
Netherlands	282.7	0.8
Canada	278.8	3.2
Germany	275.9	1.0
New Zealand	275.2	1.3
Denmark	275.0	0.7
Australia	274.2	1.0
United States	273.7	1.6
Belgium (Flanders)	271.8	3.9
Czech Republic	269.4	0.8
UK	266.7	1.8
Ireland	265.7	3.3
Switzerland (French)	264.8	1.7
Switzerland (Italian)	264.3	2.2
Switzerland (German)	263.3	1.4
France	247.0	2.7
Italy	244.4	1.9
Hungary	242.4	1.1
Slovenia	229.7	1.5
Poland	229.5	1.1
Portugal	222.6	3.7
Chile	220.8	2.1

Source: IALS

role played by the labour movement and the popular education it actively promoted, the long-time commitment to social equality and the comprehensive schools which were introduced all over the country in the early 1960s (Tuijnman and Hellström 2001).

The data in Tables 14.2 and 14.3 suggest that the range of literacy skill scores is wide in all countries. Even though some populations have higher mean scores than others, all have a significant proportion with low scores. In absolute terms, there are large numbers of adults with skills no higher than level 1 in all countries surveyed. But there are meaningful differences in how literacy skills are distributed among the populations of the countries surveyed. Adults in the Czech transition economy achieve relatively well, but this is not the case in the neighbouring countries of Hungary, Poland and Slovenia, nor in Portugal.

There are countries that have large proportions of their adult population at high literacy levels on all three scales (OECD and Statistics Canada 2000). Finland, the Netherlands, Norway and Sweden typically have the largest

Table 14.3 Per cent of population aged 16–65 at each prose literacy level, and standard errors, 1994–98

	Level 1 (s.e.)	Level 2 (s.e.)	Level 3 (s.e.)	Level 4/5 (s.e.)
Australia	17.0 (0.5)	27.1 (0.6)	36.9 (0.5)	18.9 (0.5)
Belgium (Flanders)	18.4 (1.5)	28.2 (2.1)	39.0 (2.4)	14.3 (1.2)
Canada	16.6 (1.6)	25.6 (1.8)	35.1 (2.4)	22.7 (2.3)
Chile	50.1 (1.7)	35.0 (1.2)	13.3 (1.2)	1.6 (0.4)
Czech Republic	15.7 (0.5)	38.1 (1.0)	37.8 (0.9)	8.4 (0.4)
Denmark	9.6 (0.6)	36.4 (0.9)	47.5 (1.0)	6.5 (0.4)
Finland	10.4 (0.4)	26.3 (0.7)	40.9 (0.7)	22.4 (0.6)
France	41.0	33.7	21.8	3.4
Germany	14.4 (0.9)	34.2 (1.0)	38.0 (1.3)	13.4 (1.0)
Hungary	33.8 (1.0)	42.7 (1.4)	20.8 (0.9)	2.6 (0.4)
Ireland	22.6 (1.4)	29.8 (1.6)	34.1 (1.2)	13.5 (1.4)
Italy	34.6	30.9	26.5	8.0
Netherlands	10.5 (0.6)	30.1 (0.9)	44.1 (1.0)	15.3 (0.6)
New Zealand	18.4 (0.9)	27.3 (1.0)	35.0 (0.8)	19.2 (0.7)
Norway	8.5 (0.5)	24.7 (1.0)	49.2 (0.9)	17.6 (0.9)
Poland	42.6 (0.9)	34.5 (0.9)	19.8 (0.7)	3.1 (0.3)
Portugal	48.0 (2.0)	29.0 (2.3)	18.5 (1.2)	4.4 (0.5)
Slovenia	42.2 (1.1)	34.5 (1.0)	20.1 (0.9)	3.2 (0.3)
Sweden	7.5 (0.5)	20.3 (0.6)	39.7 (0.9)	32.4 (0.5)
Switzerland (French)	17.6 (1.3)	33.7 (1.6)	38.6 (1.8)	10.0 (0.7)
Switzerland (German)	19.3 (1.0)	35.7 (1.6)	36.1 (1.3)	8.9 (1.0)
Switzerland (Italian)	19.6 (1.3)	34.7 (1.5)	37.5 (1.8)	8.3 (0.9)
UK	21.8 (1.0)	30.3 (1.2)	31.3 (1.1)	16.6 (0.7)
United States	20.7 (0.8)	25.9 (1.1)	32.4 (1.2)	21.1 (1.2)

Note: Comparable jack-knife standard errors not available for France and Italy.
Source: IALS

proportions at levels 3 and 4/5. Sweden, however, differs from these others in having the largest proportion at level 4/5 on all three scales. There are also countries that just as regularly have large proportions at low levels of literacy: Chile, Poland, Portugal and Slovenia.

Some countries differ in their ranking from scale to scale. The Czech Republic, for example, is in the middle of the ranking on the prose scale, but at the top on the quantitative measure. Conversely, Canada is in the top group on the prose scale but in the middle on the quantitative one. Hungary has a higher average on the quantitative than on the other two scales.

The average performance results for the United States and neighbouring Canada, for example, mask the fact that in both countries there is a high degree of variation in the distribution of literacy skills, with large numbers of people at both the lowest and the highest levels of literacy. Americans and Canadians at the top 25th percentile of the population distribution have a high average level of literacy compared with adults in all other nations surveyed, including Italy, Germany, Switzerland and the UK. But inequality in the range of literacy scores in North America is also among the highest of the countries studied (Tuijnman and Boudard 2001). This inequality in the distribution of literacy ability poses a large challenge to policy-makers.

The fact that range is somewhat independent of average is illustrated by the case of Denmark: the range on the prose scale is small and the average score on prose is not high, especially compared with Denmark's average on the document and quantitative scales. Conversely, Canada has a relatively high prose average but also a very large range. Variations in average and range are important characteristics of a country's skills profile. Issues of equity arise when there is a large discrepancy between the people with the lowest and with the highest literacy skills, as there are in many IALS countries.

Some conclusions

The IALS has provided evidence showing that low literacy is a major issue not only for developing countries but also for the most economically advanced OECD countries. Low skills are found not just among marginal groups, but also among significant proportions of the populations surveyed. There are important differences in the overall level and the distribution of literacy skills both within and between countries, and these differences are large enough to matter both socially and economically.

The first report on the IALS was published in December 1995, just six weeks before the OECD convened a meeting of its education ministers. The report was distributed to all ministers and their staff together with the documentation on 'lifelong learning for all', which was the theme for the meeting. Richard Riley, the US Secretary of Education, welcomed the report and congratulated the authors, but this response was not shared by all country delegations. A few were unhappy about the timing, while in many others government officials had to explain to their minister why the report did not include any results for their country. The delegation from France objected because the country had refused to let OECD publish its results on grounds that the survey was biased in favour of 'Anglo-Saxon' culture. The attention the report thus received paved the way for the eventual launch of a second wave of data collection in 1996 and a third wave in 1998.

The report also served to underline the main message of the ministerial meeting, which called on policy-makers to ensure that all citizens have access to literacy- and learning-rich environments in their homes, their communities and at work. This implies a commitment to literacy and learning in every aspect of daily life – 'life-wide' as well as lifelong. Meeting this challenge requires abandoning the conventional paradigm that equates learning with schooling. It should be replaced with one that seeks a convergence of schools, homes, workplaces and communities into mutually reinforcing environments that encourage learning in many settings, for all ages, both formally and informally, and throughout life.

But cultures of lifelong learning and literacy cannot be imposed; they must depend and thrive on a great variety of initiatives taken by different actors in many spheres of life and work. In seeking to promote such cultures, the government, both federal and state, employers, social partners, the voluntary sector and whole communities should work together and consider literacy issues in multiple dimensions. Neither federal nor state governments can take it upon themselves to invent, manage and pay for flourishing local cultures of literacy and learning. Rather, their role should be to promote learning in both lifelong and life-wide dimensions and to steer developments and allocate resources so that learning opportunities are distributed equitably and efficiently. Since public resources are best directed towards those policy domains where the social return on public investment is greatest, sound policy would see the targeting of public funds to improve foundation learning, including early childhood education and care programmes, adult basic education and workplace literacy programmes.

Notes

1. France withdrew its data in November 1995, after the comparative results had become available, with concerns about comparability. A new data collection was undertaken in France in 1998 as part of an EU-financed research study that applied the same methods and the same test instruments as were used in the original IALS. The results of this study are reported in Carey (2000: annex C).
2. The possibility that a nation succeeds in significantly altering its literacy profiles within the course of about five years cannot be ruled out. Major educational reforms, for example, can influence the literacy profiles of specific sub-populations.

References

Carey, S. (ed.) (2000) *Measuring Adult Literacy: The International Adult Literacy Survey in the European Context.* London: Office for National Statistics.

CEDE (2000) *La Competenza Alfabetica in Italia: Una Ricerca sulla Cultura della Popolazione.* Frascati: Centro Europeo dell'Educazione, and Milan: F. Angeli.

Jones, S. (1998) Measuring adult basic skills: a literature review, in A. Tuijnman, I. Kirsch and D.A. Wagner (eds) *Adult Basic Skills: Innovations in Measurement and Policy Analysis.* Creskil, NJ: Hampton Press.

Kirsch, I.S. and Jungeblut, A. (1986) *Literacy: Profiles of America's Young Adults.* Princeton, NJ: Educational Testing Service.

Kirsch, I.S. and Mosenthal, P.B. (1990) Exploring document literacy: variables underlying the performance of young adults, *Reading Research Quarterly,* 25: 5–30.

Kirsch, I.S., Jungeblut, A., Jenkins, L. and Kolstad, A. (eds) (1993) *Adult Literacy in America: A First Look at the Results of the National Adult Literacy Survey.* Washington, DC: National Center for Education Statistics, United States Department of Education.

Montigny, G., Kelly, K. and Jones, S. (1991) *Adult Literacy in Canada: Results of a National Study,* Statistics Canada catalogue no. 89-525-XPE. Ottawa: Minister of Industry, Science and Technology.

Mosenthal, P.B. (1998) Defining prose task characteristics for use in computer-adaptive testing and instruction, *American Educational Research Journal,* 35(2): 269–307.

Murray, T.S., Kirsch, I.S. and Jenkins, L. (eds) (1998) *Adult Literacy in OECD Countries: Technical Report on the First International Adult Literacy Survey.* Washington, DC: National Center for Education Statistics, United States Department of Education.

Neice, D. and Adsett, M. (1992) Direct versus proxy measures of adult functional literacy: a preliminary re-examination, in OECD *Adult Illiteracy and Economic Performance,* pp. 69–87. Paris: CERI.

OECD (1992a) *Adult Illiteracy and Economic Performance.* Paris: CERI.

OECD (1992b) *Education at a Glance: OECD Indicators.* Paris: CERI.

OECD and Human Resources Development Canada (1997) *Literacy Skills for the Knowledge Society: Further Results from the International Adult Literacy Survey.* Paris and Ottawa: OECD/HRDC.

OECD and Statistics Canada (1995) *Literacy, Economy and Society: Results of the First International Adult Literacy Survey,* Statistics Canada catalogue no. 89-545-XPE. Paris and Ottawa: OECD/Minister of Industry.

OECD and Statistics Canada (2000) *Literacy in the Information Age: Final Report of the International Literacy Study.* Paris and Ottawa: OECD/Minister of Industry.

Tuijnman, A. and Boudard, E. (2001). *Adult Education Participation in North America: International Perspectives.* Washington, DC: US Department of Education, and Ottawa: Statistics Canada and Human Resources Development Canada.

Tuijnman, A. and Hellström, Z. (eds) (2001). *Learning for Life: Nordic Adult Education Compared.* Copenhagen: Nord, Nordic Council of Ministers.

Tuijnman, A., Kirsch, I. and Wagner, D.A. (eds) (1997) *Adult Basic Skills: Innovations in Measurement and Policy Analysis.* Creskil, NJ: Hampton Press.

UNESCO (1999) *Statistical Yearbook.* Paris: UNESCO Press.

Wickert, R. (1989) *No Single Measure.* Canberra: Commonwealth Department of Employment, Education, and Training.

15

The Digital Divide and Literacy: Focusing on the Most Poor

Daniel A. Wagner

Introduction

The 'digital divide' can be broadly defined in terms of unequal possibilities to access and contribute to information, knowledge and networks. Indeed, in newspapers worldwide, the phrase 'digital divide' has become a new and dominant way to explain differences in income, education and economic development.

More recently, the digital divide has become seen as a possible 'digital opportunity' for relatively poor countries – or groups of poor people within countries – such that new and positive benefits may be drawn from the powerful *potential* capabilities of information and communication technologies (ICTs) to assist in recurrent education. Such a perspective was promulgated by the French futurist Jean Servan-Schreiber in the 1960s (Servan-Schreiber 1968). He predicted that the developing countries of the world would leapfrog the industrialized countries since primary raw materials (such as silicon, used in electronics even before the personal computer) were most abundant in the developing world. His prediction of leapfrogging did not to turn out to be accurate, but he clearly foresaw an impending digital divide that is now commonplace.

Many specialists today would agree that a digital divide exists, however defined (and there are many views on its definition, ranging from access to telephones to palm pilots), but there is less agreement as to whether the divide is getting bigger or smaller in the diverse contexts where the term is applied. As has been pointed out (DOT Force 2001), there is both good and bad news. The good news is that, in relative terms, the proportion of poor people having access to telecommunications, as well as the number of poor countries connected to the Internet and the total number of Internet users in developing countries, has been increasing steadily since the mid-1990s. The bad news is that there are still 2 billion people who have never made a single telephone call, and that the pace of technological innovations seems to increase rather than decrease the distance that separates the rich from the poor.

The changing status of literacy

The United Nations estimates that there are 1 billion illiterate adults in the world today (about one-quarter of the world's adult population), the vast majority of whom are located in the poorest countries of the world. Furthermore, recent surveys suggest that this situation is even more serious than previously believed: industrialized (OECD) countries, over the past decade, have come to admit to having very serious problems of their own in literacy and basic skills, with up to 25 per cent of adults considered to be lacking the basic skills needed to function effectively in the workforce (see OECD and Statistics Canada 1995; Tuijnman *et al.* 1997). In addition, the UN reports (UNICEF 2000) that over 100 million primary-school-age children (22 per cent worldwide) are out of school. Furthermore, when looking at access to print media, it has been found that while about 26 per cent of adults in OECD countries read a daily newspaper, only 4 per cent do so in developing countries.

With respect to literacy itself, it should be noted that current statistics are a result of changing standards and definitions that have taken place over recent decades. For many years, and continuing in numerous developing countries today, literacy was often assessed by asking a person if he or she 'could read and write' (cf. Wagner 1995). Indeed, if the OECD standard for literacy were used to measure literacy in developing countries, the number of adult illiterates in those countries would likely go up by at least two- or threefold. This seems to be in great measure due to the often poor quality of primary schooling in many developing countries (Wagner 2000) – a result primarily of the dramatic increase in access to primary school that has followed on the policies proposed at the UN Jomtien conference held in 1990.

Clearly, the problem of illiteracy and low literacy remains a major and pressing issue around the world. As we move aggressively into the information age, many specialists and policy-makers have raised not only the issue of basic literacy, but also the new term of 'technological literacy'. Interestingly, no country appears to have on record exactly what technological literacy means, probably due to the rapidly changing nature of ICT developments across the globe. Definitions will abound soon enough.

Connections between literacy and technology

We know also that educational and literacy levels play an important role in the likelihood that a person will own a computer and/or be linked to the Internet. Consider recent statistics in the United States, which describe differences between socio-economic classes (NTIA 1999):

- 61.6 per cent of those with college degrees now use the Internet, in contrast to only 6.6 per cent of those with an elementary school education.
- At home, those with a college degree or higher are over eight times more likely to have a computer than the least educated, and nearly 16 times more likely to have home Internet access.
- The digital divide for Internet use between those at highest and lowest education levels widened by 25 per cent from 1997 to 1998.
- Those with college degrees or higher are ten times more likely to have Internet access at work as persons with only some high school education.

On a worldwide basis, the statistical patterns are similar but even more stark, since the wealthy OECD countries (with 15 per cent of world population), when compared with poor countries, have:

- 90 per cent of Internet capability and traffic;
- 70 per cent of telephone communications;
- 80 per cent of world GDP;
- nearly 15 times the percentage of Internet users as in developing countries (about 30 per cent penetration versus 1.6 per cent penetration).

While data on Internet use is changing rapidly, the above data cited by NTIA, and in other more recent reports (OECD 2000), suggest that people everywhere who have less education – those who might benefit most from the Internet's educational value – are falling further behind in digital access. Similar data being gathered from around the world tend to confirm the same trends. Even so, there are some important differences to bear in mind. For example, in countries like India, not owning a PC should not be seen as completely predictive of lack of Internet access, as Internet kiosks are being set up many parts of that country, most of which have mentors or helpers to guide the illiterate in engaging in Internet communications.

In sum, the digital divide is a global phenomenon. In industrialized countries, the knowledge economy, powered by the Internet and e-commerce, has become a key driver of growth and productivity, leading to new levels of prosperity. Yet, at the same time, a *global digital divide* is growing, such that the poor and disadvantaged peoples of both industrialized and developing countries are falling further behind in education, information technology, economic and social development.

Which divide is it?

In spite of the growing interest in the digital divide, some might reasonably claim that this new divide is simply another way of describing (or just mirroring) the other well-known divides in wealth, social development, educational achievement and so forth. There is some truth to this argument. However, such a claim obscures a more complex subject.

This chapter suggests that there is an important intertwining and inevitable linkage between the digital divide and literacy. With the ICTs that we can foresee at present, it seems increasingly clear that literacy will prevail as a prerequisite when human interactivity (communication) is required, as it increasingly is. In other words, interactivity – when the individual engages in a give-and-take with information resources – will for a long time depend on print media (whether digitally provided or hard copy). If true, then the basic skills of reading, writing and arithmetic (usually subsumed under the term 'literacy') will serve as a gatekeeper that will allow some people into the digital age, and others not. In addition, there is the actual language of access, in a world where the globalized economy is increasingly dominated by the English language.

Further, even if there were no divide in access to ICT, there might yet remain a very large differential in actual use of ICT. Indeed, this result has been found frequently in many countries like the United States where access is not so difficult, but patterns of use most often follow differential patterns of literacy, ethnicity, socio-economic class and (especially in poor countries) gender (NTIA 1999).

Thus, bridging the conjoined technological and educational gap will not be easy. In the developing world, disadvantaged in-school and out-of-school youth and adults are actually composed of many diverse groups, such as women, ethnic and linguistic minorities, refugees and migrants. This 'diversity divide' is one of the most important features that helps to explain why narrowly focused, middle-class-oriented, market-driven and 'one size fits all' education programmes have often met with poor results and lost resources. Indeed, even the current dominance of the English language on the Internet has had an exclusionary aspect to it in many countries, even though English is very effective at garnering economic returns for the well-educated classes. (Use of the Internet in small and minority languages is growing in some locations, but that is a topic beyond the scope of this chapter.)

In the richer half of the world's countries it is not uncommon to find initiatives in education that involve ICTs in primary, secondary and tertiary (university) education. Yet, in the poor countries, digital divide initiatives have largely been focused on secondary and tertiary education, with almost nothing for the most disadvantaged populations (in primary and non-formal education programmes) in these countries. This was one of the primary conclusions of a report on the international digital divide (OECD 2000). A main challenge from that analysis concerned how to avoid the inevitable problems and costs associated with the integration of emerging and changing technologies into educational programmes and processes that are practical on the ground, especially in impoverished settings. Literacy and public primary education programmes are susceptible to such problems, as these are areas which have been chronically underfunded, with relatively little professional development and a poor technological infrastructure. Recent advances in the application of new technologies for education and literacy are beginning to appear. Clearly, without basic literacy skills, disadvantaged populations will have serious difficulties in utilizing the technological literacy skills needed for the new knowledge economy.

Two examples of reaching the poor

While unable here to cover the broad gamut of efforts being undertaken in the digital divide worldwide, we can point to a couple of examples undertaken in this area, one in the United States and the other in developing countries (for more information, see www.literacy.org).

LiteracyLink

In the United States, the National Center on Adult Literacy (NCAL), with federal education support, is working in partnership with the Public Broadcasting Service and Kentucky Educational Television, in the LiteracyLink project to create resources for American youth and adults who wish a second chance to complete their high school diploma without having to set foot again in a classroom. Materials are being developed that will assist learners in preparing for the GED (US high school equivalency diploma).

As part of this project, a staff training and development programme has been created for adult educators who wish to improve their instructional competences in this domain. As of 2001, thousands of teachers across the United States have begun to utilize this system with an electronic community of teachers, online workshops, pre-evaluated websites, and a database of Internet-based lesson plans. This system is designed to provide teachers with specially tailored, online access to a wide assortment of existing literacy resources. A series of live satellite-based video-conferences (via the Public Broadcasting Service) is also provided to an average of 20,000 teachers and administrators annually.

LiteracyLink is nearing completion of its first five years, and an evaluation is currently being undertaken to study the following four main questions:

- What are the differences in literacy skill acquisition between those adult learners who use the online materials and practice exams and those who do not?
- Does the use of online assessment make a difference in learning literacy skills?
- What are the differences in the effective use of the online resources by students and by teachers that are attributable to particular instructional environments, such as library workstations, the workplace, or classroom instruction?
- What is the relationship of online resources and video to learning, i.e. how does the use of video in conjunction with online activities affect learning?

LiteracyLink is one of the first and most comprehensive initiatives to harness the power of the Internet to provide instruction 'on-demand' directly to adult learners, as well as through community centres, libraries, schools and homes. Through this initiative, adult learners in the United States have access to the widest range of relevant quality materials ever made available. Whether and how adult learners can take advantage of this system outside of the United States (there are no particular technical barriers except access to the Internet itself) remains to be explored.

Bridges to the Future Initiative

In developing countries, beyond issues of cost (which are declining rapidly), ICT is rather well suited to coping with the problems of basic literacy and technological literacy. First, poor people in developing countries (and many in industrialized countries as well) tend to live in dispersed geographical contexts and are composed of diverse populations of youth and adult learners. Second, there is limited and thinly distributed professional teaching expertise. And, third, there is a need to connect learners and instructors interactively in an asynchronous way that takes advantage of learners' availability outside of the classroom.

Thus, a focus on the professional development and training of teachers in developing countries (similar to what NCAL is doing in the United States) provides a relevant locus for this kind of effort, assuming the cost constraints can be met. Teachers may become intermediaries for bridging the digital divide for the tens of millions of low-literate or illiterate youth and young adults who are in school or are in non-formal education programmes in developing countries. Teacher training resources can be delivered through existing training colleges, and would comprise CD-Rom-based materials, collaboration technology for sharing materials, pupil training resources, and greater culturally appropriate and multilingual content.

Undertaken by the International Literacy Institute (ILI) – NCAL's sister organization – such a programme has just been launched under the name Bridges to the Future Initiative (BFI), which is expected to begin in India in 2002, followed by additional partner countries. To achieve the BFI in developing countries – with a focus on both literacy and technological literacy skills – a number of basic principles will guide ILI's activities:

- Making sure that learning – content rather than hardware – is at the centre of its efforts.
- Ensuring a consumer-oriented and context/culture-sensitive approach that will maintain motivation and interest.
- Taking advantage of private-sector ICT advances.
- Maintaining focus on the poor and disadvantaged (including minorities, women, rural), rather than just on communities that just want 'more' technology or who have more 'market' attractiveness.

Organizationally, the BFI is conceived of as an international public–private collaborative partnership, composed of sponsoring agencies (such as international and national corporations, foundations and international donor agencies), national operational agencies (both governmental and non-governmental), and an international secretariat for administration and coordination, R&D and training. As a collaborative partnership, BFI will need to obtain a variety of inputs from agencies and institutions worldwide and in partner nations. At the participating country level, one or more national operating agencies will be responsible for BFI implementation in that country.

Among the various digital divide initiatives in developing countries, the BFI has a number of key features that enhance its potential impact. Most importantly, it is a collaborative effort that seeks to reinforce existing government structures (rather than replace them), and enhance mainly those areas of public education that are most in need of assistance (e.g. teacher training). In economic jargon, the BFI is trying to replicate the JIT (just-in-time) concept with the equivalent JEH (just-enough-help) in education – providing ICT-based resources when and where needed.

Future directions: keeping the focus on the most poor

There are many reasons why efforts to help the poor in the digital divide domain have not been successful to date. Most important is the tension between what will bring market value to the private sector and what is simply of use for poor people. That is, commercially viable ICT-based programmes for the poor are rare, while purely philanthropic efforts by ICT corporations are seldom well conceived or sustainable.

Nonetheless, efforts such as the BFI and others will begin in the next few years to show how ICT can support rather than reduce the well-being of poor people in either wealthy or poor countries. To understand how this will happen, several principles need to be kept in mind, including the following:

- *Even in poorest sectors, ICT is now too cheap to ignore.* While once it could be said that ICT would take money away from other lower-cost technologies (such as chalk and blackboards), new approaches will likely demonstrate the utility of ICTs when properly used.
- *Advanced ICT tools may be more cost-effective for the poor than for the rich.* It was often thought that old ICTs (e.g. radio) were necessarily the best route to reaching poor people, while advanced ICTs were cost-effective only for the relatively rich. The example of the cellular phone has dispelled that proposition. The Grameen Bank effort in Asia has shown that even the poorest people can find value and resources to support a system of cellular communications, both for personal and community development. Ironically, in wealthier countries, one could easily argue that cell phones have less value than in poor countries precisely because the former has ubiquitous access to wired phones and the cellular network is more one of simple convenience than of necessity.

- *Learning technologies must have learning and content at their core.* Many of the most egregious mistakes in the digital divide arena concern an overly narrow focus on ICT, without a commensurate focus on learning and content. Projects within the digital divide must first and foremost be about learning, and about culturally appropriate content. No amount of hardware and access can be a substitute for content, and huge losses of costly infrastructure have been incurred when this principle has been ignored.

- *ICT tools must be consumer-oriented and context/culture-sensitive.* Consumer sensitivity is a longstanding buzzword of marketing in the private sector, yet it seems often to be forgotten in supply-side projects which try to marry ICT and education. Especially when focused on the poor, it is crucial to pay close attention to consumer interests and values, which also mean language, ethnic and other cultural dimensions. The poorest people in most countries have an overrepresentation of people from ethno-linguistic minorities. Thus, development of materials designed for these people is essential, even if the start-up costs are greater on a per-unit basis.

- *Literacy and technology are becoming interdependent – they are tools of the same generic sort.* Neither is an end in itself, but each can amplify human intelligence and capability. New literacy programmes need to take advantage of the power of ICT, but ICT work will require an ever more skilled population of workers and consumers. Societies that do not work on both of these dimensions together and with some degree of synergy will fall further behind in the race to close the digital divide.

- *Corporate involvement is essential in order to take advantage of latest ICT tools.* Educators and businesspeople tend to live in different worlds. While some effective collaborations can be found, the alliance is usually a fragile one at best. In the digital divide domain, this must change for the better. Neither side can undertake effective projects to bridge the digital divide without the other. Indeed, government and non-governmental agencies must learn to collaborate better as well. The key here is the private sector which is developing ICT, which knows which advances will be coming down the road, and which will be able to 'pass down' large numbers of newly obsolete PCs which can be quite serviceable among the poor. Similarly, educators (including social scientists) often have or can gain access to knowledge about what is needed from the ICT community in order to achieve effective educational consequences. Again, one without the other will doom most ICT and education projects.

- *Focus on the bottom half of the digital divide (the top half will take care of itself).* As we enter the first decade of the twenty-first century, it is not unusual to find digital divide initiatives that provide more access to universities, secondary and primary schools. However, in a great many (perhaps the majority) of these cases, the recipients are those who are already in the middle or upper classes of their respective societies. This is especially true in developing countries where it is assumed that only middle-class communities can make appropriate use of ICT. The challenge is to stay focused on the poor – otherwise the digital gap will simply increase further.

In sum, working with new technologies to enhance the education and livelihood of poor people is one of the most exciting and challenging areas of development work today. To be effective in this complex domain is more difficult than might at first appear. Yet, with a set of good principles, and a reasonable level of support, a great deal can be achieved – indeed more than has ever been thought possible before.

References

DOT Force (2001) *Digital Opportunities for All: Meeting the Challenge. Report of the Digital Opportunity Task Force.* Washington: World Bank/UNDP.

NTIA (1999) *Falling Through the Net: Defining the Digital Divide.* Washington, DC: US Department of Commerce.

OECD (2000) *Learning to Bridge the Digital Divide.* Paris: OECD. Based on 1999 roundtable held at University of Pennsylvania in Philadelphia.

OECD and Human Resources Development Canada (1997). *Literacy Skills for the Knowledge Society: Further Results from the International Adult Literacy Survey.* Paris and Ottawa: OECD/HRDC.

OECD and Statistics Canada (1995) *Literacy, Economy and Society: Results of the First International Adult Literacy Survey,* Statistics Canada catalogue no. 89-545-XPE. Paris and Ottawa: OECD/Minister of Industry.

Servan-Schreiber, J.J. (1968) *The American Challenge.* New York: Atheneum.

Tuijnman, A., Kirsch, I. and Wagner, D.A., (eds) (1997) *Adult Basic Skills: Innovations in Measurement and Policy Analysis.* Cresskill, NJ: Hampton Press.

UNICEF (2000) *The State of the World's Children.* New York: UNICEF.

Wagner, D.A. (1995) Literacy and development: rationales, myths, innovations, and future directions, *International Journal of Educational Development,* 15: 341–62.

Wagner, D.A. (2000) *Global Thematic Study on Literacy and Adult Education.* Paper prepared for the World Education Forum, Dakar, Senegal.

Wagner, D.A., Venezky, R.L. and Street, B.V. (eds) (1999) *Literacy: An International Handbook.* Boulder, CO: Westview.

16

Learning Cultures and the Pursuit of Global Learning Norms

Donald Hirsch

Can learning be compared across cultures?

Sixty-four per cent of British women do it, but only 23 per cent of Belgian men.[1] Irish women do it for an average of 72 hours a year; French-speaking Swiss women for only 13 hours.[2] A Dutch 13-year-old does it for 1067 hours a year, an English one for 720 hours.[3]

What determines children's and adults' learning habits in different countries? The above figures, crude indicators of time spent in formal learning, show that these habits differ widely across national boundaries. At the same time the figures mask still greater differences in the character and structure of learning opportunities in each country.

This chapter explores the importance of specific learning cultures, in societies in which learning and knowledge are being seen as increasingly central to meeting aspirations – whether individual or collective ones; whether social or economic. As Castells points out in the prologue to his magisterial trilogy on the The Information Age, information in its broadest sense has been critical in all societies – he gives as an example the role of scholasticism in mediaeval Europe. But we are now in what he terms an informational society in which 'information generation, processing, and transmission become the fundamental sources of productivity and power . . . However, the actual content of "informational society" has to be determined by observation and analysis' (Castells 1996: 21). So it is important to think whether learning systems and cultures will contribute to the concentration or the dispersion of access to different types of knowledge. Will globalization create a convergence in the way people learn, or will differences persist and yield comparative advantage to certain countries or regions?

These are big questions that cannot be fully answered in a short chapter. My aim here is to consider them at three different levels, and with respect to topics that have been discussed internationally in recent decades: first, the extent and nature of adult or continuing education and training structures in different countries; second, lifelong learning in different cities; and third, learning as a development tool for various regions. I conclude by pointing to the paradoxical relationship that derives from a general tendency for learning to play at least some role in reinforcing a distinctive regional or local culture.

Before looking at these three aspects, the issue of learning cultures needs to be put into context. Why, if at all, should we be concerned if our country's citizens are not participating in as much learning as our neighbours? Learning has always been a central feature of civilized cultures: the means by which their collective wisdom is developed and passed on. Much learning is of course not formally organized – from when as babies we find out how to suckle, we spend our lives learning in ways that we may not even be aware of. Yet conscious learning, whether through formal institutions such as schools or through less organized attempts at self-improvement, also plays an essential role in our lives. Until relatively recently in our history, it was largely the preserve of elites, for whom schooling and higher education was often an essential initiation into a class or profession.

In the past century and a half, the goals of organized learning have taken on a wider social dimension. Most obviously, universal basic schooling came in the twentieth century to be seen as an essential feature of societies that aim to extend opportunities for social and economic participation to all citizens. Even in the twenty-first century, basic literacy, associated with access to primary education, continues to be the common currency of participation in learning in many parts of the world.

Yet most OECD countries are going through a second industrial revolution of learning, in which more is being demanded of learning systems. Those who set the goals for such systems want them simultaneously to open themselves up to the whole population and to contribute to a sophisticated set of competencies adapted to a complex world. The currency is no longer basic literacy or primary education for all children, but 'lifelong learning for all' (OECD 1996).

In post-industrial 'knowledge-oriented' societies, then, learning is becoming more central to people's lives (and not just in their childhood), and at the same time far more complex. The statistics on adult learning at the start of this chapter, for example, are rough estimates of the amount of time people spend on continuing education and training, based on survey questions about their participation in such activity over the past twelve months. But participation in what, exactly? An hour of organized learning is not a homogeneous unit.

Like many of the more tangible outputs of the first industrial age, learning could be relatively easily quantified when it was defined mainly in terms of basic schooling. In the Soviet Union, for example, the mass literacy campaigns of the 1920s and 1930s caused a rapid rise in proclaimed literacy rates, from around one in five adults to four in five within less than a generation (Kabatchenko and Yasnikova 1990). Until relatively recently, the fact of having spent a certain number of years at school, rather than any direct measure of ability, was taken as evidence that an adult was literate. So universal schooling and universal literacy were taken as the same thing, and any exceptions to their attainment by the whole population of advanced industrial economies were considered of marginal interest.

Today, when we talk about access to learning for all, we generally mean much more than basic education leading to literacy in a narrowly defined sense. We have learnt to value a wide range of different kinds of learning – in different settings, at different ages, and producing varying results in terms of competency. In this more heterogeneous context, national, regional and local cultures may produce highly varied styles of learning. Primary schooling may be relatively similar everywhere, but different adults in different places learn in very different ways, whether through municipal evening classes, voluntary study circles or company-sponsored training.

Yet we hesitate to respond to such diversity only by saying, as we may once have, 'let a thousand flowers bloom', and '*vive la différence*'. It is highly significant that, having moved beyond a focus on basic schooling and learning to read and write, we have found it necessary to re-invent the concept of 'literacy' with new meanings (see the contributions by Tuijnman and Wagner in this volume).

The International Adult Literacy Survey in the 1990s (OECD 2000b) was the first concerted attempt to measure adult competencies in a systematic way across OECD countries. To economists, it represents a rough and ready attempt to quantify human capital in the adult population. But the aptitudes that it assessed, in dealing with written materials in real world contexts, are highly relevant to adults' ability to function in twenty-first century environments not only as workers, but also as voting citizens and as consumers. Much the same can be said of the competencies – again expressed as literacies even though they cover mathematical and scientific as well as reading domains – first measured in 2000 by the OECD's Programme for International Student Assessment (OECD 1999).

Why are these competencies being called 'literacies'? Because there is today a sense that learning, whatever else it might do, should produce a *common* set of abilities that people in any advanced country need, in order to make the most of their lives. The ability, in confronting everyday problems, to do things such as follow a written argument, weigh up scientific evidence, or recognize the meaning of graphically presented information in an everyday problem, are seen as universally important outcomes of lifelong learning.

This analysis has become quite deeply embedded in the international paradigm of lifelong learning, at least as perceived at the policy level in OECD countries. To accept it has quite profound implications. It makes it possible, in principle at least, to create tools to assess the extent to which learning that takes place over people's lives is producing some desired outcomes. Pursuing such measurable outcomes is very different from aiming simply to create a system that opens up as many learning activities as possible to people of all ages. In theory it could allow governments and others to take a view of the relative efficiency of learning of different kinds in strengthening core skills. Equally, it makes it conceivable that the answer to the question heading this section is yes: learning *can*, at least in these terms, be compared across cultures.

Here, three caveats must be firmly registered for those who worry that this will all lead towards an excessively utilitarian and narrow view of learning (although these caveats do not mean that such worries are entirely unfounded):

• First, valuing certain common learning outcomes is not the same as saying that pursuit of these outcomes should dominate education and training provision. For example, enabling individuals to pursue their own interests may be seen as highly desirable in itself, regardless of whether this leads to improved general 'competencies'.
• Second, the 'literacies' which are being measured are wide areas of competency that could be arrived at by many routes, and not easily taught through a specific curriculum.
• Third, experience suggests that it is precisely strong learning cultures, which are different from one place to another and not easily replicable, that encourage people to engage in active learning throughout their lives and lead them to acquire and retain strong literacy skills.

The following three sections consider such cultures and the role that they play, through three prisms that have been held up in recent years to the 'provision' of lifelong learning.

National systems of adult learning

In the 1970s Jarl Bengtsson and others at the OECD set out the importance of giving people opportunities to continue learning through their lives, rather than just putting stress on initial education in childhood (OECD 1973). 'Recurrent education', 'continuing education', 'lifelong education', and finally the formulation that has had the greatest influence, 'lifelong learning', each puts a somewhat different complexion on this basic idea of seeing initial schooling not as a self-contained episode but as the start of a lifelong journey. While such an idea ultimately has many implications, including the attitude of mind of individuals and the orientation of educational curricula, in the first instance it raises the question of the provision of opportunities. How can education and training systems be adapted to enable individuals to learn when, where and what they want, rather than shoehorning them into a set of institutions controlled by educational suppliers?

The answer to this question has turned out to depend not so much on a set of common ideals, as enunciated by OECD and others from the 1970s onwards, as on national and local learning cultures. For example:

- Bengtsson's native Sweden has a strong tradition of adult study circles, which depend not on policy decisions and state funding but on voluntary effort that would be hard to transfer elsewhere. It also has an inclusive view of entitlement that has led to municipal upper-secondary education, for example, to be offered as of right to adults as well as to teenagers (Swedish Ministry of Education, www.utbildning.regeringen.se/inenglish/educresearch/adulted.htm)
- Employer-based training traditions vary greatly from one country to another. So, for example, Japanese companies have a strong ethos of providing learning opportunities for their own workers, in ways that are quite separate from any aspects of the public education and training system (Okamoto 1994). In contrast, countries with public training levies – imposing charges on any firm that does not invest a certain amount in training of its own workers – make worker training a matter for public rather than purely private concern.
- In the United Kingdom, adults have for many years been going to a wide range of evening classes in one of many national systems of adult education. Yet in neighbouring France, there is no major organized equivalent. Since the early 1990s, however, governments in the UK have tried to concentrate subsidy for such courses on those that are of direct vocational interest, leaving adults who want to study non-vocational subjects to pay through their own resources (Finger and Asún 2001).

Opportunities, then, are influenced by a combination of national habits, institutional arrangements and public funding decisions. There are important limits to how far best practice can be replicated around the world, although that does not prevent some degree of emulation. Japanese companies' commitment to their workers, for example, depends on strongly-held attitudes in the corporate culture that cannot be directly exported. But in the 1990s, partly as a result of observing this culture in British branches of Japanese multinational companies, some UK employers took on this ethos to the extent that they found it worthwhile to allow employees to engage in education and self-development within the company's time, even when it did not directly involve training for work (NIACE, www.niace.org.uk/research/EDP/edphist.htm). A harder aspect to export, typical of German-speaking countries, is the provision of courses by employers' and trade union organizations. This can involve a large organizational input from these bodies, which in many other countries do not command sufficient resources to make such a contribution.

But what of public policy and public funding? Here too there are constraints, determined sometimes by political cultures. In times of fiscal prudence, it is harder to establish for the first time a set of institutions or instruments that seem to increase the burden of the state than it is to continue to fund existing provision. That is why France would find it as hard to set up a comprehensive adult education network as Britain would to introduce a general training levy.

On the other hand, there are now a number of global influences that help create a common agenda which at least causes many countries to change in similar *directions*. For example:

- **Technology** presents similar new opportunities for learning everywhere. New distance learning techniques, developed in Australia to serve remote outback communities, can be adapted to a completely different purpose – say, linking up several workplaces with a community college – in an urban setting somewhere else in the world. The opportunity that technology gives to deliver learning when and where people want it is a common one that is starting to create new learning cultures everywhere.
- **Information and guidance** are being recognized as absolutely critical elements in making sense of a vast network of learning opportunities that is replacing ordered institution-led provision (Bartlett and Rees 2000). Comprehensive services such as the UK's LearnDirect can be expected to become the new gateways to learning. This potentially changes the culture of accessing learning, putting the consumer into the driving seat rather than making her or him dependent on what they find along a predetermined route.
- **Integration** of different kinds of learning is becoming a common paradigm. With recognition of the importance of generic skills has come the realization that it is not so easy to categorize learning as relevant 'for work', 'for leisure', and so on. Efforts are growing to give course credit across institutions, and to make fewer distinctions between the kind of education and training found in different sectors. For example, it may not be long before classes in negotiating skills mix parents with senior managers in a single course (which may include some students wearing both hats). Such integration should start to make what you learn less dependent on what kind of track you are channelled down and more on your individual learning needs. An important consequence could be that which institutions exist in your national culture will make less difference in the past than what and how you learn.

City strategies for lifelong learning

Cultures of learning, then, are partly dependent on the ways in which education and training are organized. But supply does not automatically create its own demand: the motivation and incentives for learning are critical both to participation rates and to how much people gain from participating (Hirsch and Wagner 1995). How do people relate learning to their own lives and to their local environment? To answer this question, a sub-national perspective is helpful. Cities, which can have a strong influence on people's identities and interactions, seem a good place to start.

Early in the 1990s, the concept of the 'educating city' was developed by a Congress of Educating Cities, which now brings together some one hundred cities around the world to exchange experiences. This movement is based on the concept that education depends not just on learning institutions but on people interacting with their local environment. The OECD (1993) report on city strategies for lifelong learning, written for the second Congress of Educating Cities in Gothenburg, took this analysis a step further. It suggested that the city and its identity can help in various ways to link together various forms of learning to help foster a local culture of participation. In some cases this has been part of a concerted strategy to improve the city's fortunes – an example is Pittsburgh after the collapse of its steel industry. In others there is a set of conditions rather than a conscious strategy, as in a city like Vienna. Here, a strong sense of cultural identity interacts with long-standing traditions of providing various opportunities to learn, including an extensive network of 'people's high schools' with trade union and employer bodies providing adult education and work-oriented learning.

As the 'learning city' idea has spread, has there been a transfer of best practice internationally, or the development of global paradigms for what a learning city should be? At one level the answer is no. At best, the result has been a new awareness that the city can be an important force in developing learning cultures, rather than any common model of how it should do so. In the United Kingdom, many places have awarded themselves 'learning city' status; this can mean anything from a marketing tool for the local further education college to a dynamic coalition of employers, local authorities and voluntary agencies. No tangible common set of characteristics defines a learning city.

Yet while every 'learning city' translates this idea in its own specific cultural context, there are, again, some common directions in which learning cities try to move. In particular, learning cities may seek:

- Coordination rather than isolation. Learning need not be dominated by a set of self-contained institutions, but can be greatly enhanced by links among institutions and between different kinds of public and private organization.
- To bring together learners of more than one type, for example, through projects that help people of different generations learn from each other or alongside each other.
- To relate learning to the local context and environment, and sometimes situate it outside educational institutions.
- More specifically, to relate learning to the particular economic, social and cultural context of one's city.
- Ultimately, to discover ways in which the city itself can learn – for example, by discovering new economic roles after the decline of a traditional industry.

Some of these principles challenge fundamentally the ways in which learning has been organized in a city, and create new features of learning systems that are common across international boundaries. A good example is public-private partnerships. The influence of the private sector in bringing new ideas into education is not only a global phenomenon, but can also be an instrument for spreading ideas and practices across frontiers through multinational companies. It is significant in this respect that in the world of business and commerce, cross-national organizations play a far more important role than any that exist in the education world. So links between business and education increase the scope for global forces to affect the latter.

Learning regions and economic development

A third and more recently developed concept is that of the learning region. To some extent it is an extension of the idea of the learning city, analysing how a sub-national area can use its advantages and identity to promote broad learning partnerships that improve its future prospects. But the concept of the learning region developed by the OECD (2001) is particularly orientated to the perspective of economic development.

The imperative for the learning region is particularly strong and direct. In the global economy, certain regions are emerging as winners, the most frequently cited being Silicon Valley in California. Like in the 'industrial districts' first identified by Alfred Marshall (1920: 267–77), success depends on the presence of a range of resources and conditions that give advantages in certain areas of production. In the case of twenty-first century regions, crucial factors include strong human resources and an infrastructure of commercial and educational organizations that is favourable to innovation. Potentially, the quest for regional winners may be a zero-sum game in which every winner creates a loser. But insofar as each learning region is trying to find an appropriate role or niche in an integrated world economy, this is not necessarily the case (Maskell 2000).

Against this background, there are reasons both why the culture of a learning region should be distinctive and why certain common characteristics are suggested. If Andalucia, a poor but rapidly-developing Spanish region considered as a case study by the OECD, simply tried to emulate Silicon Valley, it would surely fail. Yet this does not prevent it from developing certain niche markets in creating an economic profile that takes it beyond its dependence on agriculture and tourism. In doing so, it is bound to exploit advantages such as a pleasant climate where people want to live and work, and a large pool of low-cost service labour that can help support developing industries.

The commonalities come, as with cities, from certain underlying principles of development that regions can learn from each other. These include:

- Strengthening links between learning institutions and businesses at a region-wide level, with an awareness of which are the most promising industries that need supporting with scientific expertise.

- Putting into place where possible the conditions needed for innovation, which may include support for small knowledge-orientated businesses or the availability of venture capital.
- Above all, encouraging *networks* that enable people to pool their knowledge and expertise across a region.
- Making the most of one's cultural identity, not just through direct means such as selling history to tourists, but also by using a common understanding of a region's past and future that helps people to work together.

The last two of these principles can potentially interact powerfully: learning networks will be much stronger if built on the principle of a common heritage. In some regions identified by the OECD, such as Oresund in Sweden and Denmark, a spirit of civic and corporate cooperation is already strong, and that can be built on. In others, such as Kent Thameside in the UK, there is no prior regional identity but large, new infrastructure developments can potentially help create one.

Conclusion – global approaches to localism?

The above analysis points to a paradoxical conclusion. The distinctiveness of local learning cultures is a powerful force in helping to move towards a paradigm of lifelong learning, not least because an identity with such cultures can help to motivate individuals to participate in education and training beyond compulsory education. Yet the very trends that are helping to promote these local cultures constitute a set of common principles which between them give learning certain global characteristics – or at least cause change in common directions.

These commonalities derive their power partly from some globalizing forces such as the Internet, but also from the shared sense that learning is a high-stakes business for individuals, communities and nations in a globally competitive economy. Three perceptions in particular are driving change in the way that learning is organized:

- First, that at the heart of success in knowledge societies is the mastery of certain general competencies, rather than the acquisition of specific factual knowledge or technical know-how.
- Second, that new demands on people's lives, as workers, citizens and consumers, require people from all walks of life to use such general skills in flexible ways, and to continue to learn.
- Third, that the detached environment of the classroom can only go part of the way to creating the competencies required. This view directly contradicts a long strand of thinking, from Plato to Oakeshott, centred on the school or academy as a detached and self-contained institution.

OECD societies thus worry, for example, about the forty-year-old who lacks communication skills or has not mastered the basic principles of a computer, and risks becoming a member of a new disadvantaged, potentially excluded, class. For this reason, cultures around the world find it important to engage such a person in learning, most commonly in ways that are closely related to his or her everyday life and experiences.

How will this engagement in learning take place? In a huge multitude of ways, which continue to draw largely from local traditions and institutions, as well as being informed by some of the new international thinking in which OECD/CERI and Jarl Bengtsson have been central for three decades. It is of course impossible to give relative weights to the importance of these local influences for stability and global influences for change. Yet we may ponder whether, for example, learning in Gothenburg in 2002 has more in common with learning in Gothenburg in 1972 or learning in Adelaide in 2002. It is at least a fair bet that, after some climatic adaptation, a twenty-first-century Gothenburg student may feel more at home in the latter. Not least because Sweden has been the quickest to take on board that other global imperative for success in the modern world: speaking English.

Notes

1. OECD (2000a: 201) – per cent of employed adults who have participated in job-related continuous education and training in the previous year.
2. OECD (2000a: 201) – average hours of job-related continuous education and training in the previous year by employed adults.
3. OECD (2000a: 237) – intended instruction time.

References

Bartlett, W. and Rees, T. (2000) The variable contribution of guidance services in different types of learning societies, in F. Coffield (ed.) *Differing Visions of a Learning Society, Research Findings Volume 1*, pp. 139–66. Bristol: The Policy Press.

Castells, M. (1996) *The Information Age: Economy, Society and Culture, Vol. I: The Rise of the Network Society*. Cambridge, MA and Oxford: Blackwell.

Finger, M. and Asún, J. (2001) *Adult Education at the Crossroads*. Leicester: National Institute for Adult and Continuing Education.

Hirsch, D. and Wagner, D. (eds) (1995) *What Makes Workers Learn: The Role of Incentives in Workplace Education and Training*. Cresskill, NJ: Hampton Press.

Kabatchenko, M. and Yasnikova, L. (1990) *Eradicating Illiteracy in the USSR*. Geneva: International Bureau of Education.

Marshall, A. (1920) *Industry and Trade*. London: Macmillan.

Maskell, P. (2000) Social capital, innovation, and competitiveness, in S. Baron, J. Field and T. Schuller (eds) *Social Capital, Critical Perspectives*, pp. 111–23. Oxford: Oxford University Press.

OECD (1973) *Recurrent Education: A Strategy for Lifelong Learning*. Paris: OECD.

OECD (1993) *City Strategies for Lifelong Learning*. Gothenburg: Gothenburg City Education Committee.

OECD (1996) *Lifelong Learning for All.* Paris: OECD.

OECD (1999) *Measuring Student Knowledge and Skills: A New Framework for Assessment.* Paris: OECD.

OECD (2000a) *Education at a Glance 2000.* Paris: OECD.

OECD (2000b) *Literacy in the Information Age.* Paris: OECD.

OECD (2001) *Cities and Regions in the New Learning Economy.* Paris: OECD.

Okamoto, K. (1994) *Lifelong Learning Movement in Japan.* Tokyo: Ministry of Education.

Part 6

A Swedish Coda

17

Adult Education Policy in Sweden 1967–2001: From Recurrent Education to Lifelong Learning

Kjell Rubenson

Introduction

Despite all the policy rhetoric about lifelong learning and the evolving knowledge society in most countries the majority of citizens are excluded and there exist major class and ethnic inequities in participation in adult education (Belanger and Tuijnman 1997; OECD 2000). While these inequities exist in all countries, comparative data suggest that public policy can be somewhat effective in moderating inequality in adult education participation and highlight the relationship between the state and its citizens. Thus, as Carnoy (1995) points out, there are crucial differences in what adult education attempts to do and can do in different social-political structures. He states: 'Ultimately, these differences depend heavily on the possibilities and limits of the state, since it is the state that defines adult education and is the principal beneficiary of its effective implementation' (Carnoy 1995: 3). These possibilities and limits of the state are thus a key issue in understanding the form and content of adult education. In this context it is of interest to take a closer look at the situation in Sweden as it is one of the countries with the highest participation rates in adult education and where, in relative terms, the inequities are smaller than in many other countries (OECD 2000).

Sweden has had a long and important tradition of adult education dating back to the breakthrough of the popular movements at the end of the nineteenth century. However, it was not until the 1960s that adult education became central to Swedish educational and labour market policies. This chapter analyses government policy over a 40-year period with regard to context, reform ideology, strategies and, where possible, outcomes. The discussion focuses on four distinct periods reflecting significant shifts in policy context, objectives and strategies: 1960–69, 1970–75, 1976–1991 and 1992–2001.

The 1960s: adult education becomes a central policy arena

Policy context

The very selective, hierarchically organized parallel school system was seen as a bastion of the old class system that Sweden's Social Democrats set out to erase. While the early groundwork for establishing comprehensive schools was being laid, the issue of intergenerational equity was raised. The school reforms of the 1950s and early 1960s led to a rapid expansion of the Swedish educational system. The result was an ever widening gap between the older generation, who had received a minimal education, and the new generation, who had received nine years of compulsory education and who increasingly chose to continue on to secondary school. As a consequence, the argument that the people who were paying for the increase in primary and secondary education should have their share of the increasing educational resources grew stronger (TCO 1964; LO 1969).

The democratization of the educational system was not the only basis for the 1967 reform. It also was heavily influenced by contemporary human capital ideas, widely embraced within policy circles. The situation in Sweden – whose population had an educational attainment resembling Portugal's and a labour market resembling West Germany's – was seen as most problematic. Research had shown that there existed a large intellectual reserve in the adult population that was well equipped to undertake secondary and higher education (Härnqvist 1958). It was against this background that the Swedish parliament launched its adult education policy in 1967.

Reform strategy

The two major innovations of this reform were the introduction of municipal adult education, which would offer education equivalent to that offered by primary and secondary schools, and the creation of television and radio programmes for educational purposes. As a result of such changes, popular adult education was displaced from its former unique position and incorporated into the overall system of adult education. No longer was adult education a marginal activity. The creation of special departments of adult education within the Ministry of Education and the National Board of Education, and a separate post in the national budget, made it a distinct and separate part of the educational system.

The 1967 adult education reform had its roots in the same elitist concept of equality that guided the restructuring of higher education. The basic idea informing this strategy was that everyone should have an equal right to an education regardless of social background, gender or place of residence (OECD 1967). The concept is elitist in that it implicitly argues that society ought to offer higher/adult education to those who aspire to it and who are able to benefit from such education. The starting point for the 1967 reform was the increased demand for education on the part of those individuals psychologically inclined and socially equipped for study. Evening-class students served as models for the target group of the newly introduced municipal adult education. These students belonged to the so-called pool of talent – they had a high level of aspiration, they were motivated to study, and they were often successful in their self-tuition. The 1967 reforms were not aimed at reaching new target groups but were designed to cater to the increased demands of this existing group. They can be seen as an attempt to tackle what Patricia Cross (1981) termed 'institutional obstacles to participation', and thereby to help transform the demand for adult education into actual participation. Neither psychological nor situational obstacles to participation were addressed in 1967. The desired results of the reform were an increase in participation by the so-called intellectual reserve and an increase in human capital.

1970–75: a radicalization of adult education policy

Policy context

The debate which accompanied the 1969 reform of adult education made the Swedish Confederation of Trade Unions (SCTU) and the Swedish Central Organization of Salaried Employees take an increasing interest in adult education policy. The SCTU's report (LO 1969) proposed two main themes behind its attention to adult education: equality and justice. These early ideas were developed further in a subsequent report (LO 1971), documenting that adult education had been used primarily by those already well prepared and that, accordingly, there were few advantages in adult education for the trade union collective. Trade unions demanded that high priority be given to measures aimed at neglected groups. 'A just distribution in the field of adult education does not mean equal shares for everyone, but more for those that have received less' (LO 1971: 206). Labour's demand for action in the adult education field was not an isolated event but part of the general radicalization of the trade union movement at the end of the 1960s.

Korpi's analysis of working classes in welfare-state capitalism shows that the reformist strategy of Swedish social democracy came to be questioned (Korpi 1978). The wildcat strikes of the late 1960s strengthened labour's support for radical changes in working life. This development should be seen as a reappraisal of the labour movement's relationship to the question of economic democracy. When the Social Democrats came to power in 1932, the issue of direct state control over the means of production gave way to issues of social democracy, particularly to the emergence of the welfare state. Politics had come to be based on the assumption that the possession of political power would create sufficient opportunities to make fundamental changes in working life without necessarily abolishing private ownership of the means of production.

The trade unions called for measures to democratize political and cultural life to bring about cultural changes to parallel those in working life. The Workers' Educational Association and the SCTU demanded that the government set up a committee to experiment with various outreach models to increase participation of the undereducated in adult education. The government reacted promptly to these demands. In Government Bill 1970:35, a change of action was announced: in further reforms of adult education one of the most important issues would be how to reach those who have little or insufficient education.

Following Korpi's argument, a shift in the balance of power between social collectives and classes can be supposed to influence and reflect both the distribution of opportunity between different classes in society and the social consciousness of the people. The increasing social power of the trade union movement in Sweden explains the state's altered ways of acting in adult education matters. Ambitions for adult education to act as an agent of social reform emerged simultaneously with growing cynicism about the ability of formal schooling to effect social reform.

There were warning signs that childhood education reforms had not had the equalizing effect the government anticipated. From this perspective, we can see the intense focus on adult education as an attempt to broaden an earlier strategy aimed at remodelling class society by remodelling childhood education. The early 1970s offered an alternative strategy for social change based on a resocialization of adults, rather than the socialization of children. There are parallels between this approach and those of literacy campaigns, in which initial efforts are directed towards adults since literate parents seldom have illiterate children.

From 1970 to 1975, the tenor of government policy became more pronounced: the overall aim of adult education policy was to bring about parity in standards of living. The government's concept of what resources were necessary to provide for an adequate standard of living was informed by the definition offered by the Royal Commission on Low Income. The Commission considered resources of 'money, property, knowledge, psychological and physical energy, social relations, security, etc., at the disposal of the individual with the aid of which the individual can control and consciously govern his living conditions' to be vital. Thus, adult education was intended to achieve a redistribution of those resources through which individuals could control their lives. To do so, it was necessary that those with limited resources be recruited and that education, directly or indirectly, promote the creation of these resources.

Reform strategy

The government's strategy during the first half of the 1970s was to come to terms with bias in adult education recruitment by implementing a comprehensive package of measures. This strategy included social benefits for adult students and subsidies for outreach activities. Support need not be financial alone – it can be any form of compensatory action aimed at helping students overcome their psychological and situational obstacles to study. Ultimately, recruitment was and remains an issue of creating demand for education among groups traditionally disinclined to study.

A focus on outreach activities and study assistance for adults informed the selective measures presented in the 1974 bill on adult education. These outreach activities were meant to change adult attitudes. The package of measures – consisting of laws on the right to study leave, the position of shop stewards, state subsidies for outreach activities and study assistance for adults – was in complete harmony with the stated goals of the bill. There was remarkable optimism in the politicians' emphasis on the ability of education to create the resources through which individuals can command their lives. The texts of government bills often refer to the collective tradition and to structural changes in society. The democratization of working life is seen as a motivating factor in individuals' demands for adult education. It would be wrong to maintain that changes in adult education ignored issues of power and social control.

The central role of adult education in the government's efforts to equalize the opportunity structure during the 1970s is reflected in the amount of state subsidies that went to this sector. During the first half of the 1970s, adult education did well in comparison with the other sectors. For example, while actual resources for adult education increased by 76 per cent, resources for higher education decreased by 19 per cent (Olofsson and Rubenson 1986). The increase mainly occurred in the popular adult education sector, which saw a dramatic expansion. Thus, the allocation of resources reflects the central role of popular adult education in the democratization process.

1976–91: fiscal crises, internal efficiencies and an end to the radical period

Policy context

Once more there was a change in adult education policy. Two major factors underlie this change: the right-of-centre parties' assumption of power and a serious deterioration of the Swedish economy.

The major provision in Government Bill 1975:23 redistributed cultural and economic resources based on the assumption that continuously expanding finances would bear the related increase in cost. In reality, the situation was far different: the growth rate declined, inflation increased and the government deficit soared. In this environment, there was no room for new ventures in adult education. Instead, the government reduced its funding for education.

The Social Democrats' resumption of power in 1982 did not lead to a return to the expansionist and radical period of the early 1970s. On the whole, the policy for which the preceding government had set out the basic principles was continued. The growing discrepancy between reform ideology and actions of 1976–82 was just as marked in the 1982–91 period, if not more so. A large public deficit forced the government to undertake severe austerity measures. More importantly, there was a questioning of and a gradual shift away from the 'Swedish model' (Petersson 1991). Instead of being seen as a solution, the public sector increasingly had come to be regarded as the problem. Other changes included a shift away from centralized social organization in many fields. The power of the labour movement weakened, particularly that of the SCTU, the strongest proponent of social equality. During the 1980s, Swedes changed their values, placing more emphasis on personal freedom and less on equality. Support for the trade unions weakened and generally there was a shift away from collective solidarity. Between 1981 and 1990, the share of the adult Swedish population that had confidence in the labour unions and gave priority to the values of equality dropped from 23 per cent to 12 per cent (LO 1991a, b).

During the 1980s, the relationship between adult education and the economy, as well as working life, again took precedence. In Swedish policy documents, the link between higher and adult education, and technological change and economic growth became a common theme.

Reform strategy

Adult education policy during the 1980s was to a large extent shaped by deteriorating government finances. Consequently, much of the focus was on making the system more effective by eliminating duplications. Report after report gave serious attention to closer coordination between regular high school education and municipal adult education, where adults could complete the equivalent education. Similarly, the link between municipal and labour market training was emphasized. The existing structure with a unified comprehensive policy strategy for the whole adult education sector stood in strong opposition to the emergent public policy strategy of decentralization.

Government Bills 1990/91:68 and 1990/91:82 were an attempt to address the policy pressures and drastically changed the structure of adult education policy in Sweden. The process that began in 1967, when adult education became a unified policy area, was abandoned. From 1967 to 1991, popular adult education and municipal adult education had been governed as the two main components of adult education, and the bureaucracy was organized accordingly. As a result of the 1991 reform, municipalities would no longer receive separate funding for municipal adult education. Instead, they would be allocated a general block grant for youth and adult education. Popular adult education was moved out of the National Board of Education and given its own independent board under direct control of the popular movements, while labour market education came under the auspices of the Ministry of Labour. The result of the discussions during the 1980s for closer coordination of adult education was a paradoxical decision by which adult education ceased to be an independent policy area. This was reflected in the fact that there no longer was a special post for adult education in the budget and no adult education unit in the revised National Board of Education. These changes were in line with a new accent on child and youth education as opposed to adult education.

The 1991 reform also tried to address the uncertainty that had evolved around the role of popular adult education in the overall strategy. The 1967 reform, which unified the adult education area, had created tensions regarding state intervention into this sector. A free-standing governing board for popular adult education – which sets its goals and directions and assumes responsibility for governance while the parliament restricts itself to setting the goals for state subsidies – was created to revitalize the popular movements and strengthen their influence on popular adult education. Government Bill 1990/91:82 (p.6) presented the following reasons for providing state subsidies for free and voluntary popular adult education that is self-governing:

- Stimulates democracy, equality, and international solidarity and understanding.
- Starts from the individual's own voluntary search for knowledge.
- Is characterized by democratic values and cooperation.
- Aims at strengthening individuals' ability to influence their own life, and to be able, together with others, to change society in accordance with their values and ideas.
- Helps develop a popular culture.
- Stimulates the development of an idea-oriented adult education within the popular movements.
- Helps provide all, particularly the educationally disadvantaged, with good basic knowledge.
- Helps stimulate further search for knowledge.

The stated policy change in popular adult education should be seen in the context of what had happened to this sector during the 1980s. Under the right-of-centre parties' term of office, municipal adult education received marked increases in resources and a larger share of the total amount spent on adult education. This trend continued after the Social Democrats resumed power. In the 1976/77 budget, popular adult education received almost three times as much money as the credit-oriented municipal adult education. By the 1989/90 budget, the latter received a slightly higher subsidy. This development is significant, given the importance placed earlier on popular adult education as an instrument with which to reach disadvantaged groups.

Unlike the period between 1970 and 1976, there are no declared changes of goals found in official documents for 1976–91. However, as the focus on redistribution of resources was partly replaced by concerns for economic efficiency and internal structures, the discrepancy between stated goals and policy strategy grew during this period. This is reflected in participation figures. From 1974 to 1979 there occurred a slight relative increase in participation among disadvantaged groups (Olofsson and Rubenson 1986). This positive trend came to a halt around 1980, partly explained by the fact that there was no further expansion in resources earmarked for reaching these groups. The expansion in adult education came almost entirely to depend on developments in employer-sponsored education which dramatically shifted the landscape of adult education. Between 1975 and 1993 the participation in popular adult education went down from a high of 15.4 per cent in 1979 to 9.8 per cent in 1993. During this period the relative proportion of adult education students that went to popular adult education declined from 42 to 25 per cent. Employer-sponsored education saw a gradual increase from 5.2 per cent in 1975 to 14.5 per cent in 1993 and the relative proportion for employer-sponsored education went from 17 to 42 per cent (Rubenson 1996). This brought the role of employer-sponsored education into the centre of adult education policy discussions.

1992–2001: the economy takes precedence

Policy context

The radical reform of 1991 that broke up adult education as a policy area had left an uncertainty about its direction. In conjunction with an OECD review of the Swedish educational policy, the examiners noted that the accent now was on child and youth education and not, as previously, on adult education. As data started to become available in the late 1980s on who received employer-sponsored education and training, it became evident that it was very unevenly distributed and that the trade union (LO) collective was not well represented. Within the trade union movement control over education and training of the workforce came to be one of the most central issues. Unable to bridge the unions' demand for state policy and the employers' unwillingness to see stronger regulations, the government presented a national strategy for how to improve the human capital, focusing primarily on employer-sponsored education and training. The Parliamentary Committee on Competences presented a series of reforms, some of which involved a stronger presence of the state in employer-sponsored education and training. With a new right-wing government that stressed deregulation of the labour market, this suggestion was rejected and the whole proposal fell.

Until now the Swedish discussions on increased participation by the workforce in adult education and training and the competitiveness of the Swedish economy had taken place under full employment. The labour market conditions quickly eroded in the early 1990s. As a consequence, the debate shifted from employer-sponsored education and training to the role of adult education and training in fighting unemployment. The response by the newly re-elected Social Democratic government was to introduce the Adult Education Initiative (Government Bill 1995/97:222), not as an educational bill but as a cornerstone in a bill entitled 'Special strategies introduced in order to halve the unemployment by year 2000'.

Reform strategy: the Adult Education Initiative

The Adult Education Initiative (AEI) is a massive five-year programme for adult education established in 1997 in which all municipalities participate. The project comprises some 110,000 new educational places per year for adults, mainly in municipal adult education. Over the five years, its aim is to reach 550,000 adults – 15 per cent of the labour force. With an average yearly cost of €3700 per student, the total investment in the five-year programme will be close to €2 billion.

The AEI signals a fundamental broadening of the Swedish tradition of active labour market policy. Instead of expanding the traditional labour market training programmes with their strong vocational focus, the AEI is attempting to raise the general level of education of unemployed adults. Aiming to elevate the educational level in the adult population, the Initiative focuses mainly on expanding municipal adult education and provides a central role for the municipalities. However, while the AEI is a joint task for the state and the municipalities, it is financed via a special state grant.

The AEI contains several measures aimed at helping to reach adults who traditionally do not participate in adult education and training. Thus, there are a number of different ways for students to finance their studies. For the majority of students, the most advantageous study support is the special education grant, which was introduced at the same time as the AEI. The grant is primarily intended for unemployed persons who have not completed a three-year upper secondary programmme and who intend to study at a compulsory or upper secondary school level. In order to reach persons with little or no experience of adult education and help them to start studying, more targeted recruitment and information activities are put in place.

Some general findings so far are:

- There is overwhelming evidence that the AEI has been very successful in reintroducing adult education as an area of public policy.

- The special state funding is key to the success of the AEI and the experiment has shown the need for a centralized coordinated effort.
- The AEI has been more successful in creating coordination between the labour market training system – which is under the state and municipal adult education and the vocational programmes in high school – than with employer-sponsored activities.

As the AEI progressed, there were increasing concerns that the adult education sector had become almost exclusively colonized by the economic crisis and that the promised broad reforms and renewal of the adult education sector were not forthcoming. It was against this background that the government introduced a much awaited reform bill on adult education.

Government Bill 2000/01:72: a new direction for Swedish adult education

By 2001, the general policy-making scene had again changed considerably. After some very difficult years with high unemployment and drastic cuts to the public sector, the Swedish economy was once again healthy and large budget deficits had been replaced by solid surpluses. Government was now in the enviable situation of being able to make choices about spending priorities. In anticipation of future demographic changes and demands on the welfare system, the focus shifted to the participation rate in the economy. At the end of 2000 the rate stood at 77.5 per cent for the labour force in ages 20–64. The goal set by the government is to raise this level to 80 per cent by 2004.

In a fundamental shift from the traditional Social Democratic position on adult education, Government Bill 2000/01:72 stresses that it is essential to consider the needs of the individual as the starting-point for planning social measures. Adult education and training has so far been too concentrated on treating the individual as part of a collective with a common background and common needs, with teaching organized in prepackaged forms. Therefore the challenge for state-supported education and training is to cater for everyone on the basis of individual wishes, needs and requirements. Some of the language in the Bill is reminiscent of the general neo-liberal discourse that has informed the policy directions of lifelong learning. The fundamental strategy for the state is to govern the choices of autonomous citizens in their capacities as consumers, parents, employees, managers and investors. Increasingly, competition is enhanced by transferring public funds to private-sector educational providers. As Gordon (1991, cited in Marginson 1997: 83) argues, the idea of life as 'the enterprise of oneself' means that each person can be regarded as continuously employed in that enterprise. Consequently it is the responsibility of individuals to make adequate provisions for the creation and preservation of their own human capital. Investment in learning and its financing are an individual responsibility. Differences in participation patterns strengthen the role of lifelong learning in the positional competition. An ideology that sees no role for the state in promoting the public-good function of adult education leaves participation to market forces.

While the notion of a training market is central to the AEI and the 2000/01 Bill, the discourse is different from the neo-liberal one in that the state is clearly a player. Resources allocated for outreach activities, counselling, availability of courses and financial support can be seen as the base of a state-supported infrastructure for lifelong learning. Further, the Bill introduces a number of proposals aimed at improving the opportunity for people with functional disabilities to participate in lifelong learning.

With the exception of financial support, it is the municipalities that are responsible for ensuring that this support organization is in place. The Bill contains a number of proposals aimed at promoting this development. The state determines the goals and certain guidelines for adult education and training. The state defines the frameworks that safeguard equivalence and statutory rights. The state also provides limited funding for certain purposes. The individual organizes his or her own learning with the assistance of the municipal authorities, folk high schools, study organizations, other education providers, employers, trade unions and many others, not least those participating in lifelong learning.

The Bill notes that popular adult education has an important role to play in lifelong learning and the acquisition of a broad education, and must be independent and not subject to commercial forces. The government holds that liberal adult education can and should function as a counterweight to the commercialized, elitist and segregating forces that are so apparent in today's society. However, the actual resources connected with the Bill are mainly allocated for municipal adult education and not for popular adult education. On the contrary, by stressing lifelong learning as an individual project, the collective efforts of the social movements through their study associations are further reduced and the traditional link between civil society and popular adult education weakened.

Concluding remarks

This chapter underlines the close relationship between adult education policy in Sweden and developments in the broader social, economic and political spheres. These are more visible and noticeable than is the case in the formal educational system. This can be explained by the long history of popular adult education and the practice since the 1950s of linking policies for full employment, active labour market policy and adult education. The radical reform of the 1970s, with its emphasis on study circles, reflects the first tradition. The recent decline in public support for popular adult education and collective efforts mirrors the changing value pattern in Sweden towards a more individualistically oriented society. The economic imperative is clearly visible in the policies of the 1960s and reappears with full force in the late 1980s. From a Gramscian perspective, the recent broad societal acceptance of the economic imperative driving adult education can be understood in terms of the hegemonic dominance that this idea has achieved in today's society. The 'rule of ideas' is translated into structures and activities as well as values, attitudes, beliefs and morality, and becomes the 'common sense' of society.

It is interesting to look at Swedish adult education in the context of welfare state theory. Thus, public policy on funding regimes and provision of adult education can be understood in terms of various forms of welfare states (see Esping-Andersen 1989). The liberal welfare state with its means-tested assistance and modest universal transfers caters mainly to a clientele of low-income dependants and sees adult education mainly as way of getting people off welfare. Participation is left mainly to market forces and entitlements are strict and often associated with stigma. The social democratic welfare state, according to Esping-Andersen, rather than tolerating a dualism between state and market, and between working class and middle class, promotes an equality of the highest standard not an equality of minimal needs. The state takes a more active role in adult education and is more concerned about inequalities in participation. This line of thinking dominated the radical period of the early 1970s. While it was on the retreat during the 1980s and first half of the 1990s, the notion never fully disappeared, and the AEI and the 2000/01 Bill signal a return, but now with a stronger emphasis on the individual.

During the 40-year period covered in this chapter there has occurred a major shift in the adult education landscape. The balance between popular adult education and formal adult education has shifted, with the latter growing in importance. However, the most dramatic change is the enormous growth in employer-sponsored activities. To understand adult education today is to understand the impact of the 'long arm of the job'. The altered landscape signals that the potential of adult education practices as an instrument in the counter-hegemonic struggle is being weakened. However, it also raises the broader question of what benefits the various forms of adult education have for individuals, community and society.

Looking at individual opportunity structures, there is strong evidence that municipal adult education has served women well in terms of income, employment and access to higher education (Alm-Stenflo 2000). But data on employer-sponsored education reveal that there are major inequalities in access to this kind of education which is linked to work hierarchy and the nature of the job (OECD 2000). Not only does the rate of participation differ greatly by level of occupation but so does the nature of the educational or training activity. Those in higher positions more often follow academically oriented, often externally organized courses, while unskilled workers receive some shorter form of on-the-job training. Further, the former have jobs that provide richer chances to learn new things on the job. These differences are more marked in the private than in the public sector (Xu 2000).

The present shift in Sweden from recurrent education to lifelong learning as the organizing principle for policy-making highlights the issue of the wider benefits, not only of formal and non-formal learning but now also of informal purposeful learning. To think about lifelong learning in this broad, all-encompassing way is a change of Copernican magnitude with broad consequences for how Sweden addresses lifelong learning for all. It raises enormous challenges for public policy. Within this perspective the very core of lifelong learning is the informal or 'everyday' learning, positive or negative, which occurs in day-to-day life. Here, the issue is the nature and structure of everyday experiences, and their consequences for a person's learning processes, ways of thinking and competences. What challenges do people face? What possibilities do these challenges create not only for restrictive forms of learning, but also for investigative learning promoting new ways of acting? Approaching lifelong learning in Sweden from this perspective, it is not enough to look at the infrastructure that Bill 2000/01:72 establishes, nor the new measures to address prior learning assessments that are being put in place. Instead, we have to look at the very nature of the welfare state and the structure of working life. The question is to what extent working life, civil society and democratic traditions lead to the curriculum of everyday life inspiring and requiring all citizens to be active learners.

References

Alm-Stenflo, G. (2000) *Inkomst och sysselsättningseffekter av kommunal vuxenutbildning.* Stockholm: SCB Temarapport 2000:1.
Belanger, P. and Tuijnman, A. (eds) (1997) *New Patterns of Adult Learning. A Six-country Comparative Study.* Oxford: Pergamon.
Carnoy, M. (1995) Foreword: How should we study adult education?, in C.A. Torres (ed.) *The Politics of Nonformal Education in Latin America.* New York: Praeger.
Cross, P. (1981) *Adult as Learners.* San Francisco: Jossey-Bass.
Esping-Andersen, G. (1989) The three political economies of the welfare state, *The Canadian Review of Sociology and Anthropology,* 26:1, 10–36.
Härnqvist, K. (1958) *Beräkning av reserver för högre utbildning.* Stockholm: Swedish Public Printer.
Korpi, W. (1978) *Arbetarklassen i välfärdskapitalismen.* Stockholm: Prisma.
LO (1969) *Fackföreningsrörelsen och vuxenutbildningen.* Stockholm: Prisma.
LO (1971) *Vuxenutbildning, Fakta-erfarenheter-förslag.* Stockholm: Prisma.
LO (1991a) *Rättvisan i vågskålen.* Stockholm: LO.
LO (1991b) *Det utvecklande arbetet.* Stockholm: LO.
Marginson, S. (1997) *Markets in education.* St Leonards: Allen & Unwin.
OECD (1967) *Educational Policy and Planning: Sweden.* Paris: OECD.
OECD (2000) *Literacy in the Information Age.* Paris: OECD.
Olofsson, L. and Rubenson, K. (1986) *1970-talets vuxenutbildningsreformer.* Stockholm: HLS 9/85.
Petersson, O. (1991) Democracy and power in Sweden, *Scandinavian Political Studies,* 14(2): 173–91.

Rubenson, K. (1996) Studieförbundens roll i vuxenutbildningen, in *SOU 1996*:154, 3–63.

TCO (1964) *Utbildningspolitiskt program för tjänstemannarörelsen.* Stockholm: TCO.

Xu, G. (2000) Participation in employer-sponsored adult education and training in Sweden (1975–1995). Dissertation, University of British Columbia, Vancouver.

Index

The Society for Research into Higher Education

The Society for Research into Higher Education (SRHE) exists to stimulate and coordinate research into all aspects of higher education. It aims to improve the quality of higher education through the encouragement of debate and publication on issues of policy, on the organization and management of higher education institutions, and on the curriculum, teaching and learning methods.

The Society is entirely independent and receives no subsidies, although individual events often receive sponsorship from business or industry. The Society is financed through corporate and individual subscriptions and has members from many parts of the world.

Under the imprint *SRHE & Open University Press*, the Society is a specialist publisher of research, having over 80 titles in print. In addition to *SRHE News*, the Society's newsletter, the Society publishes three journals: *Studies in Higher Education* (three issues a year), *Higher Education Quarterly* and *Research into Higher Education Abstracts* (three issues a year).

The Society runs frequent conferences, consultations, seminars and other events. The annual conference in December is organized at and with a higher education institution. There are a growing number of networks which focus on particular areas of interest, including:

Access	Learning Environment
Assessment	Legal Education
Consultants	Managing Innovation
Curriculum Development	New Technology for Learning
Eastern European	Postgraduate Issues
Educational Development Research	Quantitative Studies
FE/HE	Student Development
Funding	Vocation at Qualification
Graduate Employment	

Benefits to members

Individual

* The opportunity to participate in the Society's networks
* Reduced rates for the annual conferences

- Free copies of *Research into Higher Education Abstracts*
- Reduced rates for *Studies in Higher Education*
- Reduced rates for *Higher Education Quarterly*
- Free copy of *Register of Members' Research Interests* – includes valuable reference material on research being pursued by the Society's members
- Free copy of occasional in-house publications, e.g. *The Thirtieth Anniversary Seminars Presented by the Vice-Presidents*
- Free copies of *SRHE News* which informs members of the Society's activities and provides a calendar of events, with additional material provided in regular mailings
- A 35 per cent discount on all SRHE/Open University Press books
- Access to HESA statistics for student members
- The opportunity for you to apply for the annual research grants
- Inclusion of your research in the *Register of Members' Research Interests*

Corporate

- Reduced rates for the annual conferences
- The opportunity for members of the Institution to attend SRHE's network events at reduced rates
- Free copies of *Research into Higher Education Abstracts*
- Free copies of *Studies in Higher Education*
- Free copies of *Register of Members' Research Interests* – includes valuable reference material on research being pursued by the Society's members
- Free copy of occasional in-house publications
- Free copies of *SRHE News*
- A 35 per cent discount on all SRHE/Open University Press books
- Access to HESA statistics for research for students of the Institution
- The opportunity for members of the Institution to submit applications for the Society's research grants
- The opportunity to work with the Society and co-host conferences
- The opportunity to include in the *Register of Members' Research Interests* your Institution's research into aspects of higher education

Membership details: SRHE, 76 Portland Place, London
W1B 1NT, UK Tel: 020 7637 2766. Fax: 020 7637 2781.
email: srhe@mailbox.ulcc.ac.uk
world wide web: http://www.srhe.ac.uk./srhe/
Catalogue: SRHE & Open University Press, Celtic Court,
22 Ballmoor, Buckingham MK18 1XW. Tel: 01280 823388.
Fax: 01280 823233. email: enquiries@openup.co.uk

THE ADULT UNIVERSITY

Etienne Bourgeois, Chris Duke, Jean-Luc Guyot and Barbara Merrill

In most universities there are now more adults as students than young people straight from school. Yet many universities continue to act as if no such change had taken place. *The Adult University* examines theoretically and practically key issues of broader participation in higher education. It asks:

- What are university access policies and how do they connect with practice; do universities behave in ways which encourage or thwart wider access?
- How do adults experience universities; and how far do universities adapt to assist adults?
- What can universities realistically do to improve both the access to and experience of university for adults.

This is a genuinely international study by a transnational team which is grounded in research into two institutions in two major European university traditions. Its focus is both on national systems and local interactions, on macro level policy and students' own voices.

The Adult University is essential reading for all those interested in the development of our mass higher education system. It points to ways in which individual universities and the system of higher education could and should evolve in advanced industrial societies.

Contents
Introduction – Changing to survive: the modern university in its environment – Are universities organised to facilitate access and participation? – Adult students: getting in and keeping out – Staying in and coming to terms – Innovation and the university: the struggle for adultification – The adult university: from adult education to lifelong learning? – References – Index.

c.192pp   0 335 19907 0 (Paperback)   0 335 19908 9 (Hardback)

MANAGING THE LEARNING UNIVERSITY

Chris Duke

This book debunks prevailing modern management theories and fashions as applied to higher education. At the same time it provides practical guidance for a clear and easily understood set of principles as to how universities and colleges can be re-energized and their staff mobilized to be effective in meeting the growing and changing needs of the global knowledge society. It is anchored in knowledge of management and organizational theory and in the literature about higher education which is critiqued from a clear theoretical perspective based on and tested through long experience of university management and leadership.

Chris Duke offers challenging advice for managers in tertiary and higher education – from self-managing knowledge workers who may feel themselves to be the new academic proletariat, through to institutional heads, some of whose attempts to manage using strategic planning, management-by-objectives and other techniques seriously unravel because they fail to benefit from the talents and networks which make up the rich 'underlife' of the institution. Loss of institutional memory and failure to tap tacit know-how and mobilize commitment through genuine consultation and shared participatory management inhibits organizational learning and generates apathy – or drives staff dedication and creativity into oppositional channels.

Managing the Learning University indicates how higher education institutions can link and network their internal energies with external opportunities and partners to be successful and dynamic learning organizations. It points the way to enabling an enterprising and valued university to thrive in hard times, and to be a community where it is actually a pleasure to work.

Contents
Introduction: Who manages what? – Changing universities – Managing and people in postmodern times – Managing what abiding university? – Managing through cooperation – Managing the academic enterprise – Managing people and resources – Managing communication and using information technology – Is the learning university manageable? – Bibliography – Index – The Society for Research into Higher Education.

176pp   0 335 20765 0 (Paperback)   0 335 20766 9 (Hardback)